A volume
in
DOCUMENTARY HISTORY
of
WESTERN CIVILIZATION

The Low Countries
in Early Modern Times

The Low Countries in Early Modern Times

edited by

HERBERT H. ROWEN

WALKER AND COMPANY

New York

First published in the United States of America
in 1972 by the Walker Publishing Company, Inc.

Published simultaneously in Canada by Fitzhenry &
Whiteside, Limited, Toronto.

ISBN: 0-8027-2035-8

Library of Congress Catalog Card Number: 72-80544

Printed in the United States of America.

Volumes in this series are published in association
with Harper & Row, Publishers, Inc., from
whom paperback editions are available in Harper
Torchbooks.

Contents

Preface

In our own day the three countries which have emerged out of the late medieval and early modern complex of provinces in the Netherlands—Holland, Belgium and Luxemburg—are all obsessed by a sense of smallness. They know that they are not and cannot be powers of the first rank, whatever the abilities and endeavors of their people and whatever the policies of their governments, simply because they have too little territory and too few people as compared to such states as France and Germany, not to speak of the giants like the United States and the U.S.S.R. Yet both Belgium and Holland have a keen awareness of past greatness; they remember when these provinces by the North Sea were economically and politically among the giants of Europe. It is the purpose of this book to give a glimpse of that past through documents; but the scope of the work compels the editor to accept a series of self-imposed limitations. The medieval period, when the provinces of Flanders and Brabant—the heart of what is now Belgium—were at their most prosperous and most powerful, is not included, partly for reasons of space and partly because it lies outside the editor's field of competence. The origins and significance of the separation of the country into the Dutch Republic and the Spanish (later Austrian) Netherlands during the Revolt of the Low Countries are observed; but once it has occurred, the history of the United Provinces in the North is stressed, for it was there that the Dutch Republic became a great power during the seventeenth century. The separate history of the South is only sketched after the break of 1579.

Within these limits, the editor has sought to give a view of a variety of historical events and developments, and the documents are as divergent in character as he has been able to manage, extending from state papers to satirical pamphlets, from general accounts and histories to personal correspondence. Only the briefer documents could always be given in full; others, even when quite extensive, are often selections. Only two of the documents were originally written in English; the others have been translated from Dutch and French, in several cases from Latin, and in one from the Italian. Generally, where a published translation was available, it has been used; but some of the sixteenth century translations would require a modern reader virtually to re-translate them, and the editor has preferred to give a version in modern English, sacrificing authenticity of tone to clarity of meaning. About three-fourths of the translations have been made by the editor especially for this collection.

H. H. R.

Introduction

The Low Countries in the early modern era were at the center of historical events of the greatest importance. Out of the congeries of provinces and lands that lay athwart the lower reaches of the three great rivers—Rhine, Meuse, Scheldt[1]—that run into the North Sea through Europe's greatest delta, the Burgundian dukes in the late Middle Ages had created a major power; modern historians call it the "Burgundian state" although its strength lay primarily in the Netherlands and not in ancestral Burgundy, in eastern France. Its strength came from the wealth created by its productive activities—shipping and fishing, trading and manufacturing, and the most advanced agriculture in Europe. But the Burgundian state was a political structure with dubious stability; it lacked a history, its constituent elements had loose interconnections of interest, or, put another way, a particularly vigorous localism. In addition, some of the provinces only came under Burgundian rule in the first part of the sixteenth century, when the house of Burgundy had already merged into the greater dynasty of Habsburg, whose dominions spread from Germany and southeastern Europe to Italy, Spain, and all the way to furthest Asia and the Americas. The Burgundians—or the Habsburgs, as we must call them from the time of Charles V, the first to inherit all these possessions—began to create a more unified state out of the Low Countries. They put central institutions of political, financial, and judicial control over the varied local and provincial authorities; but they also linked this new country with a maze of varied and often

1. Since this is the river called the Escaut in French and the Schelde in Dutch, the languages of the countries through which it flows, it is strange that English should insist upon the German name, Scheldt. But as that name has become accepted usage, it would be pedantry or an excess of Netherlandish zeal to attempt to change it.

conflicting interests in which its own special needs were easily forgotten. This was the situation in the early sixteenth century when we pick up the story of the Low Countries, especially after Charles of Habsburg was elected Holy Roman Emperor in 1519: their duke and count, their ruling prince born among them at Ghent in 1500, was now also emperor and king of Spain. Would he rule for them, or rule them for others? That was the question which the accidents of dynastic marriage had placed before them and before him.

It was a question which, as it turned out, could not be answered unequivocally. The special quality of Charles V's reign in all his dominions was that he ruled for none of them specifically. His highest loyalties went to Christendom, in the Roman Catholic form in which he had been brought up, and to his dynasty, the house of Habsburg. Yet there were uniformities in his overall policy—notably the steady pressure for the creation of more centralized and efficient government—which were of the highest importance for the Netherlands. There he continued the program of territorial aggrandizement and integration begun by the dukes of Burgundy, adding to the provinces already under his rule those which lay to the north and east, Friesland, Utrecht, Overijssel, Groningen, and Gelderland. These later became, with his inherited provinces of Holland and Zeeland, the seven United Provinces of the Dutch Republic. Some of the provinces accepted his rule voluntarily, but Gelderland fought bitterly against his domination until 1543. At the same time he moved to give greater unity to the government of the Low Countries, placing a central administration over the local and provincial authorities in 1531; it consisted of the governor-general, under his reign always a female member of the house of Habsburg, and three "Collateral Councils," the Council of State, the Privy (or Secret) Council, and the Council of Finances. His control within the provinces was strengthened by the appointment of lieutenants, called *stadhouders* in Dutch (which we shall hence-forth translate as "stadholder" because these officials came to play a unique role in the government of the later Dutch Republic). He carried forward the unification of the Netherlands as a single country by giving it a special position within the Holy Roman Empire as the Burgundian Circle (1548), bound to Germany by the flimsiest of legal ties. He also ordained by a "pragmatic sanc-tion" that it would be an indivisible heritage, subject to a single law of inheritance. To the extent that the needs of his supranational ambitions or those of his other dominions did not interfere, Charles favored the interests of the Low Countries, especially of the commercial and industrial classes. In general, a wide prosperity prevailed in the country. Antwerp replaced Bruges as the center of European trade; the river port near the mouth of the Scheldt became the warehouse and even more the trading and banking center of the continent. The industrial towns, especially in Flanders, continued to be prosperous, although with more difficulty than in earlier centuries, as competition in the cloth trade developed elsewhere, notably in England.

Charles would not brook any of the traditional rebelliousness, especially of the Flemish cities. He crushed the 1539–1540 rising in Ghent without compunction and deprived the city of its privileges and self-government, a warning to other cities not to follow its bad example. But his political practice fell short of absolutism, in the sense of the exclusion of the provincial States[2] and the States General from participation in government. He preferred to use these assemblies for his own needs, persuading and bludgeoning them into granting him extraordinary taxation for his various wars. He even strengthened the institution of the States General because the deputies from the provinces, meeting in Brussels away from their own capital (except for the Brabanters), could be more effectively bullied and even made to disobey the imperative mandates laid down by those whom they represented, the towns and noble orders in the provinces. Charles governed in general with a noteworthy combination of deftness and firmness; he was both feared and loved by most of the people, although obviously much less loved by those, like the Ghenters and Gelderlanders, who felt more of his iron hand than his velvet glove. Although the Protestant Reformation made its entry into the Netherlands under his reign,

---

2. Any historian of the Low Countries in this period must decide how to distinguish the "state," as a country and political organization, from "States," the representative assemblies. In French one word, *état*, is used for both, in the singular for the former and the plural for the latter; both forms are usually capitalized. In Dutch, the word *staat* is similarly employed, except that the singular is not usually capitalized while the plural, standing for the assembly, is; the word *stand*, plural *standen* (the same as the German *Stand*, plural *Stände*) is used rather in the sense of the socioeconomic "order." In this book, I shall follow the Dutch usage as more explicit than the French, leaving the singular in the lower case and capitalizing the plural.

there was no resistance to the measures to repress heresy which he proclaimed.

The situation changed drastically when Emperor Charles decided to lay down his great offices and to turn them and his possessions over to his son, who became Philip II of Spain, and his brother, Emperor Ferdinand I. In the division of the heritage that followed the abdication of 1555, the Netherlands were given to Philip. Under the government of Philip II, who was a Spaniard to his fingertips, the tensions which the emperor had easily been able to deflect or defeat came to a head. The new king went off to his native Spain to live as soon as he could manage, never to return; but he was intent upon governing these Low Countries where his father had been born in the same way that he ruled Spain itself— autocratically and bureaucratically, although with the welfare of his subjects (as he saw it) in mind. He left behind as governor-general his half-sister, Margaret of Parma, with the guileful Cardinal Granvelle as her chief guiding spirit and the effective prime minister of the whole country. Granvelle scorned the nobility, and not least the great nobles like the count of Egmont and the Prince of Orange; for him they were arrogant wastrels living beyond their means, "overmighty subjects" in the English phrase. The advice of the Council of State, where they held a majority of seats, was disregarded. The king and Granvelle, like Charles V before them, wanted a more effective government; but where the emperor had flattered the nobility, fed their vanity and their depleted treasuries, and obtained their grateful services in war and governance, the new monarch wished obedience on his own terms. He would not even leave them the outward appearance of being the king's principal servants and great men in their own right; he favored jurists for native-born councilors and foreigners like Granvelle for political tasks. Never one to separate difficulties and meet them separately, Philip also obtained the consent of the papacy for a reorganization of the church hierarchy in the Netherlands, which would provide a closer tie between bishops and the people than had existed. It would also enable the repression of Protestant heresies to be sharpened, ending the evasions which had been possible under the former, much looser web of church government. And the immediate losers, in terms of revenue and influence, would be just the nobility, which was accustomed to monopolizing the wealthy abbeys for its younger sons; while the new bishops, who would be given the principal abbeys to supplement their income, would thereby obtain a voice, and represent the king, within the provincial States. Such a policy might have succeeded had the nobility been isolated from the other classes of the country, and the object of their suspicion and hatred; but there was no such clear-cut conflict of classes in the Netherlands between merchants and nobles, and the king, by striking at their interests simultaneously, brought them closer together. Equally significant was that the decades of the 1560s were hard years for the Netherlanders; bad harvests in the countryside raised the price of bread at the same time that languishing trade meant unemployment and low wages.

1566 became a "Year of Hunger" in the people's memories, but it was likewise a "Year of Wonders" because it marked the start of the revolt of the Low Countries against the king. It began as a refusal of the great nobles in the Council of State to continue to serve unless their advice was accepted, Granvelle and the Spanish troops were withdrawn, and the religious persecution was removed. It became a broader movement of resistance of the lesser nobility, the "Compromise" of 1566. The combination of such resistance of the upper classes, the traditional governing class of the country, with the outbreak of Calvinist outrages against the churches (the "Image-Breaking") drove Philip II into a rage. He decided to put an end once and for all to the impertinences of these Netherlanders who refused to obey him, and sent the Duke of Alva with a powerful army to the Netherlands. Alva, who reached the Netherlands in December, 1667, replaced Margaret of Parma at the head of the country as governor-general.

Alva quickly won what seemed like a complete triumph over the resisters, the rebels, and the heretics. The little armies with which the Prince of Orange, William I, whom history knows as "the Silent," sought to defeat Alva were crushed like cockleshells. A "Council of the Troubles" took over punishment of offenders; its victims included the counts of Egmont and Hoorn, among the most notable of the country's noblemen, and many thousands of simpler people. Alva introduced a capital levy and a ten percent sales tax on the Spanish model, the notorious "tenth penny" which was never collected because the provinces bought off their obligations with lump payments. It was only in 1572 that sea rovers nominally in the Prince of Orange's service captured the seaport town of Den Briel at the southwestern tip of Holland; then, in combination with Calvinist militants, they swept away the government of Catholics and loyalists in one town after another in Holland and Zeeland, until little remained under Alva's control there but the great port of Amsterdam. Meanwhile the Prince of Orange, failing in another sortie out of Germany against Alva, made his way to Holland instead of fleeing back into Germany.

A new period ensued in the history of the revolt. Alva, distracted by orders to support the Catholic extremists in France after the Bartholomew's Eve massacre, failed to recapture the lost provinces in the North. His successor, Requesens, was more successful at first, but ultimately his grip too was weakened not only by the ability of the rebels to dominate the waterways of the delta country but also by the bankruptcy of the Spanish treasury, which left his troops without pay and in mutiny. The plunder and murders perpetrated by the Spanish troops in Antwerp in 1576 led to a revival of the military resistance in the southern Netherlands. A political basis was created for the aims sought by the Prince of Orange—to expel the Spaniard; to reunite the Low Countries under one government with the participation of the States in the provinces and the States General in Brussels, with the nobility preponderant; and to establish a regime of religious toleration. This policy was embodied in the Pacification of Ghent of 1576. But grave and ultimately insuperable obstacles lay in the way of achievement of these aims. Philip II was unwilling to concede them, and his strength was still enormously greater than that of the often squabbling provinces in the Netherlands, where he now sent his half-brother, Don Juan of Austria, to rule for him. The Calvinists were willing to accept the principle of religious toleration for the rest of the country but not in Holland and Zeeland, where they had established their stronghold and excluded Catholics from government. The Catholic rebels for their part were discontented over this violation of equality of faiths and they were also jealous of the preeminence achieved by Orange as political and military leader. The Catholic "Malcontents" were able to persuade Archduke Matthias of Habsburg, brother of Emperor Rudolf II, to come to the Netherlands as governor-general by the nomination of the States General, in competition with Don Juan; but Orange easily maintained his leadership against the rivalry of the young man, whom he brought under his own influence. The situation changed again with Don Juan's death, when Philip sent to the Low Countries a general of extraordinary political as well as military gifts, Alexander Farnese, Prince of Parma.

Parma saw his task not only as defeating the military forces of the rebellion but also as winning back the loyalty and affection of all the Netherlanders whom Calvinist passion or implacable political hatred did not make irreconcilable. He began by a methodical reconquest, taking one city after another as he drove northward toward the line of the great rivers. His most magnificent achievement as a general was the capture of Antwerp, the huge and well-defended port on the Scheldt, in 1585. But politically it was only a partial, and in a sense even a Pyrrhic, victory. For it served only to confirm the endeavor of the rebels to consolidate their independent power, and it led to the shift of most of the commercial and financial activity of Antwerp to Amsterdam, which had accepted the rebel cause in 1578. William the Silent was gone by now, for he had been assassinated in 1584, at the behest of Philip II, who had placed Orange under the ban in 1580. But the United Provinces, as the northern provinces were beginning to be called since they had formed a Union at Utrecht in 1579, had proclaimed the deposition of Philip in 1581. This loss was compensated in part by the return of the southern provinces to the king's allegiance, beginning with the Union and Treaty of Arras in 1579, Parma's outstanding political achievement. In return for their obedience, Parma abandoned the effort to establish Habsburg government in the Low Countries upon the basis of absolutism and systematic centralization; in effect, he used Catholic loyalty to recapture dynastic allegiance. But in so doing, he deepened the chasm which military and political events were opening up between the northern and southern Netherlands, and he prepared the way for the eventual emergence of two separate nations and states, the forerunners of the modern countries of Holland and Belgium.

From the year of the two unions of Utrecht and Arras, the North and South went separate ways, one to prosperity and power such as the region had never known, the other to a loss of ancient wealth and strength. In the North, the decade after the Union of Utrecht was one of political uncertainty and groping toward a definite form of government. At the same time the work of economic growth moved on, with Dutch ships crossing the European seas in greater numbers and Dutch merchants taking on the work of Europe's middlemen par excellence. In the last years of his life,

William of Orange endeavored to gain protection for the Low Countries from France, and he never accepted the ideal of an independent nation limited to the North. But the episode of the Duke of Anjou's government as "lord of the Netherlands" was a tragic miscalculation, and the attempt of his successors to persuade Elizabeth of England to play the same role was even less successful. The governor-generalship of the Earl of Leicester (1585–1587) was a fiasco, and its most important achievement was the unintended one—at least unintended on Leicester's part—of confirming the Dutch in the determination to make their country effectively independent. The Dutch Republic emerged in the proud "Ten Years" from 1588 to 1598 as an equal sovereign member of the European community of states.

Internally the new state developed a system of government by the States of the provinces and the States General, with the Prince of Orange as a military and political leader, with the offices of captain-general and stadholder. (Actually, William the Silent's successor, Maurice of Nassau, was his second son and did not become Prince of Orange until his elder brother, Philip William, who remained loyal to the Habsburg king, died in 1618.) But the republican form of government was of the aristocratic type, for the provincial States spoke for hereditary nobility in the landward provinces and for patrician governments in the towns, the self-perpetuating *vroedschappen* ("the wise men," as the town councils were called); not only was there no election from below, a rare enough way to choose rulers anywhere in Europe, but the States of Holland even forbade the towns to permit the guilds to share in the work of city government. On the other hand, the stadholders, although governors of the provinces by the appointment of the provincial States, were in fact much more like the elected monarchs of central and eastern Europe, but without the royal crown or title. The tension between the aristocracy of the towns and the house of Orange became one of the permanent elements of the Dutch political structure for the entire life of the republic of the United Provinces; but it was a tension over where the primary initiative and effective guidance of the country's policies should lie, not over the form of society. What was unusual about the Dutch situation was the passion which the common people, until the second half of the eighteenth century, felt for the house of Orange, their need for a mythic personal leader at the head of the state, their resentments against the wealthy patricians for whom they worked and who ruled directly over them, and, for the Calvinists, their religious fervor. The princes, on the other hand, felt themselves to be the born national leaders, quasi dynasts who had a birthright to be elected to the posts of stadholder and captain-general; and none of those who followed William the Silent, whatever their other, sometimes not inconsiderable gifts, acquired his sense of compassion for those he led. On the contrary, their view of the world was far more like that of the patrician regents who were their political rivals—a world of men possessing power and property with a God-given right to rule and prosper, and beneath them multitudes of the poor and the powerless, with a God-given duty to toil and obey. The regents competed with the Princes of Orange not in order to change the world in which they lived, for that was a notion strange and senseless to both sides, but to gain more of the benefits for themselves, and in the sincere belief that the policies they pursued were more beneficial for all but a handful of soldiers and courtiers because they were directed toward the maintenance of peace, civic calm, and economic well-being.

In foreign affairs, the Republic became one of the major powers of Europe by 1598, achieving recognition by such allies as England and France, partial acknowledgment of its effective independence by Spain in the Twelve Years' Truce (1609–1621), and full legal recognition at the Peace of Münster (Westphalia) in 1648. During the seventeenth century it moved far past Venice as the leading republic in Europe, and by mid-century and into the first decade of the eighteenth century it was one of the three or four greatest powers in Europe, able on more than one occasion to face the greatest on nearly even terms. But it was a power that rested upon essentially fragile foundations—too little territory, not enough people, sources of wealth ultimately dependent upon the goodwill or the weakness of outsiders, and a ramshackle constitution that took something close to political genius to make work well. But it was not until the War of the Spanish Succession that these handicaps proved beyond repair; until then the Republic possessed generals of the first order in Maurice of Nassau and Frederick Henry, admirals renowned and feared like the Tromps and De Ruyter, and political leaders of notable ability such as Oldenbarnevelt, De Witt, and William III.

Meanwhile, the country's economic life prospered as an amazed

Europe watched and was envious. Sometimes, it seemed that war, the usual enemy of commercial prosperity, served the Dutch rather than hindering them; for they enlarged their shipping and their trade during the seventeenth century—Holland's "Golden Age"— to become Europe's carriers and merchants with a predominance verging on monopoly. That prosperity was centered in Amsterdam, but it spread over most of the territory and most of the economic life of the country, more thinly in the less favored inland provinces like Gelderland and Overijssel than in the coastal provinces. Cultural life responded both to the spiritual energies released by the nation's great achievements and to the availability of resources for maintaining the life of art and the mind; yet only painting, of all the professional arts, achieved the highest level, while literature remained the activity primarily of amateurs, men who did not earn their livings by it.

Political life during the two centuries of the Republic's existence was anything but calm. The constitutional ambiguities of the regime of the Union of Utrecht fostered crises rather than limiting them, because the distribution of sovereign powers among so varied a group of entities, with a membership of several thousand, with disputed and overlapping powers, meant that major political controversies became as much battles over where legitimate power lay as over what should be done. This was illustrated in the first great controversy which racked the United Provinces after Leicester returned to England in 1587. The relations between Maurice and Oldenbarnevelt, the political leader of Holland as Land's Advocate, were already exacerbated by the conclusion of the Twelve Years' Truce over Maurice's protests; they turned drastically worse when Oldenbarnevelt, in affirming the sovereign rights of the province of Holland to settle the acrimonious conflict between Arminians and Gomarians in the Reformed church, and to aid the province of Utrecht in doing the same, challenged Maurice's military authority as commander-in-chief for the Union. It was a challenge that was won by Maurice, who wielded not only military might but also had the support of a host of forces envious of Holland's predominance within the Union and of Oldenbarnevelt's leadership within the province. Yet, after Oldenbarnevelt's execution in 1619, nothing fundamental changed. Maurice had defeated an opponent, but he was not interested in reforming the political structure of the Republic.

Frederick Henry, Maurice's half-brother who succeeded him in 1625, not only rounded out the territorial acquisitions of the United Provinces but also began such a strong shifting of the leadership of the country to the stadholder and away from Holland's regents that a constitutional change de facto if not yet de jure was in the making; if brought to culmination, it would have made the Republic into a monarchy, although probably a limited, not an absolute one. The alarmed Hollanders therefore resisted his son, William II, who became stadholder in 1647, all the more vigorously, and forced through the peace of Münster with Spain in 1648. But it almost became a Pyrrhic victory, for in 1650 the Prince of Orange came very close to wresting full control away from his adversaries in Holland in a military coup d'état. But his failure to take Amsterdam by surprise and force compelled him to accept a partial victory. Although his open foes had to abandon political life, the regents of Holland were thoroughly frightened. With William's sudden and unexpected death in November, leaving behind only a posthumous son—William III—the defeated party acted on the unforeseen opportunity, took over political leadership, and ran the country for twenty-two years.

The first stadholderless period (1650–1672) also bore the marks of a partial victory. The Hollanders reaffirmed their provincial sovereignty and persuaded four of the other provinces to join them in refraining from naming the infant William III to his forefathers' posts; but they did not otherwise reform the country's fault-ridden constitution and they did not remove the house of Orange from Dutch life. William III grew to manhood under the aegis first of his mother, a royal princess of England until her death in December 1660, a half year after the restoration of her brother, Charles II, and then of his grandmother, while those about him taught him both that the stadholdership and captaincy-general were his of right and that he was of royal blood, born to rule. The common people and the lesser provinces continued to give their affection and their support to the scion of Orange, and recurring riots and conspiracies lent weight to their feelings. Nonetheless the regime, which we call "republican" because it knew no stadholder, remained essentially stable and in control until the French invasion of 1672; for it was led by a gifted statesman, Holland's councilor-pensionary John de Witt, who was able to make the system work with extraordinary efficacy. But the war of 1672, in which England was allied with France, began with disaster. The French armies swept over the Republic from the east until they were halted by the inundation of the "water-line" between the Zuider Zee and the Rhine-Maas river system. De Witt fell from power in the midst of a quasi insurrection on behalf of the Prince of Orange, and he was slain in a political lynching that sated the people's vengefulness and gave William III, recently made stadholder (he had been captain-general since early in the year), a potent weapon of terror against any lingering resistance to his authority. William became the center of the European opposition to the aggrandizement of Louis XIV and used the Republic as the base for his military and diplomatic policies. In 1688 he took the lead in the overthrow of his uncle and father-in-law, James II, in England's "Glorious Revolution," and the next year became King of Great Britain (with his wife, Mary, as Queen regnant). As stadholder-king, he led both the United Provinces and Britain through the Nine Years' War (as the Dutch call the "War of the League of Augsburg" of 1689–97), the partition negotiations which followed it, and into the War of the Spanish Succession that began in 1701. But it was a war fought without him, for he died the next year.

Another stadholderless period intervened, for the patricians of Holland in particular, as well as in the other provinces, had come to resent bitterly William III's domineering government. But again there was no constitutional reform, and the nearly five decades of government without a stadholder did not remove the domination of Dutch foreign policy by the continuing English alliance or the renewed supremacy of the patrician aristocracy within the country. The weakness of the stadholderless regime was not only political, but also economic. Because the Republic had fallen far behind England and France as a trading and shipping power it was exposed during the War of the Austrian Succession (1740–1748), and Orangism revived and struck back, using the familiar weapon of popular rioting. William IV, of the junior branch of the house of Orange that had governed continuously in Friesland and Groningen, was made hereditary stadholder in all the provinces in 1747. But it was a success that proved costly, for the idea of fundamental political reform, sparked by the new philosophy of the Enlightenment, took hold in the United Provinces and, by making both the stadholder and the urban patricians its enemies, united them in resistance to the reformers. The last stadholder, William V

(1766–1795), was a weak-willed man of little political intelligence, quite like that Louis XVI who was to go down to destruction with the French monarchy. And his wife, Wilhelmina, a princess of the Prussian royal house, was as strong-willed, haughty, and willing to bring in foreign armies to put down domestic revolt as France's Marie Antoinette. Thus the Patriot movement, as the reforming forces were called, moved to cut down the stadholder's influence during the '80s, but was crushed by Prussian military intervention in 1787. The Patriots took their revenge when France invaded the country in 1795, overthrowing the two-century-old regime of States, stadholder, and the Union of Utrecht and forming the Batavian Republic. With that act, the modernization of the Dutch nation began.

The parallel history of the southern Netherlands during those two centuries can be told far more briefly, for it is a history of a country without independence, a victim of repeated invasions, a puppet of the great powers. Philip II, having reconciled himself to the defeat of his absolutist aspirations which Parma's policies made explicit, gave the country to his daughter Isabella and her husband, Archduke Albert. They ruled as well as they could, neither truly independent of Madrid nor wholly subservient to it, and they sought to advance the interests of their subjects no less than those of the House of Habsburg. Not as much can be said of their successors, lesser figures who were more commanders of the Spanish troops in the long and recurring wars with France than political leaders. The French triumphs that ended each of those wars whittled away the southern boundary of the Spanish Netherlands until what became the modern frontier between France and Belgium was achieved by the end of the War of the League of Augsburg. The economic structure of the country shifted from one predominantly industrial and commercial to one in which agriculture prevailed: but it was a progressive and even a prosperous agriculture, at least to the extent that the depredations of war permitted. The Catholic character of the country, created by the repression and expulsion of Protestant heretics, became complete, and the spiritual separation from the North almost as absolute. What later generations would call the Belgian nationality was taking form.

The shift to Austrian sovereignty under the Peace of Utrecht (1713) brought changes of degree but not of fundamental character. On the whole, the Austrians were better rulers, more interested in the welfare of their subjects in the Low Countries, than the seventeenth century Spaniards had been. But the country remained the least of their multiple and conflicting concerns, and within the provinces a considerable extent of self-government—which meant the rule of nobles, clergy, and wealthy burgesses—continued. Constitutionally, except that a different branch of the house of Habsburg reigned, little really changed from the political system accepted by Parma in the Treaty of Arras and which, ironically, was not much different from the early political objectives of the sixteenth century rebels. But the brutal intervention of Joseph II in the life of the Austrian Netherlands, in a bold effort to drag the country into modern efficiency and placid obedience, only resulted in a revolt of both conservatives and reformers. It drove out the Austrian regime in 1789–90, and created the short-lived republic of the United Belgian States. Although it was as backward-looking as the Batavian Republic was forward-looking, it too represented the final break with the old regime in the southern Netherlands.

In both countries, it was the French Revolution (and its bastard child, the Napoleonic regime) which shattered finally and irrevocably the institutions and the spirit of the old regime in the Low Countries, North and South. For all their differences in political organization, economic activity, and religious commitment, both countries had had characteristic regimes of the old kind, with frank and unabashed legal inequalities between the orders, worlds marked by hierarchy and privilege. Neither had been able to change itself greatly before change was imposed on it from outside and above; but they were ready, perhaps more so than any other countries on the European continent, even France, for the great transformations of the nineteenth and twentieth centuries.

1 Land and People

Few peoples have been so shaped by their geography, or in turn so changed the land on which they lived, as the Netherlanders. This characteristic is inscribed in the very name of the country. It first appeared during the Middle Ages as a term of straight description, "the low lands by the sea," but later became a fixed, proper name as *de Nederlanden*, "the Netherlands" or "the Low Countries" in the plural, as well as in the form *Nederland*, a singular which exists in English only in the occasional archaic form "the Low Country." (The equivalent French forms are the common *les Pays-Bas* and the rare *le Pays Bas*.) The English name for the people of the northern Low Countries, the modern "Kingdom of the Netherlands," is "Dutch," reflecting their Germanic origins and speech; but its literal equivalent, *Duits*, means "German," and the Dutch refer to themselves as *Nederlanders* or *Hollanders* (after their principal province). Yet the word "Dutch" does not encompass either the Flemings—the inhabitants of Flanders, Brabant, and other Dutch-speaking regions of modern Belgium—nor the Walloons, the French-speaking inhabitants of such provinces as Hainaut and Artois who were included within the territory of the Low Countries and were thought of in the medieval and early modern period as "Netherlanders."

The following selections, contemporary descriptions of people and country, reflect this ambiguous usage. The first is specifically about Dutchmen, "Hollanders," the second about the country of the Netherlands in general.

1. The Dutch Seen by a Dutchman

The outstanding Dutch writer of all time was Desiderius Erasmus (1469–1536), the "Prince of Humanists." Born and educated in his native land, he preferred to live abroad, and he apparently never wrote in his native tongue, but only in the Latin and Greek he so loved. Yet he remained a Dutchman in character, and to some extent, describing his fellow-countrymen in the following passage, he is describing himself. The following piece is taken from Erasmus' *Adages*, first published in Paris in 1500; the translation is by a modern English scholar.

Source: Margaret Mann Philips, *The "Adages" of Erasmus: A Study with Translations* (Cambridge: The University Press, 1964), pp. 209–211.

JUST AS THE Greeks say βοιώτιον οὖς, i.e., the Boeotian ear, meaning dull and gross, so Martial in his *Epigrams*, book VI, says that
Batavam aurem means an ear which is rustic, untutored, boorish:

> It is you, you he means, that Martial
> Whose naughty jokes are plainly understood
> By one who has not a Batavian ear

So Domitius Calderinus reads, though some alter the reading
Batavam to *severam*.

The Batavi were a German tribe, part of the Catti, who migrated
owing to internal dissensions and occupied the extreme tip of the
coast of Gaul, then unoccupied, and also at the same time an island
situated between two stretches of water, washed by the ocean in
front and by the river Rhine at the back and sides. As a people they
were strong fighters, with much experience in the Germanic wars,
but also powerful through their wealth, so that the Roman military
power could not be exhausted while these people were allies of the
Empire and contributed to it both arms and men; how generously,
Cornelius Tacitus tells us in his book XX. Most scholars agree, and
the guess seems uncontradicted, that this island mentioned by
Tacitus is what we now call Holland, a country I must always
praise and venerate, since to her I owe my life's beginning. And I
would that I could bring as much honor to her, as I have little
regret in being her son! For as to that accusation of boorishness
which Martial levels against her, and Lucan's charge of savagery, I
think that either they have nothing to do with us at all, or both can
be turned into praise. For which people has not been uncultured at
one time? And when was the Roman people more praiseworthy
than when they knew no arts except farming and fighting? If anyone argues that the criticisms levelled at the Batavi long ago still
hold good today, what better tribute could be paid to my dear
Holland, than to have it said that she recoils from Martial's pleas-
antries, which he himself calls vile? If only all Christians had
"Dutch ears", so that they would not take in the pestilential jests of
that poet, or at least not be infected by them, if understood. If you
call that rusticity, we freely admit the impeachment, in company
with the virtuous Spartans, the primitive Sabines, the noble Catos.
But Lucan, I imagine, calls the Batavi "savage" much as Virgil calls
the Romans "sharp" (*acer*).

If you look at the manners of everyday life, there is no race more open to humanity and kindness, or less given to wildness or ferocious behavior. It is a straightforward nature, without treachery or deceit, and not prone to any serious vices, except that it is a little given to pleasure, especially of feasting. The reason for this is, I think, the wonderful supply of everything which can tempt one to enjoyment; due partly to the ease of importing goods (since the country stands at the mouth of two noble rivers, the Rhine and the Meuse, and is washed on one side by the sea), and partly to the native fertility of the region, intersected as it is by navigable rivers full of fish, and abounding in rich pastures. And there is a plentiful supply of birds from the marshes and heaths. They say that there is no country which holds so many towns in a small space, not large towns it is true, but incredibly civilized. As for domestic furniture, Holland is unsurpassed in neatness and elegance—or so say those merchants who travel over most of the globe. In no country are there more people who have a tincture of learning than in Holland. If there are few deeply learned scholars, especially in the classics, this may be due to the luxury of life there, or it may be that they think more of moral excellence than of excellence in scholarship. For it is certain, and many things go to prove it, that they are not wanting in intellectual power, though I myself have it only in a modest degree, not to say scanty—like the rest of my endowments.

2. The Low Countries Seen by an Italian

There is something especially fitting about a description of the Low Countries by a Florentine, for northern Italy was a land of cities, like the Netherlands, and Florence was its archetypal town. The Florentine who wrote the *Description of All the Low Countries*, from which the following selection is taken, was Lodovico Guicciardini (1521–1589), whose uncle Francesco was a famous historian of the last decades of the Florentine republic. Lodovico was a resident of Antwerp, and his *Description*, which won wide popularity, was based not only upon his readings, but upon personal observation. It was first published in 1567 in Antwerp; this translation is made from the revised edition of 1581, which is dedicated to Philip II, king of Spain.

Source: Descrittione di M. Lodovico Guicciardini Patritio Fiorentino; di tutti i Paesi Bassi, altrimenti detti Germania Inferiore. Anversa: Christofano Plantino, Stampatore Regio, MDLXXXI, pp. 7–10, 12–13, 297, 300–304. Translated from the Italian by Donald Weinstein.

By our estimate, the Low Countries altogether have a circumference a little more than a fifth as long as Italy's, that is, about a thousand Italian miles or 340 Flemish leagues. . . . This country is composed of seventeen provinces . . . in which there are 208 walled places. About 150 of these are places whose favorable circumstances have gained for them the quality of walled or privileged towns, as they are called; and there are more than 6,300 villages with belfries. There are not many other lesser villages but innumerable manors where the administration of civil and criminal justice is held by a prince, lord, or gentleman. In all, there are 60 fortresses or strongholds in the country under royal governors, with garrisons varying in strength according to their situation and circumstances.

Although the air of the country is humid and heavy, it is nonetheless salubrious and good for the digestion, and above all generative (as Caesar declares more than once). But it is generally believed that the air has become more healthful and moderate during the past 25 or 30 years, either because there are more homes and inhabitants who purge it in various ways (as is done at Venice), or for some other, more significant reason. In fact, if the people of the country did not eat carelessly and neglect themselves when sick, they would ordinarily live to an old age and few would die young. This may be seen in the plain of Kempen in Brabant, where the country is naturally infertile and still the people live to a very old age thanks to abstemiousness and hard work.

Summer is beautiful and delightful because the heat is usually not too severe and flies and gnats do not get in the nose very much, except in Zeeland, where there are far too many. There are few thunderstorms, and earthquakes are very rare because the humid climate and low ground are not conducive to them.

Winter is usually long and stormy. The weather is very cold and harsh when the North, Greek, Levantine, and Sirocco winds are blowing, but when the four opposite winds blow, which is usually more than three quarters of the time (as Caesar also noted), the cold turns into rain.

The terrain is almost wholly flat. There are few hills and even fewer mountains, except in Luxemburg and Namur and some parts of Hainaut, which are quite hilly, as is the region of Liège. In many places the ground is very sandy, as in much of Flemish Flanders and in part of Brabant. Nonetheless the land is good and fertile

everywhere, although better in some regions than others, and in
many places it is very fertile, especially for cereals and grains, as in
French Flanders, Artois, Hainaut, Liège and Gelderland, where they
are produced in abundance.

Many kinds of fruit are grown, especially pears, apples, plums,
cherries, which are mentioned and praised as early as Pliny, purple
grapes, peaches, apricots, walnuts, hazelnuts, medlars and, in some
places, chestnuts. Except for many varieties of pears and apples
which are excellent and are raised throughout the year, the fruits
lack the fragrance and flavor that they possess in Italy, as there is
not enough warm weather. It is very difficult to grow figs, al-
monds, and similar fruits because there is not enough hot weather,
and olives, oranges, lemons, pomegranates, and other noble fruit of
that kind are even harder to grow; but they are supplied in great
abundance from Spain and Portugal by sea in every season. Many
grapes of all varieties are to be found in the towns and villages, but
very few in the countryside because the climate does not seem to
be suitable for them either; however, modest amounts are grown
around Louvain, Namur and Luxemburg, and wine is made from
them, but in small quantities, and it is rather tart because the grapes
do not ripen fully. However, now that the people devote themselves to agriculture more than before and are not so sparing of
expense, it may be expected that many other places will produce
wine. It has been tried several times with modest success at Brussels, Diest, and nearby Antwerp, and in several places in Germany,
even at Cologne which has as much cold weather as most of this
country. There are trees of all kinds and of good size and quality
both for lumber and for fuel. There are not many bays, cypresses,
pines, or fir; on the other hand there are great numbers of a tree they
call the linden, the *Tiliae* of the Latins, which are similar in shape
and foliage to the elm, but taller and of more rapid growth. . . .

There is beautiful scenery in most of the countryside thanks to
the frequency and regularity of the trees and plants which are seen
virtually everywhere, as well as the many fine meadows which are
to be seen everywhere, full of every kind of cattle. Everyone
agrees that their meadows are greener and more picturesque than
ours; unless I am mistaken, this is due to the wetness of the low
ground, which causes their pastures to give excellent fodder almost
all year.

The country has domestic livestock in very great abundance for meat of every kind except buffalo. In Friesland and Holland the cattle are especially large, often indeed of extraordinary size; frequently they weigh more than 1,600 pounds local weight (that is, 16 ounces per pound, which makes more than 2,000 pounds in our weight). Indeed, one animal from Friesland which was presented as a gift at Malines to the Count of Hoogstraeten was so large and fat that it weighed 2,528 pounds local weight. This was considered so remarkable that a lifesize portrait of it was placed inside the gate of the count's palace, with the day and year of the presentation, and it can still be seen there today. . . .

The country, especially Holland, Friesland, Gelderland, and Flanders, produces a great number of big horses, proud, handsome beasts excellent for every use, and especially good for warfare, so that in a battle of lances they have no equal in strength. However, except for most of the Flemish horses, they are a bit too heavy, especially in the head, and rather hard to manage.

The woolens of the country are somewhat coarse, inferior in quality to those of Spain and even more to those of England. One reason for this besides the climate is that the pastures here are so wet and nourishing that the animals grow coats which are too thick, long, and rough.

The country produces no salt, alum, or sulfur, except in the region of Liège; nor does it have any important minerals, so that it produces no metals of any kind except iron, some lead and a bit of copper. Nevertheless, what the country lacks in nature it makes up in the abilities of its people. On every side, they see to it by their industry and diligence that they suffer no lack of anything; on the contrary, there is such an abundance of these materials as well as of everything else (as will be seen in the description of Antwerp) that the daily needs of various foreign countries are taken care of by this region.

The country produces such large quantities of madder, which here is called *garance*, that not only do they supply their own country but a large part of Europe as well. They also produce excellent woad, although in small amounts, and flax and hemp in great abundance.

DESCRIPTION OF HOLLAND

Holland is a small country but full of great and memorable things. It has many fine towns and lovely villages, great men and women, excellent cattle, immense riches and power—but we shall describe it in detail. Holland lies in the island which in ancient times was called Batavia, from Bato, the son of the king of the Catti, a people who came from Germany, according to Cornelius Tacitus. . . . Opinions vary as to how Holland got its modern name. Among those whose opinions are most widely accepted, some say that it was first called Houtland, which means "lumber country," since, according to them, the country was heavily wooded and was afterward called Holland, which sounded better. Others maintain (and I agree with them) that it is a name compounded of the two Teutonic words "hol" and "lant," which really means "concave" or "hollow country," because in many places a traveler by cart or horseback can clearly see the ground shake like something bobbing on the water. An extraordinary occurrence which took place two years ago near Haarlem shows this very clearly. A cow grazing in a field more than half a league in length fell into a hole and was found dead three days later in the gulf which is nearby to the east. This means that the cow, having passed down through the earth into water, was carried by the water into the gulf, where it re-emerged. Although it seems strange and almost impossible that a country of such size rests on water, nevertheless it is very obvious that a part, if not all, has no other foundation but water (perhaps because the country is adjacent to water) and is supported by it. This is true of the whole region known as Waterland, that is, country of water, where the town of Monnikendam is located, and some other villages near Amsterdam. In Artois, near St. Omer, there is a very large lake (which I shall talk about in due course) in which there are various rather big bits of land which look like meadows and rise above the water, and on which cattle graze; and yet the lake has neither the size nor the volume of flow to sustain such a mass, as does the ocean. But these things are not at all contrary to nature, although they may seem so; every day, when wells and ditches are dug, it is seen that the earth rests on water and, what is more, that by the grace of God the water and earth rest on air. But let us see what Pliny writes in agreement with our opinion on this question of lands and islands with great forests perched and bobbing on top of water. . . .

To the north and west of Holland is the sea; to the south are the Maas and Brabant; to the east lies in part the bay of the Zuider

Zee[1] and in part the province of Gelderland, so that it is truly the
Batavian Peninsula and not an island, as many call it and believe it
to be. It has the huge rivers Rhine and Maas which, in many
branches and tributaries that bear other names, wash it in many
places. Nevertheless, not content with these waterways, the inhabitants have supplemented nature with very great skill and labor;
they have made so many canals and great ditches everywhere that
one can travel by water as conveniently as by land between all the
towns and almost all the important villages. It is a marshy country;
it has many ponds and is full of ocean bays, while the ocean
together with the branches of the Rhine forms many small islands,
each with its own name but together called by one name, Holland,
as was said above. The air, notwithstanding so much water and
humidity, is healthy and pleasant by reason of the good breezes,
the saltiness of the sea, and the great number of dwellings and
inhabitants who purge it, as at Venice. The land is so low that
almost all the rivers and major canals where the tide enters and
carries materials with it are diked so as not to overflow the land.
For this reason it is a wonderful thing to see the water so much
higher than the ground in many places. And this country is so
watery that generally one sees few trees and fewer fruit trees in the
countryside. Nevertheless we read that in ancient times the country was full of woods and forests, as in the time of the emperors
Diocletian and Maximianus; moreover, even now in those surrounding lands which have been recovered from or abandoned by
the sea, great quantities of huge ancient trees are constantly being
found everywhere beneath the ground. These are thought to have
been torn up by storms when the ocean covered this country long
after the time of Julius Caesar. I think that this happened in the
terrible and gigantic storms and winds that occurred in the year
860, three years before Charles the Bald elevated this state to the
level of a county (as will be recounted). The result, as it seems,
was that the ground, remaining so low and covered by water most
of the time, changed a great deal.

Because of its low and damp ground, this country produces very
little wheat or rye. Nevertheless it has such a great abundance of
them that it supplies other provinces, for these grains are shipped

1. Literally, the "Southern Sea," now called Ijsselmeer, "Ijssel Lake,"
since its separation from the North Sea by an enclosure dike.—*Ed.*

here from many regions, especially from Denmark and the Baltic. The country does not produce wine and yet there is plenty of it, and more is drunk here in proportion to the number of people than in any region where wine is produced. It is brought here from many places, especially from the Rhineland. Flax does not grow in this country and yet it produces more fine linen than any other region in the world, since it obtains flax from Flanders and a certain quantity from Liège and the Baltic, although this flax is not as fine. Holland does not produce wool and yet an enormous amount of woolen cloth, especially for ornamental purposes, is woven here from wool which it gets from England, Scotland, Spain, and a little from Brabant. It does not grow lumber and yet it builds more ships and dikes and other things made of wood than perhaps all the rest of Europe, importing it from the Baltic and elsewhere. The foundation of the country's fruitfulness lies in the pastureland for grazing and feeding cattle and the districts where herds are raised; there is livestock in abundance, especially horses, oxen, and cows. The horses are large and husky; while they are a bit heavy of head, they are still handsome and of good quality, especially for warfare. They get better all the time too, because efforts have been made for some time to improve the breed with Spanish cavalry horses and other light horses which are purchased for this purpose. . . . The oxen are handsome and huge, as are the cows, whose milk is made into so much cheese and butter that anyone who has not been here and seen it himself would never believe it. In truth the value of the cheese and butter production of Holland is correctly and accurately compared to the value of the spices that come into this country from Portugal, which, as already related in the description of Antwerp, amounts to more than a million in gold per year. Nor will this seem amazing to anyone who considers the following example. A single village of Holland called Assendelft, about a league from Beverwijk and two leagues from Haarlem, has four thousand cows which each year, taking winter and summer together, produce at least eight thousand "measures"[2] of milk. The quantity of milk reportedly produced by four other villages, Oostzaan, Westzaan, Krommenie, and Krommeniedijk, not far from Assendelft, is so great that I dare not describe it. Indeed, a

2. In Italian "lotti," which Guicciardini elsewhere describes in detail in its Dutch equivalent.—*Ed.*

survey was made not long ago by some important people, among
them Jan Benninck, a member of the Council of Holland, and it
was found that the quantity of milk produced each year by these
five villages, including Assendelft, was greater than the quantity of
Rhine wine shipped to Dordrecht, the staple for the entire country,
so that this is a marvelously huge amount. A great deal of butter
and cheese is distributed, first to the adjacent regions which consume an extraordinary amount, and also to Germany, England, and
Spain. Similarly, the huge number of herds which are exported
bring a great deal of money into the region. It is easy to calculate it
from the export duty which is paid at Gouda, which amounts to
more than three thousand ducats a year. Also, a tax of considerable
size is paid which brings in more than a million, not counting what
is collected on exports from other places as well as the vast quantity which is consumed within the land of Holland itself. The
country exists principally upon its fishing and shipping, which are
unceasing and extensive. These are the native arts of the Hollanders. Holland alone uses in fishing and shipping more than 800
good large sailing ships with from one to four or five sails, most
with three, and from 200 to 700 tons burden. It has more than 600
other ships and boats which they call fishing busses, from 100 to
200 tons and over.

The circumference of the region of Holland proper is about 60
leagues. It is not so large that if a man were set down in any part of
it, he could not reach the borders in six hours. Nevertheless it has
29 walled towns. These are Dordrecht, Haarlem, Delft, Leiden,
Gouda, and Amsterdam, which are the six principal towns; then
Enkhuizen, Hoorn, Alkmaar, Purmerend, Edam, Monnikendam,
Weesp, Naarden, Woerden, Oudewater, Schoonhoven, Ijsselstein,
Vianen, Leerdam, Asperen, Heuckelum, Gorinchem, Woudrichem,
Heusden, Rotterdam, Schiedam and, the smallest, Geertruidenberg
and Zevenbergen. In addition to these walled towns, it has various
other smaller towns, as Medemblik, Beverwijk, Muiden, Nieuw-
poort, Vlaardingen, and 's-Gravezande, which in former times
were all walled but because of discord and civil dissensions or for
other reasons have had their walls in great part or entirely dis-
mantled. Nevertheless they retain their privileges and status, just as
when they were walled. The country also has more than 400
villages, many of which, although not surrounded by walls, have
exactly the same characteristics and privileges as the towns; this is

particularly true of The Hague. . . . Outside this territory Holland has under its dominion various nearby islands, the most notable of which, beginning from the north, are Vlieland, Texel and Wieringen,[3] the last being given this name from the plant called "wier" [seaweed], the plentiful supply of which is used to build and maintain many dikes. Toward the east, in the gulf of the Zuider Zee, it has Urk and Ens[4] together with some villages. In the south, from the Merwede to the mouth of the Maas, it has the islands called Voorne, Goeree, and Sommelsdijk, which is also called Voorn,[5] and Corendijk with Piershil.[6]

3. No longer an island because of the drainage of surrounding lands.—Ed.
4. These now lie on Noordoostpolder, on the east bank of the Ijsselmeer. —Ed.
5. Overflakkee.—Ed.
6. The present island of Hoeksche Waard is intended.—Ed.

II Shadows Cast Before: The Reign of Charles V

Although Netherlanders in the later sixteenth century came to see the reign of Charles V (1506–1555) as a golden time of peace and plenty, it has become clear that the elements which broke out into the flames of civil war under his son, Philip (1555–1598) were already present. Not only was the subordination of the country's interests to those of Spain implicit in the elevation of Charles of Ghent to the thrones of Germany and Spain; the prince who ruled so many dominions, and so absolutely in Spain, had little sympathy for the traditional privileges of his subjects in the Low Countries. What Philip II attempted to complete, his father began.

3. Privileges of Subjects Confirmed

When Charles V came of age in 1515, he began his personal rule, at least in form, by swearing the traditional oath to uphold the privileges of the province of Brabant upon entering the city of Leuven (Louvain). The "Joyous Entry" (*Blijde Inkomst*), as it was called, dated back to the mid-fourteenth century and had been renewed and extended frequently thereafter. Although specifically applying to Brabant, it embodied the principles upheld by the people—which in this context means the clergy, the nobility, and the commoners—of the other Low Countries provinces.

Source: Jeanne Mennes, "De Staten van Brabant en de Blijde Inkomst van Kroonprins Filips in 1549," *Anciens Pays et Assemblées d'Etats*, XVIII (1959), pp. 56–58, 64–68, 72–78, 156–164. Translated from the Dutch by Herbert H. Rowen.

CHARLES, by the grace of God Prince of Spain, the Two Sicilies, Jerusalem, etc., Archduke of Austria, duke of Burgundy, Lorraine, Brabant, Styria, Carinthia, Carniola, Limburg, Luxemburg, and Gelderland, count of Flanders, Habsburg, Tyrol, Artois, Burgundy, the Palatinate of Hainaut, landgrave of Alsace, Margrave of Burgau and of the Holy Empire, count of Holland, Zeeland, Phiret, Kieburg, Namur, and Zutphen, lord of Friesland, Upper Windischermarch, Portenau, Salins, and Malines.

To all men present and future, greetings. For as it is proper and fitting for the prince and sovereign of a land to give and bestow the grace and gift of right and privileges to his good subjects and people, and mindful of the many and great services, the affection and the loyalty which our good people, the subjects in our lands of Brabant, Limburg, and our other lands Beyond the Maas [Meuse] often gave to our forefathers, the dukes and duchesses of Brabant, of blessed memory, such as good men owe to their rightful rulers, and confident that they will continue to give the same to us, we have granted, given, and affirmed in this Entry and reception in these aforesaid lands, and do grant, give, and affirm those privileges, points, and confirmations of rights as follow below, promising and taking an oath for ourselves, our heirs, and descendants, to maintain them and to have them maintained firmly and without interruption forever.

I.

Item, firstly, that we will be good judges and true lords over them and permit no violence or arbitrary action to be done to them in any way, and that we will not do or permit anything to be done to them outside the courts and the laws, but will treat all our prelates, houses of God, barons, nobles, good people and subjects of our cities, jurisdictions and lands of Brabant and Beyond the Maas in all things through the courts and according to the rights of the cities and the benches which have authority over them, and that these judges in our aforesaid lands must hold their sessions without any delay on any pretext of commission or omission, provided that these aforesaid judges may put off trials in lordships one time but no more. . . .

III.

Item, that as duke of Brabant and Limburg we shall never enter into any obligation affecting the lordship of these lands, wage war or raise loans, directly or indirectly, except with the counsel, will, and consent of our cities and the country of Brabant. And we shall not give our pledge or seal to any other acts by which our countries, boundaries, or cities, or any of their inhabitants, or any of their rights, liberties, or privileges might be injured or diminished or our countries and our subjects harmed in any way.

IV.

Item, that we accept the title and arms of Lorraine, Brabant, Limburg and of Margrave of the Holy Empire as established, and that we shall have a seal made and engraved in accordance with the aforesaid title and arms, with signs clearly distinguishing it from our other seals; and we may not change this seal nor give permission for a new seal to be engraved on the same model, except for good reason and with the consent of the three estates of our land of Brabant. This seal must always remain within this our land of Brabant, and never be taken away, and it shall be used to seal all acts concerning our lands of Brabant and Beyond the Maas, or their inhabitants, but for no other purpose. Also, letters concerning these matters shall be written by any of our secretaries assigned to Brabantine affairs and shall be signed by four members of our Council of Brabant.

V.

Item, that during our absences we shall appoint seven worthy persons, one of whom shall be the chancellor or keeper of the seals, a native of our aforesaid country of Brabant and competent in three languages, to wit: Latin, French, and Dutch, whose duty it shall be to guard our aforesaid seal. Four of them shall be native resident property owners in our aforesaid country of Brabant, or possessors of a peerage in this our country in their own right or through marriage. The remaining two to represent us in our Council are to be selected at our pleasure, provided that they know the Dutch language.

We undertake to commit the government of our aforesaid country in our absence to these seven. And when we are in our aforesaid countries of Brabant or Beyond the Maas, we shall conduct all our affairs concerning these countries of ours with the counsel of our aforesaid Council of Brabant.

And all who are to be councilors and secretaries to us or to our successors, before binding themselves in their conciliar or other office by the usual homage, fealty, and reverence to us or our successors, must pledge and promise to our three Estates, representing the whole country, that they will never use these offices to write, witness, or seal letters by which any of our country's cities, castles, people, revenues or lordships, on water or land, lying either on this or on the other side of the Maas, would be disturbed, mortgaged, sold, alienated, diminished, burdened, or in any way encumbered, surrendered or ceded in any manner, except by consent of the aforesaid three Estates. And should it nevertheless be discovered that any of our aforesaid councilors, keepers of the seal or secretaries, in Council, office, or service has been guilty of error or misconduct, we shall correct him in accordance with the counsel of the nobles and good cities of our aforesaid country of Brabant, or of the majority of them. . . .

LXIV.

Item, we further have confirmed and ratified and do confirm and ratify all other prelates, cloisters, houses of God, barons, knights, cities, franchises, and all our other subjects and good people of our lands of Brabant and Beyond the Maas in all their rights, liberties, privileges, charters, customs, usages and practices, which they now possess and were given and granted under seal by our forefathers, the dukes and duchesses, and also those which they have followed, practiced and continued, in particular the additional letter granted by the aforesaid late duke Philip, our great-great-grandfather, to the aforementioned three Estates at the time of his Entry, as well as two other letters granted them by our said great-great-grandfather, one of the date of September 20, 1450, and the other of November 21, 1457, and promise them jointly and separately to hold and keep these for ever, for ourselves and our heirs and successors, without violating them or doing or permitting anything to be done against them in any way, and further declare for ourselves, our heirs and descendants, that we shall never allege or permit to be alleged that we are not bound to maintain the aforesaid liberties, rights, privileges, charters, customs, usages, and practices which we here in general have confirmed and ratified, on the grounds that we did not specifically and individually give, grant, or promise the previous points and articles, and we do not wish that they shall suffer or meet any harm, hindrance, or prejudice on this account. And because we intend and desire that all these aforesaid points, articles, gifts, promises, confirmations, and assurances shall continue to be observed strictly and without interruption for all time, we have therefore promised in good faith and sworn upon the Holy Bible to the prelates, cloisters and houses of God, barons, knights, cities, and franchises, and all our other good people and subjects of our aforesaid lands of Brabant and Beyond the Maas, and their heirs and descendants, that we, our heirs and successors, shall forever stand firmly by them and never do anything or permit anything to be done against them in any manner. And should it happen that we, our heirs or successors, should by our own action or that of others violate them in whole or in part, in any manner whatsoever, we consent and concede to our aforesaid prelates, barons, knights, cities, franchises and to all our other subjects aforesaid, that they need not do us, our heirs or successors any services, nor obey us in any other things we might need or which we might request of them, until such time as we shall have corrected the mistaken course hitherto pursued toward them, and have completely abandoned and reversed it; and for this purpose we will decree and declare that all officers installed in their offices in a way contrary to the Entry of our aforementioned great-great-grandfather Duke Philip[1] shall be dismissed immediately; and further that for the future, too, any innovation contrary to established custom which might be attempted shall be null and void, nor shall it be upheld in the future. All this is granted without guile.

To the contractual and perpetual establishment of these things, we have had our seal appended hereto. Given in our city of Louvain, January 23, in the year of Our Lord 1514[2] according to the style of writing of our court of Brabant.

4. A Rebellious City Crushed

No city in the Low Countries had a more turbulent history of assertive independence and domestic strife than Ghent, in Flanders. The rebellion in Ghent in 1539 was an endeavor to maintain its privileges against the centralizing and authoritarian government of the officials of Charles V, specifically against a tax to which it had not consented. What is particularly striking in this account of the rebellion by an inhabitant of Lille—whose name has not come down to us, but who was wholly on the side of Charles V—is the utilization of the dissatisfactions of the poor by a segment of the ruling patriciate as a weapon against the competing authorities; one cannot but be reminded of the relation of the Jacobins during the French Revolution to the Paris crowd.

1. Philip the Good, r. 1419–67.—Ed.
2. Old Style; 1515 New Style.—Ed.

Source: L. P. Gachard, ed., *Relation des Troubles de Gand sous Charles Quint, par un anonyme* (Brussels: M. Hayez, 1846), pp. 9–11, 17–18, 20, 27–28, 33–34, 36–40, 62–64, 153–154. Translated from the French by Herbert H. Rowen.

ALTHOUGH PEACE, that great boon for the whole country, had just been made between the Emperor, our Lord, and the King of France, the Ghenters continued to keep close watch night and day in all the streets and quarters of the town, in the civic guards' quarters and in the various guild-houses. Everyone armed himself as if there existed an open war in the Low Countries directed only against them, as if the enemy had invaded Flanders and laid siege to the town of Ghent.

To hear them talk and see them strut around, it seemed that they were not afraid of anyone anywhere who wished to cause them harm, no matter how great he was, nay, they were not even afraid of their own prince. These were the very words, or very close to them, spoken by many of the rabble and the burghers, young and old alike but mainly the youths, who are always quicker and bolder in speech than their elders. They defended whatever they said and did with petty arguments: they would act properly and justly and establish law and order in this town of Ghent, in the county of Flanders and then in all the other provinces of the Netherlands. The wicked rebels and rascals told the simple good people that better times would come, there would be more business and jobs in the country and the city, and goods would sell better than before or at the time, and that as a result of these and other measures, everything would sell at lower prices and therefore the people would live better and with greater freedom than they had had. The simple folk in Ghent and the surrounding districts gladly lent their ears, for they had always wanted freedom and were ready to believe that it would be achieved right away. But the wicked men had something quite different in mind, the very opposite of what they told the simple, good people. They did not think about what would result from their deeds but hoped only that they would bring better times; whereas those wicked rebels desired only a pretext to bring the rabble, whose only purpose was pillage, into the city and district of Ghent. Nonetheless, misled by what they had been told and hoping for better times, everyone in Ghent was ready to support these wicked men, knowing nothing of their purposes but believing and hoping that everything would turn out well. Moved by this hope, the Ghenters behaved as if they were the princes and lords of the county of Flanders who had only to say, "We want it," to have something done. And they did things contrary to the authority and supremacy of the Emperor in his capacity as Count of Flanders, who was their good prince and sovereign lord. A number of captains of the common people began to take the lead in Ghent. They sent some of their number with letters to other towns in Flanders, exhorting and inciting them not to pay their share of the contribution of four hundred thousand gold guilders but instead to join with them and to enjoy every advantage. There was no need to be afraid, they wrote, because the Ghenters would protect them against everyone.

The cities of the region were persuaded by the Ghenters' fine words and promises. Some, like Courtrai, Audenarde, and others, where great divisions and disturbances also occurred, listened and followed Ghent. Other towns which had no pretext of disorders listened to the Ghenters but waited to see whether they succeeded before they themselves acted. This also happened in a number of smaller towns. Indeed, the whole county of Flanders was then quite ready for riot and rebellion. The Ghenters had them take a count of their men and distributed them into civic guards, including men too old to do much. The Ghenters and those who joined them placed their confidence wholly in the force and strength of the civic guards, for there were great numbers of people in the Low Countries who had wanted nothing more than to become members of these companies, which would have been a great pity if they had been able to get in. But God in his mercy took his measures and did not permit it. . . .

[Description of the arrest and death of several leading burghers in Ghent at the hands of the rebels.]

It was around this time that the Ghenters, in their wicked folly, tore into a thousand pieces an ordinance and statute issued by the Emperor as Count of Flanders in the year 1515, in accordance with the Peace of Cadzand, which was called the *chalfvel*[3] (which in our language means "calfskin") because it was written on parchment, and was signed by His Majesty's own hand and sealed with his great seal. Among other things it strictly prohibited the holding of any illegal assemblies likely to result in disturbances, or even to

3. The *Kalfvel,* as the Declaration of Charles V of April 11, 1515, was called.—*Ed.*

speak such words as could create disorder, under pain of major punishments stated at length in the said ordinance. The rebels in Ghent wanted to destroy and nullify this ordinance because it specifically forbade the wicked things they were doing and wished to do, and because they did not wish to be contradicted in anything but only to hear their own mad and evil fancies, for there was no reasoning with them. This is why this ordinance brought out into the open the great wrath, chagrin, and ill-will directed not only against the Queen Regent[4] who governed the Low Countries for her brother, the Emperor, and against provincial governors and the members of her council, but also, as it appeared, against their count himself, who had issued the statute, for they put its pieces in their caps to wear, and they at once proclaimed that the statute and ordinance was henceforth void and would not be enforced, for it was not to their interest and they had violated it so gravely. . . .

Many good and notable burghers, gentlemen, officials of the Emperor, merchants and other worthy men of the city of Ghent, seeing that things were going very badly and likely to get even worse, got away as best as they could manage, but not without great peril to their lives, and their property was seized at once; but they preferred to lose their possessions in the city rather than run such danger every day from wicked men and see and hear the suffering. For there was no order or control over the common people, nor any justice save what they wanted and intended. . . .

The Emperor, who was living at this time in his kingdom of Spain, was informed by the Queen, his sister, of what was happening in Ghent, where he had been born about forty years before. His Majesty had already been informed several times of the refusal of the Ghenters to pay their share and quota in the grant to His Majesty of 400,000 gold guilders. The Emperor had written sealed letters to them about this several times but they disregarded them completely. He was also informed that the Ghenters wished to contribute soldiers from their city instead of paying their contribution in money, to which His Majesty would not consent. Whenever he received such information, he had always written to the Queen to tell her what he wanted done in this affair, for it was of the greatest importance, for whatever the Queen had done had been by His Majesty's command. There were other good reasons to act, for these were things of great importance and consequence.

4. Mary of Hungary.—*Ed.*

When the latest reports came, the Emperor again sent sealed letters to his people of Ghent, in which His Majesty ordered them explicitly to restore peace, to hold no assemblies, and to cause no disturbances or do any other things which might displease him, and to obey the Queen, his sister, on pain of incurring his indignation and receiving heavy penalties. If they did not do so, he would take measures which would cause them much sorrow and which they would never forget. As you shall hear, this is indeed what His Majesty was to do when the time and place came. The Ghenters paid little or no attention to these letters or these threats, acting like men without understanding who did not think ahead to what would come of their deeds and what would happen to them. They believed that there was no prince strong enough to defeat them and reduce them to obedience. They even refused to believe that these letters came from the Emperor, but said that the Queen had written them in His Majesty's name so as to shake and frighten them. Many believed this and hence paid no account to these letters. . . .

[Description of the unsuccessful mission of Adriaen de Croy, Count of Roeulx, to Ghent on the Emperor's behalf, in late October and early November, 1539.]

Soon after the departure of the Count of Roeulx from Ghent, where he saw that there was no good reason to hope for the situation to improve and because he feared for his own safety, the Ghenters renewed their disorders. Their riotousness was now even worse than before. Things went so badly in the town that for a time it was forbidden to ring the bells for the workers and no one opened shop, so that it seemed like High Easter in the town, with all the houses and stores closed. This caused extraordinary fear among the good people who were still in the city. Most of them wished that they were thirty leagues away, even if they could have only half of their possessions but had their wives and children and families with them, for they were every day in great peril of losing all their possessions and their lives too, which mattered most. They were never safe, day or night, and were in continual fear. Everyone kept his ears open and good guard in his house. It was a very piteous time. May God protect us every one from such things, for a people in rebellion is a very great danger. But when the Emperor came, a great change occurred. . . .

The disorders began among the common people at the instigation of these burghers, who told them many things that were not true and aroused them about different matters which the common people would never have thought of by themselves and who would not say and do the things they did without the complicity of well-informed people. It is an evil thing to arouse a people, for they do not settle back to peace when one desires. It is more important to keep a people at peace than to arouse it, for the fury of a people is no little thing and one should be on one's guard against it. But these burghers and rich men did not believe that these disorders would turn against them as happened, with threats to their lives and the looting of their wealth which was the intention of all the poor commoners. Some of these poor men did not even remain still as they walked the streets but when they met rich men told them in great envy and hatred: "On your way! The time is near when we will own your wealth in our turn. You have been wealthy enough and will be poor like us in your turn. You will know what it is to be poor and we will know what it is to be rich and to wear your fine robes, and you will wear ours, which are shabby and cheap." And they said other similar insults to the rich men, who thereupon decided to be silent and patient and speak meekly, for otherwise they were in great danger of their lives.

And when these burghers of Ghent saw that matters had come out this way and were going so badly, they greatly repented that they had put these common people in the position which they now had and they would have gladly taken it away from them if they had had any way to do it. But now it was too late, for the people had gone too far in their rebellion and had become the complete masters of the city. It was impossible to take power from them, for they wanted to know everything and to have an accounting for everything, even of many things which had happened in the city thirty years before, and of many other affairs which they searched out from the past and brought forward without any foundation or reason. Whatever they thought of, they wanted done; it did not matter whether it was good or evil. Some burghers rescued their best furnishings and records from the city of Ghent as best they could, but only with great difficulty and danger of losing everything, even their lives, which is the main thing. A close guard had been put on the city to prevent such movements, and it was strictly forbidden to transport any goods outside the city, and even burghers who lived outside in country houses were ordered to return to the city with all their goods. Those who came back were few, which was wise, for those who were able to escape with their goods did so and those who could not remained in very great danger. Some hid their goods in the ground and other secret places as best they could, while others were so frightened and at their wit's end that they hardly knew what they were doing and did not rescue anything, but were so surprised that they took no steps to save any of their things; some have even died since as a result of their fears and repeated attacks of curdled blood, with its attendant grave maladies. It was a sorry time: may God in his mercy save each and all of us from the likes of it!

These burghers had believed that this upheaval would turn out quite differently, according to their own purposes and dreams, and enabling them to accomplish aims which were not at all good. God therefore permitted events to turn out exactly contrary to their hopes, with great pain, damage, and even with danger to their lives. Thus, thinking to take revenge on others, they failed to accomplish their wicked purposes and the revenge turned upon themselves; as usually happens to those who plot the fall of others, they themselves had a fall. But, despite its bad beginning, this upheaval ended rather mercifully, for that Tuesday passed without bloodshed, which was the work of God, who had pity upon his people thanks to the prayers of some good persons, churchmen and laymen, of whom there are many in the city of Ghent. They too were in great danger from the wicked men who went about daily in bands and squads and made great threats against them and compelled them to give a part of what they demanded, which was food and drink and sometimes money; and the same thing was done to the burghers and the rich, which greatly vexed one and all, for no one gladly gives away what is his own under duress. They therefore repented of their earlier foolish opinions which had come down to them from father to son, and also of having gradually aroused the common people and having enabled them to do harm. For now they saw that everything had turned against them, quite contrary to what they had wanted, and they might not just lose their property but were in great peril of their lives, for this was what the poor common folk were moving toward.

And for these reasons and to avert all other dangers, these burghers and rich men, with the entire government and others, thereupon joined the party of the Emperor, at the side of his

adherents and the men of good will. . . . And after that day, the
rebels ceased to be as bold as before and began to quiet down a
little and be more moderate, which was a great boon to the whole
city as it awaited the arrival of the Emperor. . . . And after that
day the burghers and worthy men began to play the master more
audaciously than they had done before and the rebels began to
subside, and each drew to its own side and made excuses to the
others. This was a good beginning for the worthy men, who
nonetheless did not fail to stay on the alert and keep close watch in
their houses, ready for action if the need arose, and thus they began
to regain sway and courage. The reason that these burghers and
the like showed themselves now to be good adherents of the party
of their prince was more fear for their lives and the loss of their
goods than good will toward him, which they had scarcely ever
shown before. . . .

[The decision of the Emperor to return to the Low Countries to
take charge of affairs in person is described, then his trip across
France as the guest of King Francis I, and his arrival at Valenciennes, in the Netherlands. The Ghenters, fearing what he would
do, sent a delegation to him, which he received harshly. He then
went to Brussels, en route to Ghent, where he made his entry of
February 14, 1540, New Style.]

The Emperor entered this city of Ghent with his train at the
beginning of Lent in the year 1539 [Old Style]. The entry lasted
more than six hours, apart from the transport of supplies, which
had begun some days before, lasted all that day and continued for
several more days. Those who entered the city were eight hundred
men-at-arms of the Netherlands troops (which, with the archers
included, amounts to from three to four thousand horse), all carrying their lances at the ready; and four thousand German infantry,
almost all properly equipped, pikemen with the pikes on their
shoulders, halberdiers with their halberds, and the remainder har-
quebusiers, each with his harquebus in his hand along with everything else needed to use it. These troops, both infantry and
cavalry, were all ready and equipped for combat if the need arose.
With them came the Emperor, accompanied by many cardinals,
archbishops, bishops, and other great ecclesiastical lords and
princes, as well as many great princes, dukes, marquesses, counts,
barons, grandmasters, and lords, as well as most of the knights of
his Order of the Golden Fleece and others, and a very great

number of noblemen from every quarter and country, Spain, Naples, Sicily, Italy, Germany, as well as the Netherlands and other lands where His Majesty held sway, along with various ambassadors from our Holy Father the Pope, the kings of France, England, Portugal, and Poland, as well as from many princes of the Empire and Italy, and from the republic of Venice and other countries, provinces, and potentates; and there were also the members of His Majesty's household and his domestic officers, with the archers of his bodyguard and the halberdiers of his guard, on good mounts and well armed.

The Emperor, entering his city of Ghent in such company, with such might and on such a footing, greatly astounded and frightened the inhabitants. There was much reason for it, for this was not an Entry which gave them much pleasure but one of fear and sadness. The Entries which His Majesty had made before had not been made with such might and force but were all friendliness and pleasantness. Nevertheless the Ghenters performed their duties in the usual fashion. The members of the two benches of government, the grand dean, the dean of the weavers, the burghers and other notables and commoners of the city, went with all reverence and humility to greet the Emperor as their count, in the manner in which this had always been done, welcoming His Majesty into his city of Ghent and presenting him with its keys. . . .

[Military measures of the Emperor, followed by a delay in his announcement of the city's punishment until the arrival of his brother Ferdinand, his elected successor as emperor. Only some days later did the arrest, imprisonment, and punishment of the principal culprits begin. This was followed by the abolition of their customary law, the execution of nine prisoners, a plea of the leading Ghenters for mercy, which Charles met with warnings against the Ghenters' rebellious habits. He followed this with a decision to build a citadel within the city, followed on April 29 by the formal abolition of the city's traditional privileges and self-government.]

When the Emperor pronounced this sentence against Ghent and issued his ordinance concerning the city, the Ghenters were immensely shocked and afraid. They had good reason to be, but it gave them no comfort that they themselves were the cause of what was happening.

The sentence and ordinance were not to their advantage at all but rather greatly to their detriment. Where previously it had been the greatest city in the whole county, they now became the least. Thanks to their crimes and abuses they lost what they had loved so much and guarded so well over so many long years, their privileges, and with them all their ancient customs and usages. They were deprived of these and also of all the other powers, franchises, and liberties which they had held in such number before. The Ghenters had possessed and used these with great presumption, believing that no other city was comparable to this city of Ghent and themselves. They thought that there was no prince upon the earth great and mighty enough to dominate them and that even the Count of Flanders could do little or nothing without them. Great as they had been in their own estimation, so great now was their wrath against this sentence and ordinance made and pronounced by the Emperor to their great detriment, scandal, and reputation for all time; but none of them dared say one word of what they would have said, and what some would have done, if they dared. But the fine cavalry and infantry and the large numbers of troopers from every state, region, and country who were distributed and quartered in every part of the city prevented them from doing anything. The Ghenters were not even able to assemble to offer any riot or resistance; all their weapons and the artillery which belonged to the city or the guilds were taken from them, as were the guildhalls in which they were accustomed to meet and make disturbances, and where they kept their artillery and other weapons which belonged to them and had been kept from past wars and riots against their counts. Thus they were able to offer no resistance but could only mumble silently among themselves, but without seeming to, for they all feared for their lives; but most were very angry inside. Nevertheless they had to display patience, even if only under constraint, for there was nothing else they could do. Willingly or not, the Ghenters soon met the terms of the sentence. They handed over all their privileges, although with extreme regret, for they loved and esteemed these privileges more than anything else, which they had always thought made them the sovereigns and the superiors over everyone else.

III Origins of the "Troubles"

After Charles V, worn out by the cares of a world-wide empire, abdicated at Brussels in 1555, he was succeeded in the Low Countries, as in Spain, by his elder son, Philip II. Where the father was a man who combined stubbornness on what he saw as essentials with flexibility on tactics, the son was a narrower man, equally tenacious but lacking the familiarity with local conditions that Charles had acquired by constant travel. Philip was a Spaniard through and through, where the emperor had been a European and a dynast above all. Philip remained in the Low Countries until 1559, when the French acknowledged their defeat on the battlefield by accepting the Peace of Cateau-Cambrésis; then he sailed to Spain, never to return. He had acquired no fondness for the Netherlanders, no intimacy with the great nobles and the wider reaches of the people which could tie the nation and the king to each other by affection and understanding. He left his half-sister, Margaret of Parma, as governor-general, but the real head of his government was Antoine Perrenot, bishop of Arras, who became Cardinal Granvelle in 1561, when new bishoprics were established in the country and he was set over them as archbishop of Mechelen (Malines). All the forces that Charles V had successfuly kept down—resistance to persecution of heretics, localism and provincialism hostile to centralization within the Low Countries, and an incipient nationalism equally hostile to foreign overlordship—welled up against the person of Granvelle.

With the year 1566, the resistance of the Low Countries to King Philip's authority suddenly became deeper, broader, and edged with violence. Until then the resistance had been primarily the affair of the great nobles led by William of Nassau, Prince of Orange. They had sought to cow Margaret of Parma, to drive out Granvelle and eliminate the *Consulta* which he headed and which was the country's real government, and to bend the king to their will. They demanded that the Council of State, which they dominated, be given effective authority, and that religious persecution be halted; but in the fall of 1565, the king finally made his will known, and it was blunt rejection of their demands. While the great nobles hesitated, the lesser nobility, in the grip of economic hardships, and the common people, their miseries intensified by food shortages and soaring grain prices, acted.

5. The "Troubles" Begin

The close ties between the nobility and the merchants in the Low Countries disturbed Granvelle from the very beginning of his domination of the government in Brussels as the principal "minister" under Margaret of Parma in 1559. In August, 1559, he drew up for his own use a summary and explanation of the troubles which were already visible there. He was particularly disturbed by the alliance between the nobles and the merchants—the key political and economic forces in the country; his explanation of its origin, although unflattering to both groups, is perceptive.

Source: Cardinal Granvelle, "Mémoire des sources et causes des troubles des Pays d'Enbas, des progrès d'iceulx, pour, si après il estoit besoing en donner plus particulier compte, y pouvoir avoir recours," in: [Guillaume] Groen van Prinsterer, ed., *Archives ou Correspondance inédite de la Maison d'Orange-Nassau*, First series, vol. I (2nd ed.) (Leiden: S. and J. Luchtmans, 1841), pp. 37–39. Translated from the French by Herbert H. Rowen.

THE FIRST and the principal [cause] is the will of God and his infallible and irrefutable decision to punish the sin of insolence. This country was already too prosperous, so that the people were not able to resist luxury and gave in to every vice, exceeding the proper limits of their stations. The nobles wished to be adorned like kings and lived beyond their means. They sank into debt as a result and were no longer able to support themselves in the style to which they had grown accustomed; they found their resources eaten up by the interest which they owed to merchants. They could see no better way out of their situation than to change the government and avoid the authority of the courts of law, which would not be able to compel them to pay their debts. The authority of these courts had been greatly reduced by the wars, and the nobles possessed greater influence in public offices than was proper, and they gave harsh and outrageous treatment to the officers of the courts who came to enforce sentences upon them. The Bishop of Arras [Granvelle], seeing the harm which could ensue from such indebtedness, with the lords so much in arrears, wrote to His Majesty (as his letters will prove) that if they could be discharged of their debts for the sum of two millions, it was his opinion that His Majesty should discharge them so as to avoid greater losses, except that he feared that they would continue their superfluous expenditures in the hope that His Majesty would always accept responsibility for paying off their very exorbitant debts, and that they would not, so far as we can see, use the ransoms of the French prisoners which they had bought from the common soldiers (a practice which in truth is improper and our good fathers in former times would not have approved), and which now amount to more than two millions, to remedy their situation but would indulge instead in even more lavish expenditure. So that we may understand how large these debts were, the Prince of Orange admitted to the late Queen of Hungary[1] at Furnod[2] before she left for Spain that he owed 800,000 francs, and the expenditures which he has made since in order to build his reputation and win supporters have been much larger. Merchants also made unnecessary expenditures without limit in an effort to equal and surpass the nobles and became their companions, and the nobles accepted them and paid them honor, attending their banquets and visiting their homes, in order to obtain money from them to meet their own expenses. This is why, when the States General met at such an unfortunate time, the nobles and merchants reached agreement and took away the management of taxation from the financial officials and put it into the hands of the merchants. The merchants then lent money to the nobles and supplied pay for their soldiers, while making their own profit from the use of tax monies. Finally, when the soldiers became dissatisfied, this became a pretext for alienating the affection which the soldiers owed to His Majesty, their prince and natural Lord, and for bringing them into their own service; they made a show of compassion for them and took care of their complaints, offering aid and placing responsibility upon the king and his ministers in order to get them hated.

Great harm, especially in the matter of religion, also resulted from intercourse with foreigners, which could not be avoided because of the needs of commerce. Various Germans, Italians, Burgundians, and others among the nobles made use of the Netherlanders, turned them into dangerous men, preaching freedom to them and blinding them with a belief in their own greatness and that they did not have to accept being governed but should seek to govern themselves. No little assistance was given in opening the

1. Queen Regent Mary.—*Ed.*
2. Probably Furnes or Tournai.—*Ed.*

way to these many evils by some nobles, Spaniards and Flemings as well as others, who were brought up with His Majesty in his chamber, and who whispered into his ear that it was not proper that a prince like himself should be given to a few persons to govern and guide him, and that it would be more fitting to establish a Council of State, formed of a goodly number of the leading nobles, who understand affairs better and would direct them so as to create greater contentment among the subjects. They even put . . .[3] regarding the good Queen Mary, saying that she took it upon herself to attempt to do everything, that she wished harm to the nation, and that she could do what she wished if she remained at the head of the government of the country, and that she did not judge them according to their worth but gave her hand above all others to the Marquis de Berges[4] and that she displayed remarkable ingratitude, for he had been brought up by her as if he were her own son, and she had given the bishopric of Liège to his brother [Robert], who had in truth little merit. But the marquis understood very well that if he governed the Lady Mary, she would enable him to achieve his harmful purposes.

6. A Band of Beggarly Nobles

A group of noblemen, mostly young and mostly of the lower ranks of their order, came together early in December, 1565, in Brussels to hold Reformed religious services. From their meeting developed a league— called in the language of the time a "Compromise," because they were under a common oath—which received the support, testified by signatures, of noblemen from every part of the Low Countries, including some Catholics and a few of higher rank, notably Louis of Nassau, brother of William of Orange and a Lutheran, and Charles of Mansfeld, a Catholic. Orange himself and other magnates did not join the Compromise, but its menace compelled Margaret to seek their counsel. She permitted some two hundred unarmed members of the league to present a petition against the Inquisition on April 5; during the ceremony, Berlaymont, a magnate who remained a fervent Catholic and faithful to Philip, whispered to her that these shabby petitioners were only "beggars" (gueux, in French). The scurrilous name was taken up as an ironic boast by the leaguers, and then "Gueux" became a general name for the resisters during the next decade. The dismayed Margaret sent two distinguished noblemen to Spain to present the case

3. Unreadable in the manuscript. Probably something like "suspicions into his head."—Ed.
4. Jean, Lord of Glymes.—Ed.

against the Inquisition to the king in person. Following is the text of the oath sworn by the members of the Compromise.

Source: Lacroix, ed., *Œuvres de Ph. de Marnix de Sainte Alde-gonde: Écrits politiques et historiques.* (Brussels: Fr. van Meenen, 1859), pp. 19–22. Translated from the French by Herbert H. Rowen.

To ALL who shall see these presents, know that we who have put our signatures below have been told and have learned with adequate assurances that a host of foreigners—men without any concern for the welfare and prosperity of these Low Countries, with no care for the glory and honor of God or for the public interest but desiring only to satisfy their own ambitions and avarice even at the expense of the King and all his subjects, although they falsely pleaded their great zeal to maintain the Catholic faith and the union of the people—have nevertheless managed to win over His Majesty by their well-turned remonstrances and false teachings, so that he has been persuaded, in violation of his oaths and of the hope which he always nourished in us, not only to refrain from moderating the edicts already issued concerning religion but even to reinforce them and to introduce the Inquisition among us in all its strength. Not only is this Inquisition iniquitous and contrary to all laws of God and man, in its barbarity exceeding the worst practices of tyrants; it cannot but result in great dishonor to God's name and in the utter ruin and desolation of all these Low Countries. This would be all the more true because, under cover of a few persons' lying hypocrisy, it would destroy all public law and order and all equity, completely weaken the sanction and respect for the ancient laws, customs, and ordinances which have been observed from time immemorial, and deprive the States of the country of any freedom to express their opinions; it would abolish all ancient privileges, liberties, and immunities and thereby not only make the burghers and common people of this country wretched and everlasting slaves of the Inquisitors, who are themselves men of no quality, but would also compel the magistrates, officials, and the entire nobility to submit to the mercy of their inquiries and searches, and in the end it would expose every loyal subject of the King to continued and open peril of his life and property. Not only would the honor of God and the Holy Catholic faith (which they claim to be

defending) be gravely involved therein, but also the majesty[5] of
the King, our head, would be lessened and he would face great
danger of losing his entire state, for ordinary business would come
to a halt, the trades would be abandoned, the garrisons of the
frontier towns neglected, and the people incited to continual sedition. In a word, nothing could result from it but horrible derange-
ment and disorder everywhere.

Having carefully weighed all these things and having fully
considered and taken into account our callings and the duty to
which we are all bound as faithful vassals of His Majesty and
especially as men of gentle birth, being all in this regard His
Majesty's helpers by our prompt and willing service in maintaining
his authority and greatness and in providing for the welfare and
safety of the country, we have come to the judgment, which we
still hold, that we cannot fulfil our duty except by eliminating
these wrongs while at the same time providing for the safety of our
property and persons so that we may not become the prey of those
who wish to become rich at the expense of our blood and our
goods under the pretext of religion. For this reason we have
decided to form a holy and lawful confederation and alliance by
which we promise to bind ourselves mutually under solemn oath to
use all our efforts to prevent the reception or introduction of this
Inquisition in any way, open or concealed, under any pretext or in
any disguise whatever, whether it be called inquisition, visitation,
edicts, or otherwise, but to extirpate and eradicate it completely as
the mother and the cause of all disorders and injustices. We have
before our eyes the example of the people of the kingdom of
Naples, who have rejected it to the great relief and repose of their
entire country. Nonetheless we protest in good conscience before
God and all men that we seek nothing which may in any way turn
to God's dishonor or the diminution of the grandeur and the
majesty of the King or his states; on the contrary, our purpose is
only to maintain the King in his state and to preserve in it all good
order and law, resisting to the best of our ability every kind of
sedition, popular tumult, monopoly, factiousness, or partisanship.
We have promised and sworn and do now promise and swear to
uphold this confederation and alliance as sacred and inviolable for

5. Meaning "sovereignty," in accordance with sixteenth century usage.—
Ed.

all time, without any break, as long as we live. We take God the sovereign lord as witness of our consciences that neither in deed nor in word, neither directly nor indirectly, will we knowingly and willingly contravene this confederation in any fashion whatever. And, in order to ratify this alliance and confederation and to make it stable and firm for all time, we have promised and do promise each other full assistance with our bodies and our goods, as brothers and faithful companions, joining hands so that none among us and our confederates may be investigated, harassed, molested or persecuted in any way, either in our lives or our property, for any cause emanating from this Inquisition or based in any way upon the edicts favoring it, or indeed because of this present confederation. And, in the event that anyone, in any way whatever, visit any molestation or persecution upon any of our brothers and allies, we have promised and sworn and do promise and swear to help him with our lives and our property, and in fact to do everything we can, sparing nothing and avoiding all evasions and subterfuges, just as if we were involved in person; with a specific and quite express understanding that we will in no way be exempted or absolved from this, our confederation, because the said molesters or persecutors may try to cover their persecutions by some other pretense or pretext (for instance, if they claim that they are only punishing rebellion or some such pretext), until it has been demonstrated in fact to us that these reasons are true. We maintain this position especially because we hold that in such cases it cannot be claimed that the crime of rebellion has been committed when its source proceeds from a holy zeal and praiseworthy desire to maintain the glory of God, the majesty of the King, the public tranquility and the safety of our lives and goods. Nonetheless we agree and mutually promise that in such an event each of us will follow the common opinion of all his brothers and allies, or of those who will be given such duties, in order that this sacred union may be maintained among us and that what will be done will be more certain and stable because it is done with common agreement. In witness whereof and in assurance of this confederation and alliance, we have invoked and do invoke the most sacred name of God, the Sovereign Lord, who created the sky and the earth, as our judge who sees into our consciences and thoughts and knows that this is our decision and resolution. We most humbly pray that by His power from on high He will keep us firm and steady and give us such prudence and discretion of spirit that, always possessing good and mature counsel, we may achieve our purpose with a good and happy success, bringing glory to His name, to the service of His Majesty, the King, and to the welfare and safety of the public. Amen.

H. de Brederode, Louis of Nassau
Charles, Count of Mansfeld

7. *The Beggarly Poor*

The year 1566 was marked by famine, which reached a height during the Summer. The anxieties of hungry men heightened the fears of Calvinists—often the selfsame men—that they would not be able to continue their prayer meetings in the fields—"hedge sermons" (*hage-preken*), as they were called—when the weather worsened. On August 10 (not August 14, as in the selection) in the small town of Steen-voorde in western Flanders, a mob of Calvinists assaulted the town church, destroying stained glass, sculpture, and other works of reli-gious art. The movement, which spread with the speed of rumor and imitation to other towns and provinces, reaching Groningen in the extreme North a month later, received the name of the "Iconoclasm" (*Beeldenstorm* or Image-Breaking). It expressed both the class hatreds of the poor and the desire of the Calvinists to have assured places of worship shorn of the "idolatry" which religious art meant for them. With it, the conflict between Philip and the Netherlands took a new turn. The nobility, fearing for their own leadership within the coun-try, began to look over their shoulders in their resistance to the king; he for his part decided to crush the resistance once and for all, and sent the Duke of Alva with a powerful army of Spanish regulars to the Low Countries the next year. Alva took over command of government as well as of military repression from Margaret at the end of 1567. The following selection is a description of the Iconoclasm, particuarly in the great port city of Antwerp, by the great seventeenth-century Protestant historian of the Dutch Reformation, Gerard Brandt.

Source: Gerard Brandt, *The History of the Reformation and Other Ecclesiastical Transactions in and about the Low Coun-tries, From the Beginning of the Eighth Century, Down to the Famous Synod of Dort, inclusive.* (2 Vols.; London: Timothy Childs, 1720), Vol. I, pp. 191–194.

The plundering of the Churches, that dreadful Tumult, not unlike the so frequent Rebellions of the *Jews*, and the Storm of the

Iconoclasts, or Image-breakers, that spread it self over Greece, began in *West Flanders* on the 14th of August, 1566, the day which preceded the great Festival of the *Papists,* the Ascension of the Virgin *Mary.*

Some few of the vilest of the Mob, to whom several Thieves and Whores had joined themselves, were those that began the Dance, being hallooed on by no body knows whom. Their arms were, Staves, Hatchets, Hammers, Ladders, Ropes, and other tools more proper to demolish than to fight with; some few were provided with Guns and Swords. At first (being emboldened by the absence of the Count of Egmont, the Governour of that Province, who had been called to Court by the Regent the Lady *Margaret*) they attacked the Crosses and Images that had been erected in the great Roads of the Country; next, those in Villages; and lastly, those in the Towns and Cities: All the Chappels, Churches, and Convents which they found shut, they forced open, breaking, tearing, and destroying all the Images, Pictures, Shrines, and other consecrated things they met with: nay, some did not scruple to lay their hands upon Librairies, Books, Writings, Monuments, and even the dead bodies in Churches and Churchyards. Swift as lightning the evil diffused it self, insomuch that in the space of three days above four hundred Churches were plundered. In some places the Magistrates themselves pulled down the Images, to prevent the Mob from doing the same; whereupon, when they valued themselves for their foresight in this matter, the President *Viglius* told them, that, *insaniebant cum ratione, they had been wisely mad.* In other places, this wild rage of the Mob was curbed by power and prudent order. . . .

The Government of *Antwerp* mistrusting that in the absence of the Prince of *Orange,* who had been just then summoned to *Brussels* to the Regent, the storm against Images might blow likewise that way, the rather because of the Fair-time, and the number of strangers that resorted thither, they caused the Image of the Virgin *Mary* (which otherwise used to be exposed for a week together on that occasion) to be removed from the body of the Church into the Choir, that it might give no offence. But their good intentions produced bad effects, and their care for the publick peace was perverted to publick tumults; for the Mob observing the fears of the Government, began to grow insolent; and some of them, in a sarcastical way, asked the Image, whether her fright had driven her so far from her post? and whether she would join in crying, *Vive les Gueux,* &c.? A parcel of young Lads playing about the Pulpit, one of them went into it, and began to mimick the preaching of the Monks and Priests; some were for hearing, others for pulling him down, but he defended himself with his feet against them, till at last a young Schipper went and threw him down headlong. The Men espoused the Boy's quarrel, and one of them wounded the said Schipper with a Dagger. After much ado, by the intervention of the *Scout*,[6] and the Officers that belonged to the Church, the Mob was prevailed upon to clear the place, and the doors were immediately shut, and so remained that day.

The Magistrates, (whether it was that their courage and prudence forsook them at that juncture) tho' they had the whole night following to consider what they should do, could resolve upon nothing to stifle the smoking Embers of Mutiny. Nay, they even neglected to feel the pulse of the Citizens and Militia, whether they were inclinable to stand by them against these insolences, which threatened the quiet of the Government. However, they were not wanting to signifie the importance of this affair to the Prince of Orange their *Governour,* and to desire his advice; they also informed him, how *Herman Modet,* and others of the Protestant Teachers, had upon the same day declaimed against Idols, saying, *That they ought to be removed from our sight, as well as from our hearts.*

The next day the Mob gathering in and about the aforesaid Church, the Contentions relating to our Lady began afresh. An old woman sitting before the Choir to sell Wax-Tapers, and to receive Oblations, began to scold at the people, and throw ashes and filth at the boys, provoked, it may be, at their telling her that those wares began to be out of fashion, and that it was high time to shut up shop. The Officers of the Church seeing that as the Mob increased the quarrels did so too, endeavoured to clear the Church of them, and to shut it up, but no body minded them. The *Scout,* and the Civil Magistrates, being informed of these disorders, repaired to the said Church, and admonish'd the people to leave it, as some did, but others pretended, that they had a mind to stay and hear the Hymn of *Salve Regina;* these were told, that there would be none that day; whereupon they replied, *They would then sing it them-*

6. The Sheriff (*Schout* in Dutch).—Ed.

selves; and accordingly one was heard to begin a Psalm or Hymn in one corner of the Church, others in another, and the people ecchoed to them. Some of the young fellows had the confidence to play at ball, others to kick stones about the Church, and even to throw them at the Altars.

These were the preludes of greater evils. Some thought, that if the Magistrates left the Church, they might draw or carry away the Mob after them; therefore the Burgomasters repaired to the Council Chamber; but finding they could do nothing by fair means, they resolved to raise the Militia, and disperse the people by force. In the mean time they caused the Church doors to be shut, all but one wicket, to let out the remainder of the people; and the *Scout* having laboured to dismiss those that stay'd without, went again into the Church, and endeavoured, together with some others of the Magistrates, to clear the place, but was opposed by some of the Ringleaders with stern countenances and rebellious language. In the meanwhile, a great Mob rushed in at the little Gate, and the *Scout* was forced to quit the Church. The moment he was gone, they fell to singing Psalms with open throats. The Treasurer, and other Officers of the Church having secured the Holy Reliques and other Trinkets, fled after him. Then all the rest of the Rabble that were without, forced their way in, and broke open all the doors; wherefore the *Scout* and other Magistrates went thither again, but being terrified at the numberless concourse of people, and the shouts and noise that echoed from the Church, they retired immediately to the Stadthouse, thinking themselves very happy if they could save that; which did not remain unthreatened. In the mean while the Rabble was every where up, the Burghers houses and shops all shut, and as the Sun declined, the breaking, robbing and plundering increased.

The Virgin's Image, that had been carried about in procession but two days before, was the first sacrifice to their fury. The Chappel in which it stood was entered by force, and the Idol thrown down and dashed to pieces, all the people roaring, *Vive le Gueux*, and demolishing all the Crosses and Images that were in their way. Hurried on by the same fury, and re-inforced by fresh numbers, they flew to other Churches, Chappels and Cloisters, where they did not mishandle stocks and stones only, but living creatures too, among them the *Franciscans* fared the worst. They broke open Chambers and Cellars; staved all the barrels, and set the beer and wine a running. There was a *Carmelite,* or bare-footed Monk, that had reason thankfully to remember their pranks as long as he lived; for they delivered him from a prison to which he had been confined about twelve years. Neither did they spare the prisons of the Civil Magistrate; releasing several out of them. They likewise forced the Convent of Nuns; who fearing worse things, made their escape, and retired to their friends, abandoning their Lodgings to the fury of the Mob. . . .

At day-break, these destroyers of Images sallied out of the Town, and fell to plundering the Abbey of St. Bernard, and other Religious houses round about, sparing none that were in their way or sight; whilst those of their Gang that staid within made an end of all that remained there. Three days this epidemical rage lasted, which grew up to this height of insolence through the cowardice of the Magistrates. Add to this, an incident which made the Mob yet more bold: Some people of quality and estates, armed with pistols and daggers under their cloaths, mixing with them and lurking in corners and by-places of the Town, terrified all that were inclined to oppose them; overpowering the Watches kept by the Inhabitants. Besides, the chiefest of these durst not exert themselves; such as were *Papists,* suspecting that the *Protestants* had unanimously plotted their ruin, durst not stir for fear of being fallen upon: And on the other hand, the *Protestants* fearing these disorders would be revenged upon them, thought they did enough in keeping a watchful eye on the *Romanists.* In one thing however they all agreed, *viz.* in keeping the Rabble out of their houses and from their coffers; and accordingly the *Roman Catholicks* of the *Low Countries* have since been often reproached by the *Spaniards,* with having had more regard to their own Temporal concerns than to the interest of the Church and Religion.

8. *Against Spain, in the King's Name*

The Prince of Orange, who had been horrified at the image-smashing episodes, was no less appalled by the rule of terror which Alva introduced into the Low Countries. Alva's triumph would mean defeat for the aspirations of the magnates, an end to all loving-kindness in matters of religion, and destruction of self-government in the Netherlands, in the sense that its policy was made by Netherlanders in the interests of the Netherlands and not of Spain. William of Nassau took up the challenge and became the leader of the resistance. It was a cause which he would find he could shape only in part, and which would shape him

in ways he hardly anticipated in 1568. It transformed the proud magnate, amiable and not a little arrogant, that he had been, into a tough
leader of a desperate cause, stubborn and compassionate, ready to die
for principles and flexible about the means of realizing them. William
the Silent—the "taciturn" of the French epithet *"le Taciturne"* indi-
cates a man who kept his own counsel, not one who spoke little—was
in the making. Orange (as he is often called, after his sovereign principality enclaved in southern France) became a rebel reluctantly, and his
commission given to his brother, Count Louis of Nassau, on April 6,
1568, to act with armed force against Alva and his troops, employs the
common device of claiming to act on behalf of the king against the
king's commander.

Source: [Louis-Prosper] Gachard, ed., *Correspondance de Guill-
   aume le Taciturne, Prince d'Orange,* 6 vols. (Brussels: C.
   Muquardt, 1847–1866), Vol. VI, pp. ii-iv. Translated from the
   Dutch by Herbert H. Rowen.

WILLIAM, by the grace of God, Prince of Orange, Lord of
Nassau, Katzenellenbogen, Vianden, Dietz, and Baron of Breda,
Diest, etc. To all who shall see or hear these presents, let it be
known that out of the great affection which we do bear for the
King of Spain, our gracious lord, and for His Majesty's hereditary
Netherlands;
   And in order to prevent the ruin and desolation of these lands,
which are being assaulted by the Spaniards, whose steady purpose
it is only to bring them and hold them in intolerable slavery,
sorrow, and misery under their government, despite the contracts,
leagues, and privileges which they violate every day, upon which
the prosperity of this country is wholly dependent and which His
Majesty has affirmed, confirmed and sworn by solemn oath, so that
the result is great and unspeakable antipathy to His Majesty and
harm and loss for these lands;
   And because the Spaniards further endeavor by promulgation
and renewal of edicts to extirpate the pure word of God, so as to
achieve more effectively their designs and aims in other, adjacent
lands, as we have seen in France, where the realm was thrown into
uproar when some liberty of religion was permitted;
   And because, as these purposes have moved toward accomplishment, these Low Countries have faced the danger not only of
being robbed of their contracts, leagues, and privileges, but also of

being so enslaved that no one could be sure of life or property, or indeed even of the honor of his wife and daughters;

And because the Spaniards, using false accusations and slanders, banned all those who fled the country so as to avoid their tyranny, and imprisoned others who stayed but were under any suspicion whatever, thus by a single stroke gaining the upper hand in the country and making provision for themselves by means of confiscations;

And because these are all things which should not have to be borne by those who bear affection to the service of His Majesty and the prosperity of their country, in view of the great loyalty which its inhabitants have always displayed;

Therefore, having been earnestly beseeched by the inhabitants of the country of both Protestant and Roman faiths to take action with the counsel of the Estates General of the country for the service of His Majesty and to protect the freedom and liberty of everyone in his religion and conscience, we have asked and begged our dearly beloved brother, Louis, Count of Nassau, to contend against these conditions with such soldiers as he shall have need of, and we hereby give him power and authority to do this as well as to recruit and bring into his service for his greater success such additional soldiers as he shall need, after he has, with God's help, won success in these endeavors. At our request, he has accepted this task out of love and affection for the King and for the Low Countries. We therefore call upon one and all to favor, help, and assist him in the performance of these tasks, as a duty in the service of His Majesty, their own welfare, and that of their fatherland, and we shall gladly consider all such actions to have been done as if by ourselves.

In witness whereof, we have placed our name below and caused our privy seal to be attached thereto. Given at Dillenburg, on the 6th of April in the year of Our Lord 1568.

9. The "Beggars" Take the Offensive

For the next four years Alva seemed all-triumphant and near to total and final victory. Orange's attempted incursions with armies of German hireling troops failed; the repression of heretics and rebels by Alva's "Council of Troubles" continued unimpeded. But unpredictable circumstance intervened. Nowhere did Alva's authority appear firmer than in the northern Netherlands, most distant from Orange's base in

Germany; yet it was there that the Spaniard's doom began. Early in 1572 a band of semi-piratical "Water Beggars," preying upon shipping in the Channel and the North Sea under commission from the Prince of Orange, were barred from their English bases by Queen Elizabeth, who feared Spanish reprisals. The roving *Gueux de Mer* found the little Holland port of Den Briel (The Brill, as the English called it), on one of the mouths of the Rhine, without a Spanish garrison; they captured it on April 1, and then a combined movement of fierce "Water Beggars" and vehement Calvinists took over one town after another in Holland and Zeeland, seizing the chance that Alva had left few troops in the two provinces. The Prince of Orange, at his ancestral castle of Dillenburg in Germany, responded to the opportunity too. On April 14 he issued a call to the inhabitants of the Low Countries to rise against Alva.

Source: Gachard, *Correspondance de Guillaume le Taciturne, Prince d'Orange.* Vol. VI, pp. 297–300. Translated from the Dutch by Herbert H. Rowen.

WE, William, by the grace of God, prince of Orange, count of Nassau, etc., banneret of Breda, Diest, Grimbergen, etc., burggrave of Antwerp, etc., lieutenant general of his Royal Majesty in Holland, Zeeland, Friesland and Utrecht, seek for each and every estate, lord, knight, nobleman, captain, bailiff, sheriff, steward, burgomaster, alderman, tax receiver, guild, trade, civic guard and its officers, and burgher, and for all the good inhabitants of the Netherlands of every station, freedom and deliverance from the present enslavement by cruel, foreign, and bloodthirsty oppressors.

We suffer with all our heart over the multitudinous and excessively cruel violences, the excessive burdens, taxes of ten, twenty, and thirty per cent, and other imposts, exactions, burdens, seizures, slayings, expulsions, confiscations, executions, and innumerable other unparalleled and intolerable inflictions, intimidations, and oppressions which the common enemy, with his Spaniards, bishops, inquisitors and other dependents, continues daily with unprecedented novelty and violence to inflict upon you, your wives, and your daughters, and your souls, bodies, and goods. After so many years, this now grows steadily worse under the name of His Royal Majesty, but without his knowledge, in violation of his oath, and contrary to the liberties and privileges of the country, although in fact at the instigation of Cardinal Granvelle and the Spanish Inquisitors, whose purpose it is to put into effect the decisions of the

Council of Trent and the Inquisition of Spain. These events are so public and well known, especially to you who see, fear, and suffer them yourselves that I do not need to give any broader account of them.

You know and the whole world knows with what diligence and cost of money, difficulties, and troubles, we have worked these last four years in order to restore to each and all of you, and to our beloved fatherland, your former freedom, prosperity, and wealth, and to deliver you from foreign tyrants and oppressors, for the sake of our own conscience and the fulfilment of our oath, which binds and obligates us to you for the true service of the King, the liberties of the country and the deliverance of the oppressed; and also to enable you to enjoy the freedom of your consciences and of the word of God, in proper obedience and true constant service to his Royal Majesty, without having to bear any longer these fears, anxieties, persecutions, slayings, robberies, and harassments by the tyrants, the Spanish foreigners, the inquisitions, bishops, and the edicts.

As a member of the community of the Netherlands, we would long since have aided you and brought you to that favorable condition, with God's grace, if you had not been made blind and deaf by the inordinate fear, the vain hopes, and false temptations instilled in you by governors who were put in place by the enemy and are truly betrayers of the fatherland and sworn servants of the tyrant; if until now you had not been negligent for so long in helping and supporting us to achieve your own welfare and deliverance. We hope that you now understand this better and will acquit yourself more adequately and give us more help, especially since you now see the great opportunities which we have at this time and which draw you on, and you know that we have not faltered but have ceaselessly sought by all feasible means to achieve these aims. Now various lords and friends are ready to offer us renewed help and assistance on sea and on land. Indeed, the enemy has already suffered notable damage from ourselves and our collaborators, who have entered this country and taken over various harbors, cities, places, and districts which have placed themselves in our hands for their deliverance on behalf of his Royal Majesty. They have shown what each and every one of you should do if you do not wish to draw perpetual harm upon yourselves, through your own guilt, bringing yourselves and your descendants into perpetual slavery and peril of soul, body, and property. For it is greatly to be feared that if you do not take advantage of this favorable situation, when the common enemy suffers from a shortage of troops, with many sick, and a shortage of ships and supplies, and when we already hold so many streams and waterways that the enemy finds it difficult to move about, then God will never again grant such a great opportunity. For you will have shamefully and evilly scorned and wasted the means which He sends to you so that you can now easily attain the freedom of His word and your consciences and of your fatherland, your bodies, wives, children, and the preservation of your privileges, rights, and goods, all in the true service of the King. We ask God in His grace to spare you all these evils and to give us and you His blessing, and strength and prosperity. With these, after expelling the tyrannical oppressors, together we shall see the Netherlands in their ancient freedom, governed again without any violence, with proper obedience to the King and security for your consciences, and according to the advice of the States General. To achieve this, if you will help by giving yourselves over into our hands, we wish to contribute all our strength; but if you do not do so and bring shame, violence, and grief upon yourselves, we do not want to have the fault laid upon us. Given at Dillenburg, April 14, 1572.

GUILLAUME DE NASSAU.

10. A New Regime Starts

Encouraged by the events in Holland and Zeeland, a revolutionary assembly met at the city of Dordrecht in mid-July. It called itself the States of Holland, but the historic body of that name had never assembled before on its own initiative, as it did now. Its purpose was to provide leadership for the movement of resistance to Alva upon a legal basis, and it proclaimed that it was the "lawful States of Holland," but it was in reality a new basis of law that was being created, the emergence of what were already in fact although not yet in name new rulers for the country. To a considerable extent, they were the continuation of the old local and provincial authorities; and the political issue of the revolt was of course precisely whether the king could govern without them and against them. But they were not yet a clear-cut majority of either people or governing class; such important towns as Amsterdam were to hold out for years against the authority of the revolutionary States and the Prince of Orange. William set the tasks for the new assembly in instructions given to Philip of Marnix, Lord of Saint Aldegonde, the Prince's advisor who was the chief instigator of the Dordrecht meeting; these were read to it on July 19. The assembly recognized William as stadholder in Holland, although the king had named someone to replace him.

Source: Gordon Griffiths, ed., *Representative Government in Western Europe in the Sixteenth Century* (Oxford: Clarendon Press, 1968), pp. 430–431. Translated from the Dutch by Gordon Griffiths.

INSTRUCTION AND ADVICE for Sir Philip of Marnix, Lord of St. Aldegonde, &c., commissioned by my gracious lord, the Prince of Orange, to go to the city of Dordrecht on His Grace's behalf and there to address the assembly of the Estates as directed and charged by His Grace.

I. First: whereas the Estates and commissioners of the neighboring cities, summoned to meet in the city of Dordrecht on the 15th of the month of July, have resolved to take up the problem of the common government of the country, the above-named commissioner of His Grace will maintain that they should with one voice decide to recognize His Grace as Governor General and Lieutenant of the king over Holland, Zealand, Friesland, and the bishopric of Utrecht, as he has heretofore been, and to which he was by His Royal Majesty legally and properly commissioned, regarding any unconstitutional or other violations or alterations of the customs and rights of the country as not having intervened.

II. That they should in addition decide how they may be united with the other countries and provinces in this matter, though the other countries have not had His Grace for their governor, yet accept him as first-ranking member of the Estates General of the country, responsible for protecting the country from foreign tyrants and oppressors and restoring its ancient rights and privileges, and thus should also recognize him as their protector and, in the absence of His Royal Majesty, as their head and worthy to be so. . . .

VI. The assembled Estates and deputies of the cities should also debate and ordain the best and most suitable measures to provide for the problem of His Grace's warships, that good and lawful order and regulations be established and maintained aboard them and over their commissioned officers; and similarly over the governors, captains, commanders, and other commissioned officers; and over the soldiers and others on land, who hold any command or commission from His Grace within the county of Holland, or are elsewhere in his service, that a good praiseworthy order and government be established and maintained, for the protection and defense of the country, and with the least possible burden upon the inhabitants and citizens, and with a view to a good union and accord among all classes.

VII. And that to this end all Governors, lieutenants, and commanders, both general and particular, shall maintain good agreement and correspondence with one another, and so likewise the cities with one another.

VIII. They should further debate and ordain the best and most suitable measures by which the ancient privileges, rights, and usages of the cities, which may have been withdrawn and abolished under the tyranny of Alva or at other times, might be restored and re-established in their essence, union, power and respect, in accordance with the privileges and rights which the king has sworn to maintain in the land; the above-named commissioner shall further declare on behalf of His Grace and explain to the assembly that His Grace has no other purpose than to see that, under the lawful and worthy government of the King of Spain, as Duke of Brabant, Lorraine and Limburg, Count of Flanders, Holland, Zealand, &c., the power, authority and prestige of the Estates may be restored to their former state, in accordance with the privileges and rights which the king has sworn to maintain in these countries; without which Estates His Grace will not do or order anything which could be injurious to the generality or in anywise concern it.

IX. On the other hand he hopes that the Estates there assembled will bind themselves and promise the others never to enter into any accord, agreement or compact, be it with the king himself, or with anyone bearing the orders or commission of His Majesty, nor to do or decide anything else concerning the generality, without securing His Grace's advice, consent, and agreement upon it, and including His Grace, so far as His Grace agrees that this be done.

X. His Grace for his part will also undertake and bind himself not to act nor to permit action of such a kind, without the advice and consent of the Estates, or at least the majority of them, or without including the Estates and countries, whenever and to whatever extent they desire.

XI. To this end the Estates there assembled and the deputies of the cities should take an oath to His Grace between the hands of His Grace's commissioner to be true to him forever and not to betray him, to stand by him and to help him with all means available to them, and to observe the foregoing points truly in all their parts. So also the commissioner for His Grace shall promise them by oath to protect, defend, and uphold the above-listed points respectively, so far as they concern His Grace.

11. The Goals of the Prince of Orange

William the Silent, unable to score a success on the battlefield, went in 1572 to Holland "to find my grave there" but determined to fight on against Alva and what he represented. For a little while Alva seemed to be gaining the upper hand again; he was able to send troops into the North and recapture some of the towns seized by the rebels, notably Haarlem. But the ability of the "Water Beggars" to keep command of the waterways enabled the rebels to continue the fight, and the resistance did not cease. The Emperor attempted to persuade the two sides to make peace. The following letter by the Prince of Orange is a reply to his brothers, John and Louis of Nassau, to whom terms were suggested; it sums up pithily a whole range of issues: William's new commitment to Calvinism; his hatred of the Spaniards; the need to pay, or pay off, the mercenary soldiers on whom he depended; his distrust of Philip II; and, not least, his skepticism regarding assistance from Elizabeth of England.

Source: William of Orange to Counts John and Louis of Nassau, February 5, 1573, in: G. Groen van Prinsterer, *Archives*, First Series, Vol. IV (Leiden: S. and J. Luchtmans, 1837), pp. 49–51. Translated from the French by Herbert H. Rowen.

MY DEAR GOOD BROTHERS, Counts John and Louis of Nassau, etc.,[7]

I have received your letter and learned what the situation is from it as well as from the report of the person you sent to me. I cannot thank you too much for your many good offices on my behalf and the trouble and labors which you undertake. To answer the points that you raise, you know quite well that it was never and is not now my intention to seek the slightest advantage for myself. I have only aspired and claimed to seek the country's freedom in the matters of religious conscience and government, in which the

7. The greeting is given here as in the address at the end of the letter, rather than as in the formal opening, "*Messieurs mes frères.*"—*Ed.*

foreigners tried to oppress it. I therefore see nothing else to propose but that it be permitted to practice the Reformed religion according to the word of God, and that this whole country and state return to its ancient privileges and liberty. To achieve this the foreigners in the government and the army, especially the Spaniards, must be driven out. But it will be most necessary of all that the King or the country pay off and satisfy the cavalrymen and soldiers who served me in this cause in two campaigns. If we are granted these points and given good assurances on them, then people will indeed see that I want nothing more than peace and public tranquility, and that I am not stubbornly pursuing some foolish notions of my own. The whole difficulty lies in the fact that although such assurances have been repeatedly given in the past, those who gave them also took oaths not to keep such contracts, being confident that they would be absolved from them by the Pope and therefore were not bound by them. I should be pleased if the Princes [in Germany] personally conferred among themselves on the means which could be proposed to give us good assurances. In view of the fact that for myself I confess that I can find no such means, at least none such as would be at all acceptable to the King, I therefore beg you to deliberate upon this matter. If you find something feasible, I will not fail on my part to accept it and to do what I can to persuade the States of the country to do so.

As for what you write about your coming here, I do not find it either expedient, or befitting your persons, or of advantage to the cause, to put yourselves in danger. It seems better to me that you go to Emden and then come by sea aboard two or three good, well-equipped ships.

As for the Queen of England, the Ambassadors of the States have written me that she did not want to get involved and that there was no hope there. Nonetheless, although they had decided to return at once, they have remained for a long period, so that I do not know whether there has been a change of opinion, but I do not expect it. I will not fail to inform you of what I hear. Now I recommend myself most affectionately to your good graces and pray God to keep you, my brothers, in His holy safeguard and protection. Written at Delft, this fifth of February, 1573.

Your most good brother,
at your service,
WILLIAM OF NASSAU.

IV For Religion and Liberty

From the beginning of the resistance and the revolt, two causes had been inextricably tangled in their origins and their course. One was *religion*, which meant the place of Calvinists and other Protestants in society and the state; the other was *liberty*, which meant not only the rights and privileges of local and provincial authorities, but also those which belonged to each man individually against the intrusions of the new governments no less than those of the old authorities. The debates and struggles which marked the interrelationship of religion and liberty in these decades of Netherlands history already carried much of the burden of the passions and the ambiguous, or multiple, meanings which these large words were to bear in later times and in other lands down to our own day.

We may see this by looking first at the special role of the Calvinists in the revolt—so special, indeed, that modern Dutch Calvinists still look upon the rebellion, and the Dutch state and nation which emerged from it, as deeply and truly their own and no one else's. The Calvinists were part of an international movement of religious transformation and reinvigoration which, despite the initial distaste of Calvin himself for political violence, became a powerful revolutionary force transcending the boundaries of single states. Moved by a fervent conviction that they and they alone possessed the truth of God's word (a conviction shared, to be true, with most other religious groups of that time), they sought to gain freedom of religion at the cost of tremendous exertions and a readiness for sacrifice. But it was freedom for themselves, as, in their own eyes, the only true church; it was not freedom for those who held false doctrines, neither Catholics (in their invective, "Papists"), nor Mennonites (the peaceable Anabaptist group that replaced the turbulent revolutionary Anabaptists of earlier decades), nor Socinians (who denied the doctrine of the Trinity), nor Lutherans, first of Protestant denominations. For these passionate Calvinists freedom for religion meant repression of Papism and Socinianism as abominations, and at the very least restriction of the rights of worship of Mennonites. The most essential task of the state, in their eyes, was to serve God's church against its enemies; and the meaning of the revolution to which they devoted their goods and their lives was to put "pious men"—that is, good Calvinists—in the seats of power.

William of Orange, himself born a Lutheran, raised a Catholic and committed to the broad religious sympathy and belief in tolerance associated with the name of Erasmus, found, especially after the crisis of 1572, that he needed the Calvinists—irreconcilable haters of the Spaniards—as the key political force for continued resistance. He became a member of the Reformed church but clearly with the reservation that he would not abandon his Erasmian openness in matters of religion as well as his belief that the revolt was primarily political in character, and that religious freedom, however important, was only one of the liberties for which the Netherlanders fought. He relied heavily upon the staunchness of the Calvinists but endeavored to blunt their readiness to persecute fellow-Christians. He hoped, by a feat of political wizardry, to persuade Calvinists and Catholics to live together in peace and a modicum of harmony in a united Netherlands where the Spaniard no longer ruled.

At stake, of course, was not so much whether the state which was emerging from the revolt would have an established church as what kind of state church it would be: whether one to which all subjects and citizens would be required to belong (as was the age-old tradition in almost all of Christian Europe), or one church acknowledged as the true Church, so that the state restricted government posts to its members, favored it alone with government support of its ministers and its edifices, but permitted other churches which were not politically disloyal to have freedom of belief and (with some restrictions) of worship. Since the Calvinists were committed to the former notion and the Prince of Orange to the latter, and yet they were also committed to each other by the urgencies of the rebellion against a powerful foe who would spare neither if victorious, the course of events remained during William's lifetime, as thereafter, confused and ambiguous, a source of conflict within the anti-Spanish camp.

12. The Stings of Religious Hatred

The Calvinist loathing for Roman Catholic faith and practices received its classical statement in the Low Countries in a satirical diatribe, *The Bee Hive of the Romish Church*, by Philip of Marnix, lord of Saint Aldegonde (1540–1598). It was written first in French in 1567, the year when Saint Aldegonde's brother, John of Marnix, lord of

Thoulouze, one of the earliest nobles to go over to Calvinism, was killed in battle near Antwerp. Two years later Saint Aldegonde, in exile in East Friesland, translated it into Dutch. As *De Bijenkorf der Heilige Roomsche Kercke* it became one of the most widely effective Calvinist tracts, for in it vituperation and hatred are expressed with great literary power. It is written as a parody of an allegorical defense of the Roman faith by a Catholic churchman. The following selection is taken from an English translation published in England during the early seventeenth century.

Source: Philip of Marnix, Lord of Saint Aldegonde, *The Bee Hive of the Romish Church*. Translated into English by George Gilpin the Elder. (London: John Dawson, 1623.), pp. 350–356.

Now FOLLOWETH further the exposition and declaration of the Bee hive, and the description of the Bees, the Honie and the Honie combe, with all things belonging thereunto.

The first Chapter.

Whereof the Bee hive is made.

The Bee Hive then, wherein our Bees dwell, swarme, and make their honny, is made with tough and strong Wicker, or Oziers of *Loven*[1] and *Paris*, plaighted and wrought together. They commonly call them at *Loven, Sophismata* or *Quotlibeta*, and are found for the most part, by the Basket makers of the Romish Church: namely, by *Iohannes Scotus, Thomas de Aquino, Albertus Magnus*, and other such like, which have beene very expert and cunning in this Arte.

These rods thus woven or plighted together, must for the more securitie bee bound also with grosse *Iewish* or *Thalmodician* cables, and then over that draw a clammie or cleaving morter plaster, made of olde rubbish or chalkie dust (wherewithall the auncient olde decaied councels were wont to bee mortered and dawbed) being good and small beaten to pouder, and wrought very thinne, with a little chopt straw, which the Apothecaries call, *Palea Decretorum*, wetting and often moystening the same with scumme of the auncient Doctors: and also mingled among the same some new chalke of *Trent*, and so wrought together with sande, which is digged out of the decayed welles of mens superstitions, or of that

1. Louvain or Leuven, in Belgium, seat of the great Catholic University.— *Ed.*

old sande which the Heretikes were wont to bind their argumentes with all. Here under you may also mingle some Jewes lime, or *litumen,* which is a very tough and cleaving substance, wherewithall the citie and Towre of *Babylon* was wont to bee bounde, and it is drawne out of the poole and dead sinke of *Sodom* and *Gomorre:* For herewithall thou shalt make such an excellent morter, that neither the heate of the Sunne, nor shewers of raine, will bee of force to moisten it, or make it to splitte. The masters of the Bee hive, who love to have it somewhat garish to the eye, use besides all the rest to make snow white *Gypsus,* or a kinde of playster of white biblish Marble stone very finely grounde in a *Lovanist* or *Parisian* Mill, beeing wrought with excellent strong durtie decrees, & so stroke over with a whiting brush or pincell, and then painted with all manner of gallant pictures and brave Images: for that makes a gaye shew, and causeth the Bees the rather to enter into it.

The ii. Chapter.
Declaring the first originall of these Bees.

Concerning the first originall of Bees, are sundry opinions amongst the learned. Some amongst the Poetes, as *Higinius,* and others say, that there was a woman, named *Melissa,* whom *Iupiter* did transforme into a Bee. And it seemeth partly, that our bees be of a feminate disposition. The other, as *Euhemerus* sayth, that they are proceeded of Hornettes and Horseflies, which did norish and feede *Iupiter,* beeing in a cave, in the land of *Creta,* and that he (for that cause) did endue them with honnie. Which fable therein doth agree with the truth, forsomuch as the idol *Iupiter,* and all other idols are nourished and maintained with the honnie of our bees, and by them brought acquainted into the world. Some suppose, they were first founde in *Thessalia,* which is a very fertile soyle of all manner poysons and sorcerers necessaries: the other say, in an Island named *Quea:* other some, upon a mountaine *Himettus.* In summe, whatsoever it be, thus much is of it, that our Bees are exceeding olde: for Moses mentioneth, that in *Egypt* were such a sort of Bees, *David* declareth also of a swarme of such Bees, which had environed him about. And *Esaie* speaketh of the Bees in *Assyria,* and *Chaldea.* Yet notwithstanding, our Bees doe somewhat differ from those. For, these were first bredde at Rome, in the dayes of *Numa Pompilius,* and continued many hundred yeeres after, and are marvellously encreased: yet after that, the first kinde beeing almost worne out, they are growne to another kinde in the days of *Phocas* the Emperour of Rome. But we will permit this to the iudgementes of Historiographers.

The iii. Chapter.
Of the qualitie and sundrie sortes of Bees.

Those Bees *Ergo*, are of sundry qualities, but are in a manner all brought into two sortes or species, according to the description of *Plinie*. For the one are domesticall or house Bees, and be conversant among people. The other are strange and odde, terrible to see to, more teastie or angry, and with a sharper sting, but withall, more diligent in their Beehive. And albeit they are conversant also amongst people, and frankely bestowe their honie, yet be they more solitarie and stranger than the other, and therefore are called with the Greeke word *Monachi*,[2] that is to say, dwelling solitarie or by themselves, and are knowne from other, by a hoode which they weare on their heads. Wee will terme the first tame Bees: and these wilde Bees.

Furthermore, they are both divided into foure manner of sortes or kindes, after the description of *Aristotle* and *Columella*. Of which the very best are thick and round: they make the most hony, & keepe company next to their king, amongest which the most excellent are of a sanguine colour, as though they had redde scarlet wings. Those tend on the king, and are commonly by his side, being of both kindes, wilde and tame: the other are of manifold and sundry sortes with more varietie: but how much the neerer they approch to the king, so much the thicker and rounder they commonly grow.

The second kinde or sort resemble and are like to Waspes, Horseflies and Hornets: they make not so much hony as the first, because they come not of so good a kind. Notwithstanding, they labour earnestly, and bring also much hony into the hive. They are in a manner of the condition and nature of Horseflies and Hornets, saving that they love not so well to flie and seize on horses and kine, as they doe on sheepe. Wherein they digresse cleane from the nature of the ordinarie Honybees, which doe carefully shunne the sheepe, for feare, lest they should intangle themselves, & sticke in

2. Monks.—*Ed.*

their fleeces. But these have a good remedie for that, for they first bite away their wool, after that their skinne, and lastly doe sucke their blood, to which they are wonderfully addicted. There are also amongst these, which are as profitable in the Bee hive, as any other, by reason of their fearcenesse, for they have very fearce & murthering stinges, in so much as those beeing stoung by them, can hardly escape death. For the wound cannot be remedied with any thing, but with golden salve: they are of the generation of *waspes*, which *Aristotle* and *Plinie* doe name in Greeke *Ichneumones*, which may be interpreted Inquisitours, or after the Latin phrase *Inquisitores*, & after the saying of *Plinie* are so called, because with great industrie and diligence, they know to seeke and catch the flies, and bite off their heads, permitting them to live of that which remaines: howbeit, these our *Ichneumones* do most covet the wool and bloode of sheepe, & are marvellous bloodthirstie. They are likewise of both kinds some tame, some wilde: But the wild are alwayes more fearce & deadly. They are bredde or ingendred, after the same order which *Aristotle* doth declare of his *Ichneumones:* namely, they take very venimous Spiders, named *Phalangiae* (which are found plentifully in *Spaine* at the old Inquisitors walles & postes), and carrie those to their holes: and after they have greased them a good with filth and durte (whereunto ours use commonly Popes grease) then doe they set or broode over them, and after that sort increase their kinde.

The third sorte is by *Arlem* named *Pheres*, which signifies asmuch as theeves & rovers, because they are of an exceeding theevish disposition, and have a great large and broad belly commonly blacke to see to. These devoure great store of honie, and love exceedingly wel the smacke of Prebendes and fat beneficed hony, which the Bee Apothecaries doe tearme in Latin *Veneficia:* And therefore are called *Veneficiari*, or veneficed. They are for the most part tame, yet there are found not a few, which are of the wilde and strange disposition. And they are separated amongest them selves, each over a severall office and charge, according as the king hath appointed them. For some have nothing else to doe, but with an irksome buzzing by day and night doe swarme in their hive. But they know their rule, how and when they shall swarme, and are for that cause called *Regulares*, or by a Greeke word *Canonici*.

Touching the wilde sorte of Bees, some are called fathers, or with a *Chaldean* word *Abbas*, because they beare rule over the other Bees, like a father over his children. Some keepers, or after the Italian and French phrase, *Gardians*. Some are called the first, or in Latine *Priores*. Some Controllers, or in Latin *Provinciales*: each after his state and calling, and according to the rule and dominion which hee beareth over the other common Bees, which common Bees make the fourth and last heape or kind of Bees, according to *Aristotles* declaration, and are named in Greeke *Cephenes* and in Latin *Fungi*, that is after our language Buzzardes or Drones. These are the most unprofitable Bees, and yet the most in number: they have no sting, and will not worke, but live on the labour of the other, and chiefly the wilde Bees amongst the which some flie swarming from doore to doore, to find out baightes to fill their bagges: and therefore are called *Mendicantes*, that is to say, beggars, or begging bees: because they are of the begging order of Bees. But the tame Drones doe not flie so from house to house, but tarry in their Bee hive, and there get their commons with swarming, without labouring, or doing any good. For when they would doe any good, then doe they commonly misse, and are also for that cause called Missebees, or Massebees.

The iiii. Chapter.
Of the nature of Bees: of their ingendring, and procreation.

Further, concerning the nature of these Bees, there is a difference betwixt male and female, especially amongst the wilde. And they love to goe together, yet doe they not ingender the one of the other, but be most altogether ingendred and made of their king, like as *Aristotle* and *Plinie* doe plainely shew: for without this king, they cannot bring forth their like, notwithstanding they can brood up these foresaid wormes named *Clerus*, after they have been first ingendred by the king if *Plinie* be credible, in the sixteenth chapter of the forenamed booke of his Historie.

The v. Chapter.
What the rule and being of these Bees are touching their king.

In their rule they resemble the common sort of hony Bees, for they have all one king, and cannot abide without a king, whom they call *Papa*, as if one should say, *Pater Apum*, that is to say, The father of Bees, whereof it cometh, that we call all these Bees in the

Dutch tongue *Papen,* and with us *Papistical Priests.* For the Bees
are called in Latine *Apes.*

This king hath a sting in like maner, but he doth not occupie
himselfe abroad, because al other bees are prest to do him service,
in whatsoever pleaseth him to commaunde. And like as this king of
Honiebees hath a spot on his head: so likewise doth he carrie a
token or marke on his head, like a triple crowne: howbeit, all the
other Bees (as hath beene said) doe beare in like manner a round
white spot in the middle of their heads, in manner of a crownet.
They flie all at once about this king, and shew themselves very
meeke & obedient towards him. He goeth seldome abroad, but
when hee doth determine to goe forth any whither, it may bee
perceived long before, by the swarming and humming of the forerunners. For whensoever he goeth out, the whole swarme followeth round about him, and oftentimes they carrie him on their
shoulders, like as the honie Bees doe carrie their king.

He hath likewise certaine loyterers by him, and serviteurs which
gard him and some other of the very best, which be of a ruddie or
sanguine colour, and remaine always next to his side, and are for
that cause named *Laterales,* or *a Latere.* In summe, each one would
faine be next, for that is reputed for great honour: where he settles,
there is the host of the whole swarme and staple of the honie and
honnie combe: and such as dwell many hundreth miles thence,
bend notwithstanding their flight thitherwardes: whosoever hath
him to friend, shall in like manner finde friendship of all the whole
swarme: when they lose him, then is all their porridge spilt, and
sporte at an end: For they creepe pensively to their selles and
closets, and there buzze, or swarme so long and so much, till they
have gotten another. And if by mishap it chaunceth, that there be
two or three kings, (like as hath often beene seene,) then falles out
great schismes and troubles among them, and they bee at mortall
warres together: yea, cease not, till the one or the other be dis-
patcht and made away: like as *Virgil* hath finely set forth.

13. A New Monkery?

The conflict of attitudes between the fervent Calvinists and William
the Silent was most clearly revealed in their policy toward the
Mennonites. For the rigid and rigorous Calvinists, there was scarcely
any difference in wickedness and ungodliness between Catholics loyal
to Rome and more extreme Protestants, such as the Anabaptists. The

Mennonites continued to be persecuted in the provinces where Spanish power was re-established and Catholicism became again the sole lawful religion; but they were also the target of the Calvinists in the northern provinces. A dispute over the right of Mennonites to ply their trades in the capital of Zeeland, Middelburg, led them to appeal to the Prince of Orange for his protection. His reply, and the indignation of the orthodox Calvinists, voiced through Saint Aldegonde, are related in the following passage from Gerard Brandt's *History of the Reformation*.

Source: Gerard Brandt, *The History of the Reformation*, Vol. I, pp. 330–333.

ABOUT THIS TIME [1577] the fires were again kindled at *Antwerp* for the *Anabaptists*. The first that was burnt, was a shoemaker of *Delft;* and the next *Hans de Ruiter,* a Teacher of their congregation, with his wife and daughter.

This Sect began likewise to be ill treated by the *Reformed* on the other hand. Upon their scrupling to take the usual oaths of a Burgher at Midelburg, endeavours were used to deprive them of the freedom of the town, and consequently by this roundabout way, to oblige them to leave it. But the Prince of *Orange* granted them a Protection under his hand and seal, of the following tenor:

> Whereas a Petition has been presented to his Excellency, on the behalf of certain inhabitants of the town of Midelburg, complaining that the Magistrates of that town did, long since, cause their shops to be shut up, and consequently forbid them to follow their respective trades and employments, which are the only means they have to maintain their families; the pretence of which prohibition was, that they had not taken the oath which their fellow citizens had taken, notwithstanding that the said inhabitants remonstrated to the said Magistrates, that without ever taking the said oath, they for many years chearfully supported all civil burthens, contributions and taxes equally with other citizens and inhabitants of the said place, and were never wanting therein, or in other circumstances of their duty; and that therefore they ought not to be now molested, any more than formerly, upon that account; especially since they aimed at nothing more thereby, than to live with freedom of conscience, on account of which this present war was entered into against the king of *Spain* by his subjects, and all religious ceremonies and institutions, inconsistent with the said freedom of conscience, are still opposed: in which war, by God's assistance, the success has been such, that our religious liberties have been obtained and preserved. For which reasons it would be very unreasonable that the petitioners should be

deprived of what they themselves have helped to recover, by paying taxes and contributions, and by bearing their share of other
burdens, and by even hazarding their lives. And whereas, upon
their representing all these matters to the Magistrates, no other
answer was made them but, *that they must conform themselves
to the Polity and Customs of the said town.* Whereby the said
Magistrates seem to design not only to drive them the said petitioners with their wives and children, now residing at Midelburg,
out of these provinces, to their utter ruin; but consequently an
infinite number of others of that perswasion in *Holland* and
Zeland, who by virtue of the Placards have put themselves under
his Excellency's protection. Which proceedings can be profitable
to none, but may be very pernicious to the country, by lessening
the trade of it every where: On which accounts the said petitioners have most humbly besought and intreated his Excellency
to look down upon their case with compassion, and to give the
necessary orders therein, and especially since they are contented
to be punished as perjured persons, as often as they be guilty of
any thing contrary to the contents of the said oath.

His Excellency having taken the premisses into his most serious
consideration, and having previously advised with the Governour
and Council of *Zeland,* does ordain and decree, by these presents,
that the abovementioned petitioners shall be permitted to make
their solemn affirmation, as they have offered, in lieu of the oath,
before the Magistrates of the said town; provided that all of them
who transgress the said affirmation shall be punished as forsworn
persons. And his Excellency requires and commands the Magistrates of *Midelburg,* and all others whom it may concern, not to
burden or disquiet the consciences of the petitioners with the said
oath, or otherwise; but to suffer them to open their shops, and
follow their business as formerly. But all by way of provision, and
until it shall be otherwise ordered upon mature deliberation, and
in a more peaceable situation of affairs.

Thus signed and sealed by his Excellency
in the town of *Midelburg,* January 26,
1577.

The Subscription was
William of *Nassaw.*

And *Lower,* By my Gracious Lord the Prince.
Signed, *de Baulemont.*

And the Seal affixed to it was
of red wax with a double Label.

Notwithstanding this, some of the Clergy did all that lay in their
power, by means of *Philip de Marnix,* Heer *van Aldegonde,* to
exasperate the Prince against them; particularly at the meeting of
the States of *Holland* and *Zeland,* holden at *Dort* in *March* follow-

ing. But that which passed between the Prince and *Marnix* on this occasion, may be seen in a certain extract of a letter, written by the said Gentleman to *Jasper Heidanus*, a Minister, and bearing date from Dort, the last day of *March*. It runs thus: 'The business of the *Anabaptists* was treated of yesterday with the illustrious Prince, upon the receipt of your and *Taffin*'s letters, and really I find it much more difficult than I expected. For at *Midelburg* he gave me great hopes that all such as refused the oath should be excluded from the Burghership, or at least not admitted as formerly had been practised. Now he alledges that this cannot be done without exciting new troubles in the Church; since the States will never consent to the passing a law, which they think will by no means tend to the advantage of the Commonwealth. Nay, he further says, that this was the only cause why the Consistories or Church-meetings were formerly so disagreeable to the *States*, that they were never near putting them all down at once by a Placard. Wherefore to revive the same affair, would, as he verily thought, turn to the great damage of the Church, especially at a juncture in which many of the *Popish* Mungrels would strive to take advantage by it. When I warmly urged that those who dissolved the bands of all humane society, might fairly be cast out of it, even under the shew of preserving civil order, and at the same time subjoined, with how great danger both the Church and State might be attended by issuing such a Placard, which could not but be impious in it self; he replied pretty sharply, that their *Affirmation* might serve for an Oath, and that we ought not to press this matter further, unless we would own at the same time, that the *Papists* were in the right, in forcing us to a religion that was incompatible with our consciences. And further, that the people of *North-Holland* would never consent to, nor endure what I proposed. In short, I do not find we can do any thing in this matter, which indeed troubles me the more, in that I observe the minds of many good men so imbittered, I might say, so deeply wounded, by the intervention of I know not what unseasonable offences or scandals, that they are the less favourable to those who endeavour to promote the affairs of the Church to the utmost of their power. In truth, the Prince has reproached me, partly on his own account, and partly on account of the *States*, as if there were a design in the Clergy to lord it over our consciences, and that they were endeavouring to bring every body under the yoke of their laws and

institutions. And upon this occasion he commended the saying of a
Monk that was here not long since, who, upon several objections
brought against his religion, answered: *that our Pot had not been
so long upon the fire as theirs, whom we so much blamed; but that
he plainly foresaw that in the course of a pair of hundred years,
Ecclesiastical dominion would be upon an equal foot in both
churches.* These things make great impression upon the Vulgar,
nay, they puzzle the Wise, and if timely care be not taken, will
occasion no small mischief. Therefore, as far as in me lay, I have
both now and at all times done my utmost to remove this prejudice
out of the minds of men, by which they are alienated from us,
whether it be through the ignorance, deceit, or wickedness, of
such as maintain that we are setting up a *new Monkery*. For I
labour to convince them that we do not oppose nor condemn any
thing but what the Law of the Lord, expressed in Holy Writ,
opposes and condemns; and in other matters make use of Christian
liberty; which rule, above all others I look upon to be of very great
importance to the building up of the church; for experience, the
best mistress, has taught me so. I have likewise frequently
observed at *Brussels*, how great offence the opinion of our rigidness, which is riveted in the hearts of the *Papists*, daily occasions.
And what is there more common or usual in these our churches,
than for the chiefest of the Nobility, and infinite numbers of the
Commonalty, to keep away from our assemblies, only because they
are afraid of a new tyranny and yoke of spiritual dominion. The
Prince himself when I addressed to him, some years ago, opposed
this shield only against all my arrows. In truth, abundance of the
Germans join themselves purposely with the Heterodox, because
they dread our insufferable Rigidness.'

  This letter rendered almost verbatim from the *Latin* original,
may teach us of what importance the Prince of *Orange* and the
States of *Holland* and *Zeland* thought liberty of Conscience to be
at that time, and what it was in our *Reformation* that displeased
many in those days.

14. A Moment of Unity: Accord at Ghent

The debacle at Den Briel, with the subsequent loss of most of Holland
and Zeeland to the rebels, led to Alva's replacement in 1573 by Luis de
Requesens. Although Requesens managed to make some gains against
the insurgents, his persistent shortage of funds led to mutinies among

his troops. On the other hand, in the southern provinces which formed his base, the continuing resistance of the two maritime provinces encouraged efforts, especially in Flanders and Brabant, to reach an agreement with the Prince of Orange and the provinces of Holland for reunification of the country. Requesens' death in April, 1576, cleared the way for a meeting of delegates at Ghent in October. The looting and killings by Spanish mutineers in Antwerp (the "Spanish fury" of November 4–7) hastened final accord on November 8 of the "Pacification of Ghent." Its principles were those for which the Prince of Orange had fought for so long: expulsion of the Spanish soldiery; self-government of the country, although under limited sovereignty of Spain; religious peace upon the basis of toleration, although Calvinism would remain the established religion in Holland and Zeeland. The original signatories were followed by all the provinces of the Netherlands except outlying Luxemburg. Philip II's new governor-general Don Juan of Austria (the famed victor over the Turks in the naval battle of Lepanto) was required to swear to uphold the "Pacification" before he was accepted. For the moment, it seemed that the revolt of the Low Countries had achieved its original aims—self-rule or political liberty, and freedom in religion. But there were ambiguities in the agreement which would test its strength, particularly since the Spanish monarch himself was not ready to accept its principles and was insistent upon suppression of the rebellion at almost any price.

Source: "Traité & Confédération dite *la Pacification de Gand* entre les Etats des PAYS-BAS d'une part, & le Prince d'ORANGE avec les Etats de HOLLANDE, ZEELANDE &c. d'autre, faite à Gand le 8. Novembre 1576," in Dumont, *Corps universel diplomatique du droit des gens*, 8 vols. (Amsterdam and The Hague, 1726–1731), Vol. V, part i, pp. 278–283. Translated from the French and Dutch texts by Herbert H. Rowen.

To ALL THOSE who shall see or hear these presents, Greeting. As these provinces[3] have been exposed these last nine or ten years to a cruel war because of the Spaniards' ambition and harsh government, and because of the injustice and violence committed by them and their adherents, so that this country has fallen into extreme hardship and destitution; and in order to provide for these needs and to prevent greater trouble and the oppression and sufferings of this country by means of a firm peace and an effective pacification,

3. The original, "les Pays de deça," is the old phrase used to distinguish the Burgundian provinces in the Low Countries—"on this side"—from the hereditary provinces of ducal Burgundy and Franche-Comté.—*Ed.*

there assembled at Breda during the month of February in the year 1574 deputies and commissioners of His Majesty and of the Prince of Orange as well as of the States of Holland, Zeeland and their associates, who proposed various measures strongly conducive to such pacification. But these measures did not bear the fruit which had been expected from them, but on the contrary, instead of the relief and compassion which it was hoped His Majesty would give us, the Spaniards continued every day their oppression and impoverishment of the poor subjects and tried to reduce them to perpetual enslavement by arousing sedition among them, going so far as to threaten the Lords and the cities and seizing several places by hostile force, which they sometimes looted and burned. This is why those to whom the government of this country was entrusted have declared the Spaniards to be enemies of His Majesty and of the public good, and the States of these provinces were compelled, with the consent of these deputies, to take up arms and adopt other measures to prevent total ruin, and in order that the inhabitants of these Low Countries, being joined together in a firm peace and agreement, may by common action drive out the Spaniards and their adherents as the destroyers of this land and restore these subjects to the enjoyment of their rights, privileges, customs, and liberties, by which means their trade and their prosperity may flourish again. With the prior accord of the aforesaid Lords to whom the government of the country was entrusted, the negotiation begun at Breda for God's honor and His Majesty's service between the prelates, nobles, cities, and members of Brabant, Flanders, Artois, Hainaut, Valenciennes, Lille, Douai, Orchies, Namur, Tournai, Utrecht, and Malines, on the one hand, and the States of Holland, Zeeland, and their associates on the other, by their respective commissioners, to wit: [. . .] after the presentation of their commissions included at the end of these presents, have made and drawn up the present treaty, alliance, and firm and perpetual Union, under the following conditions:

I. First, that all offenses, slanders, misdeeds, and damages occurring as a result of the troubles between the inhabitants of the provinces included in this treaty, no matter where or how they happened, shall be forgiven, forgotten and considered as not having occurred, so that no mention shall ever be made of them and no one shall be sued on account of them.

II. In consequence thereof, the said States of Brabant, Flanders,

Hainaut, etc., as well as the said Lord Prince and the States of Holland and Zeeland and their associates, promise to maintain henceforth in good faith and without dissimulation, and to have their provinces maintain a firm and inviolable peace and friendship, and by this means to assist each other at all times and on all occasions with their counsel and deeds, their lives and wealth; with the particular purpose of driving and keeping out of the country the Spanish soldiers and other foreigners who have attempted, without any recourse to law, to deprive Lords and Nobles of their lives, to appropriate the riches and wealth of the country, and to reduce and keep the common people in perpetual enslavement. And in order to furnish whatever will be necessary to resist those who may attempt to thwart them in these measures, the said confederates and allies promise to hold themselves ready and equipped to make all necessary and reasonable contributions and taxation promptly.

III. It has been further agreed that immediately after the departure of the Spaniards and their adherents, when everything will be quiet and safe, the two parties will be bound to promote and obtain the convocation and meeting of the States General in the form and manner in which it was held during the time of the late Emperor Charles, of praiseworthy memory, when he ceded and transferred these Low Countries to the hands of the King our Sire, in order to put the affairs of the country generally and individually in good order, concerning not only the exercise of religion in the provinces of Holland, Zeeland, and associated places, but also the restitution of fortresses, artillery, ships, and other things belonging to His Majesty, which during the said troubles were captured by Hollanders, Zeelanders, or otherwise, in such fashion as shall be found expedient for the service of His Majesty and the welfare and unity of the country. This will be done without contradiction and without interference, delay, or holding back from either side, either in regard to ordinances, declarations, and resolutions which will be taken and made in the application of these measures, whatever they may be, to which both parties submit themselves absolutely and in good faith.

IV. That henceforth the inhabitants and subjects on both sides, in any province of the Low Countries, no matter what their status, quality, or condition, will have the right to stay and reside, pass in and out, remain, and engage in trade everywhere, either for the sale

62 FOR RELIGION AND LIBERTY

of goods or otherwise, and in full freedom and security. It shall be understood that the Hollanders, Zeelanders, and others of whatever province, quality, or condition they may be, shall not be allowed or permitted to infringe in any way inside or outside the said lands of Holland, Zeeland, and the allied places, against the repose and public peace, notably against the Roman Catholic religion, or against its practice, nor to slander or annoy anyone on this cast, by deed or word, nor to commit scandals against it by similar acts, under penalty of punishment as disturbers of the public peace and in order to serve as an example to others.

V. And in order to assure that nonetheless no one be exposed to renewal of court action, capriciousness, or peril, all ordinances heretofore made and published regarding heresy, as well as the criminal ordinances made by the Duke of Alva, and prosecution and execution of sentences under them, shall be suspended until the States General shall order otherwise: but it shall be understood that no scandal will be caused, as defined above.

VI. My Lord the Prince shall continue to hold the posts of Admiral General of the Sea and His Majesty's Governor in Holland, Zeeland, Bommel and other associated places, with general command such as he now exercises, with the same judges and magistrates, without any change or innovation, except with his consent and advice, and in the towns and places which His Excellency now holds, until the States General shall order otherwise after the departure of the Spaniards.

VII. But as regards the cities and places included within his commission from His Majesty which are not now under the authority of His Excellency, this point will remain in suspension until these cities and places will be joined in this union and agreement with the other States and His Excellency will have given them satisfaction in the points concerning interests in coming under his government with regard to the practice of religion or in other matters, so that the provinces may not be dismembered and all dissension and discord may be avoided.

VIII. And meanwhile no ordinances, instructions, judgments or writs shall have force in the lands and cities governed by the said Prince except such as will have been approved or issued by His Excellency or by the Council, the magistrates, or the officers in them, without prejudice for the future to the jurisdiction of the Grand Council of His Majesty.

[Other clauses provide for the release of prisoners without the payment of ransom, and for the restitution to the Prince and all others of their property confiscated since 1566 and not yet sold or transferred.]

XIII. The columns, trophies, inscriptions, and effigies erected by the Duke of Alva putting dishonor and blame on those named above or on anyone else, shall be pulled down and destroyed.

[Further clauses establish the attribution of revenues affected by the events of the war.]

XIX. All prelates and other ecclesiastical persons whose abbeys, dioceses, foundations, and residences, although located outside Holland and Zeeland, nonetheless possess property within these provinces, shall return to the possession of these properties, as provided above for laymen.

XX. But as for religious and other ecclesiastical persons who were professed or prebendaries in these two provinces and withdrew from them, in view of the fact that most of their property has passed into new ownership, they shall henceforth be reasonably provided for along with those who have remained, or otherwise they shall be permitted to take possession of their property, but at the choice and option of the States, and provisionally until the States General shall give orders about their subsequent claims.

[Other clauses about the special position of Holland and Zeeland follow.]

XXIV. The lands, lordships, and towns on the opposite side shall not be included in this joint accord and pacification to enjoy its benefits, until they shall have joined and entered it effectively, which they may do when they wish.

Which treaty and peace negotiation, resulting from the report, approval, and acceptance of the Lords Deputies in the government of these provinces, as well as of their States, together with the Prince, the States of Holland, Zeeland and their associates, the said deputies, by virtue of their power and commission, have promised to observe, maintain, and fulfill inviolably in all the said points and articles, as well as all that the States General shall define and order in regard to it; and to obtain their ratification, swearing, signature, and sealing by the prelates, nobles, cities, and other members of the said provinces on both sides, and particularly by the said Lord the Prince of Orange, generally and particularly, within a month to the satisfaction of all. In witness whereof the said deputies present for this purpose have signed these presents in the town hall of Ghent on November 8, 1576.

15. A Second Attempt at Religious Peace

In 1577, the States General came into conflict with Don Juan because he obeyed Philip II and disregarded the Pacification of Ghent. The party of moderate Catholics in the southern provinces appealed to the young archduke Matthias of Habsburg (the future Holy Roman Emperor) to come to the Netherlands to take over Don Juan's office; his known moderation in religious matters would, they hoped, make him acceptable to the Protestants. William of Orange, who obtained the upper hand in the councils of government, accepted Matthias in order to keep the resistance to Spain united. In December, after Don Juan was declared forfeit of his office, Matthias was proclaimed the new governor-general. He made Orange his lieutenant-general, and later in the year accepted a "Peace of Religion," concluded at Antwerp on July 22, 1578, by himself, Orange, the Council of State and the States General. It was a reaffirmation of the principles of the Pacifica-tion of Ghent and made more specific provision for the avoidance of religious conflict.

Source: "Paix de Religion dans les PAYS-BAS, arrêtée & concluë, du consentment & de l'avis de l'Archiduc MATTHIAS, du Prince d'Orange, du Conseil d'Etat & des Etats Généraux, faite à Anvers, le 22. Juillet 1578," in: du Mont, Vol. V, part i, pp. 318–320. Translated from the French by Herbert H. Rowen.

IT IS WELL KNOWN to all that the tyrannical ordinances issued before this concerning religion upon the counsel and persuasions of foreigners, especially Spaniards, without the judgment of the States General having been heard, and which were thereafter enforced with great rigor and intolerable punishments, were the cause of all our present difficulties, because they resulted in the infringement of the privileges, rights, and laudable customs of the country and finally in a despicable war undertaken by the enemies of the father-land and in our total ruin and enslavement. [The failure of Don Juan of Austria to observe the Pacification of Ghent, as he had sworn to do, and his renewal of the war in the Low Countries] have compelled us to take up arms together in the protection and defense of our natural freedom. Thus it was that, in the extremities to which this war (which is the mother of all disorder and mis-fortunes) drove us, we were compelled to do and permit various things which we did not like or intend, being harmful to Religion[4] and the obedience which we owe to His Majesty, and which we would never have considered under other circumstances but which we cannot now prevent. We repeatedly remonstrated and pro-tested to this effect before engaging in this war, by letters and by ambassadors sent to His Majesty and to Don Juan. And although we lack neither strength nor courage in our own defense, yet we fear, because there is such a diversity of provinces and opinions which hinder its accomplishment, that our courage and strength will be of scant help to us unless we come together in a closer alliance, accord and unbreakable union, especially as concerns religion. For, since the so-called Reformed religion is much fol-lowed and loved in this country not only because of the war, but also because we are necessarily hosts to merchants and other residents of neighboring realms and countries like France, England, Germany, and others, who adhere to this religion, it is to be feared that if we do not grant it freedom of exercise by an amicable agreement and peace in the matter of religion (as has been done in Germany and France, who came to agreement in this respect and now live in peace and quiet, instead of in their former mutual intolerance and enmity, and thus avoided the great perils, blood-shed, and other troubles which faced them), then, in the absence of such an agreement, our common enemy, who is in our land, will find it all the easier to harm us, while, if we are held together in close union by a peaceful accord, we shall be able to defend our-selves against all troubles and dangers. We have given much con-sideration to all these things, but especially to the fact that the enemy fears nothing so much as to see us all in a good union with regard to religion, having sought above all by this pretext to keep us in disunity and discord. The situation is now such that should the enemy take our country, either by guile or by force, he will spare neither churchmen, nor Catholics, nor anyone else. We have also considered that the adherents of the so-called Reformed religion have very earnestly asked by repeated petition to be permitted the free exercise of religion, according to rules and ordinances to be agreed upon.

With the purpose of assuring the peace and repose of all, and after mature deliberation not only with the deputies of the States

4. I.e., the Catholic religion.—*Ed.*

General but also the States of each province individually, we have ordered and do order by these presents the following points, without prejudice to the union of these provinces, who should not change their attitude or break with each other because of this ordinance, especially since no one is compelled to change religion or to accept such freedom if he does not approve it.

[The first eleven clauses provide for freedom for both religions under specified conditions.]

XII. And in order to avoid all irritation and disputes, it is forbidden to compose, sing, or publish any slanderous songs, ballads, refrains, or other defamatory pamphlets or writings, or to print and sell them, on either side.

XIII. It is also forbidden to all ministers, readers, and others who preach publicly, whatever their religion may be, to speak or use any words tending to arouse trouble and sedition; but they shall conduct themselves in courteous and modest fashion and tell their listeners only such things as edify or instruct them, under the aforesaid penalties.

XIV. We further forbid, under the same penalties, all soldiers of any religion to wear any badges which might offend the others or incite them to quarrel or controversy.

[Further clauses regulate feast days, to the advantage of Catholics except in Holland and Zeeland; provide for equality before the law, with rapid administration of justice; and confirm self-government in the towns.]

V The Creation of the Dutch Republic

The goals sought by William of Orange in the Pacification of Ghent and the "Peace of Religion"—the unity of the Netherlands upon the basis of religious toleration and the expulsion of the Spaniards—continued to prove elusive. The Spanish commander-in-chief and governor-general who took over from Don Juan in October, 1578, was Alexander Farnese, Duke of Parma, who combined extraordinary political and military gifts. He began a methodical reconquest of the Low Countries which in seven years drove the Prince of Orange and his supporters out of the southern Netherlands. At the same time he softened the policies of his master so as to win back to Philip II's allegiance the Catholics who opposed Orange's predominance. But Parma could not dislodge Orange from his stronghold north of the great rivers in the provinces of Holland and Zeeland. Thus a fateful separation of the North and South began to take shape, the origin of modern Holland and Belgium as separate states.

The first steps in this development were the two "unions" of 1579, the Union of Arras in which Parma regained the support of the Walloon provinces and the Union of Utrecht by which Holland, Zeeland, and other northern Provinces combined to stiffen their defenses and form a "narrow union" of the provinces in which Calvinism prevailed. Events then moved swiftly. Philip II put the Prince under a ban of outlawry the next year, to which the States General (in which Flanders and Brabant were still represented, but not the provinces of the Union of Arras) responded by making the Prince of Orange the effective head of government and by casting off the sovereignty of Philip (1581). The next years brought the attempt of William the Silent to obtain sorely needed assistance against Parma's campaign of reconquest by making the French duke of Anjou a constitutional sovereign over the Low Countries, which failed because Anjou wanted absolute power; the assassination of the Prince in 1584 and the capture of Antwerp by Parma in 1585; the governorship-general of the Earl of Leicester (1585–1587), who sought vainly to create an authority in opposition to that of the States of Holland. Then came the famed "Ten Years" of 1588 to 1598, during which the provinces of the Union of Utrecht turned boldly to full self-government, under the political guidance of John van Oldenbarnevelt and the military leadership of Maurice of Nassau, William of Orange's second son (the first, Philip William, had been abducted to Spain while a student at the university of Louvain). The Spaniards were held at the river lines, all the northern provinces recaptured, and a reconquest of territory to the south begun.

After Parma's death in 1592, the Spanish power diminished, and the States General, now reduced to authority in the northern provinces, were recognized as an independent state by France and England. In the South, Philip II, near death, gave the Low Countries to his daughter Isabella and her husband Archduke Albert of Austria. Albert, after vainly attempting to regain the allegiance of the Dutch by far-reaching concessions or at least to achieve terms of a satisfactory peace, finally accepted a truce in 1609, to last twelve years. The independence of the States General of the United Provinces of the Netherlands—the Dutch Republic, as we call it—was an accepted fact, although not yet acknowledged in law by Spain.

16. As if a Single Province

The movement of the Catholic and conservative elements, especially in the southern provinces, toward a reconciliation with Philip II, which culminated in the Union of Arras (see below, no. 47) of January 6, 1579, was paralleled by a movement of the provinces where the Calvinists and the spirit of hostility to Spain moved strongly toward formation of their own "closer union." It was not directed against the States General as such, but was conceived by William of Orange as a means of strengthening the central national body; but his brother, John of Nassau, who led the negotiations as governor of Gelderland, was a passionate Calvinist and approved the provisions of the ultimate agreement which granted freedom only to the Reformed faith in Holland and Zeeland, while granting the other signatories the right to determine which religion would be favored under conditions of general toleration. The final negotiations, conducted at Utrecht, led to an agreement signed by Holland, Zeeland, Utrecht, Gelderland, and the rural districts of Groningen on January 23, 1579. During the months which followed and into 1580, the Union was signed by several Flemish towns, notably Ghent and Bruges, and by the more important Brabant cities except Brussels. William the Silent, displeased by the religious clauses, did not sign it until May 1579. The political terms were those of a perpetual alliance of existing sovereign states; but it was more than just an alliance of the traditional kind, for central bodies of government, the Council of State with primarily executive functions, and the States General, were established or continued, and no member had the right of secession. Yet the Union also proclaimed that the sovereign rights of the individual provinces remained intact. The resulting ambiguity made disputes over authority a virtual certainty, and the stadholders "now in office" were empowered to decide such cases. There was no intention to create a new state nor to create a new constitutional arrangement of power; yet the Union of Utrecht remained the fundamental law—one might almost say, the substitute for a constitution—until 1795, when the Dutch Republic was extinguished.

Source: "Verhandelinge van de Unie, Eeuwig Verbondt ende Eendracht tusschen die Landen, Provintien, Steden en Leden van Hollant, Zeelant, Utrecht, &c. binnen de Stadt Utrecht gesloten, den 23. January Anno 1579," in du Mont, V, i, pp. 322–327. Translated from the Dutch by Herbert H. Rowen.

WHEREAS, since the Pacification made at Ghent, by which almost all the provinces of these Netherlands bound themselves to help each other with their lives and goods in order to drive out the Spaniards and other foreign nations, together with their adherents, we have discovered that these same Spaniards under Don John of Austria and their other chiefs and captains have endeavored and still daily endeavor to bring these provinces as a group and individually under their subjection, tyrannical government, and slavery and to divide and dismember these same provinces by arms and wily practices and to destroy and subvert the Union created by this aforesaid Pacification, with the aim of the utter ruin and downfall of the aforesaid lands and provinces, in which enterprise they persevere, having recently solicited certain cities and quarters with letters and attacked and invaded others, to wit, Gelderland, with arms,

  THEREFORE the members for the Duchy of Gelderland and County of Zutphen, the counties and lands of Holland, Zeeland, Utrecht, Friesland, and the districts between Eems and Lauwers[1] have found it wise to unite and bind each other more closely and specifically, not in order to split away from the aforesaid general

1. The *Ommelanden* of Groningen province, that is, the "surroundings" which did not include the city of Groningen itself. The full name of the province was *Groningen en Ommelanden* ("Groningen and Surroundings"), or *Stad en Lande* ("City and Countryside").—*Ed.*

Union made by the Pacification at Ghent, but in order further to strengthen it and to take measures against the troubles which may come upon them from the wiles, attacks, and violence of their enemies, by determining how and what each of these provinces will do in such a case and acting to protect them against the violence of their enemies. And to prevent further separation of the aforesaid provinces and individual members while the others remain in the aforesaid general Union and Pacification of Ghent, the deputies of the aforesaid provinces, with the full authority granted by their principals, have decreed and concluded the following Points and Articles, without thereby in any way desiring to secede from the Holy Roman Empire.

I.

Firstly, the aforesaid provinces will form an alliance, confederation, and union among themselves, as they do hereby form an alliance, confederation, and union, in order to remain joined together for all time, in every form and manner, as if they constituted only a single province, and they may not hereafter divide or permit their division or separation by testament, codicils, donations, cessions, exchanges, sales, treaties of peace or marriage, or for any other reason whatsoever. Nevertheless each province and the individual cities, members, and inhabitants thereof shall each retain undiminished its special and particular privileges, franchises, exemptions, rights, statutes, laudable and long practiced customs, usages and all its rights, and each shall not only do the others no damage, harm, or vexation but shall help to maintain, strengthen, confirm, and indeed protect the others in these by all proper and possible means, indeed if need be with life and goods, against any and all who seek to deprive them of these in any way, whatever it may be. It is fully agreed that differences which now exist or may develop hereafter between some of the aforesaid provinces, members or cities of this Union, concerning their particular and special privileges, franchises, exemptions, rights, statutes, laudable and long practiced customs, usages and rights, shall be decided by means of the ordinary courts of justice, by arbiters, or by friendly agreement, and the other lands or provinces, cities and members thereof shall not interfere, as long as the parties submit to procedures at law, unless they intercede for the sake of agreement.

II.

[The Alliance and Union is to be maintained against attempts upon it made in the name of the Peace of Ghent or under the pretext of re-establishing Roman Catholicism, removing any innovations introduced since 1558, or overthrowing the present Union of Utrecht.]

III.

That the aforesaid provinces shall also be bound to assist each other in the same way and to help each other against all foreign and domestic lords, princes, lands, provinces, cities or members thereof, who seek to do them, as a group or individually, any harm or injustice, or wage war upon them. But it is agreed that assistance given by the Generality of this Union shall be provided with knowledge of the situation.

IV.

Item, in order to assure the aforesaid provinces, cities and members thereof more effectively against all violence, the frontier cities and others where this shall be found necessary in any provinces, shall be maintained and fortified at the cost of the cities and provinces in which they are situated, with the Generality providing one-half of the costs. Provided that if it shall be found expedient to build several new fortresses in any of the aforesaid provinces, or to rebuild or tear down any that now exist, then the costs shall be borne by all the aforesaid provinces in common.

V.

And to provide for the expenses which shall be found necessary in such cases as the above for the defense of the aforesaid Provinces, it is agreed that there will be introduced, raised, and leased to the highest bidder every three months or at other convenient time, in all the provinces upon the same footing for their common defense, various taxes upon all kinds of wines, beers of domestic and foreign brew, the grinding of corn and grain, salt, gold, silver, silk and woollen cloth, livestock and cultivated land, slaughtered beasts, horses, oxen sold or exchanged, goods weighed at public scales, and all other goods which it shall be unanimously agreed hereafter to tax. In accordance with the ordinance to be drafted and adopted upon this matter, the revenues of the domains of his Royal Majesty shall also be employed for these ends, after deducting the charges upon them.

VI.

These revenues shall be increased or decreased only by unanimous decision, according to the needs of the situation, but shall serve only the common defense and the expenditures placed upon the Generality, and they shall not be diverted to any other use. . . .

IX.

Item, that no treaties of truce or peace shall be made or wars begun, nor any taxes or contributions be raised affecting this Union in general, except with the general advice and consent of the aforesaid provinces. But in other matters affecting the maintenance of this Confederation and the results and consequences thereof, decisions shall be made according to the opinions and votes of a majority of the provinces included in this Union, which shall be counted according to the existing practice of the States General but only provisionally until other arrangements are ordered by the common decision of the Allies.[2]

Provided that in the event that the provinces cannot reach agreement in matters of truce, peace, war, or taxation, then the difference will be referred to and provisionally submitted to the stadholders now in office in the aforesaid United Provinces, who shall bring the parties to an agreement or make their own decision in the conflict, as they shall deem proper. It shall be understood that if the stadholders themselves cannot come to an agreement in such matters, they shall name impartial assessors or deputies of their

2. The Dutch word *bondgenoten*, "allies," is used in the Union of Utrecht and during the entire subsequent history of the Dutch Republic for the member provinces, not for foreign allies, usually designated as *geallieerden.–Ed.*

own choice, and the parties shall be held to accept the decisions made by the stadholders in this manner.

X.

None of the aforesaid provinces, cities, or members thereof may make any confederation or alliances with any neighboring rulers or countries, without the consent of these United Provinces and Allies.

XI.

It is agreed that if any neighboring princes, lords, lands, or cities desire to join with the aforesaid provinces and enter this Confederation, they may be accepted only by common advice and consent of these provinces.

XII.

The aforesaid provinces shall be required to adhere to the same valuation of coinage, that is, the rate of monetary exchange, according to such ordinances as shall be made thereupon at the first opportunity, and it may not be changed except by common agreement.

XIII.

As for the matter of religion, the States of Holland and Zeeland shall act according to their own pleasure, and the other Provinces of this Union shall follow the rules set down in the religious peace drafted by Archduke Matthias, governor and captain-general of these countries, with the advice of the Council of State and the States General, or shall establish such general or special regulations in this matter as they shall find good and most fitting for the repose and welfare of the provinces, cities, and individual Members thereof, and the preservation of the property and rights of each individual, whether churchman or layman, and no other Province shall be permitted to interfere or make difficulties, provided that each person shall remain free in his religion and that no one shall be investigated or persecuted because of his religion, as is provided in the Pacification made at Ghent. . . .

XVIII.

Item, none of the United Provinces, or cities or members thereof, shall impose any taxes, convoy fees, or similar burdens, which shall be detrimental to other Provinces, except by common agreement, and none of the allies may be taxed more highly than the inhabitants of a province itself. . . .

XXIV.

To assure its more exact performance, the stadholders of the aforesaid provinces who are now in office and their successors, as well as the magistrates and chief officials of each Province, City, and Member thereof, shall be required to swear on oath to follow and maintain this Union and Confederation and each Article therein, and to have others do the same.

XXV.

The same oath shall be taken by all civic guards, confraternities, and corporate bodies in any cities or places of this Union.

17. The Need for Effective Central Power

Resistance to an astute and resourceful captain such as Parma required a concentration of efforts and a common plan of action under one leadership. But such a structure of government conflicted with one of the principal driving forces in the opposition to Philip of Spain—the resistance to centralization. The difficulties faced by William of Orange in uniting the efforts of the towns and provinces in a common endeavor against what was ultimately one danger are illustrated in a remonstrance which he presented to the States General on January 9, 1580.

Source: Gachard, Correspondance de Guillaume le Taciturne, Vol. IV, pp. 196–200, 202, 204. Translated from the French by Herbert H. Rowen.

GENTLEMEN, since I have often told you in person and (as your journals will testify) have warned in writing about the straits into which we would fall if you did not make prompt provision to meet the situation, I think that I will have sufficiently done my duty if I make no further mention of this. I am sure that you and those who will have knowledge of what has taken place will consider that I have fully performed according to my oath in this respect.

But I see that I have not yet advanced the welfare and security of this country as much as I had desired, because of shortcomings which, I believe, do not lie in yourselves, gentlemen, for you have probably done as much as you could, within the limitations of your instructions, but which lie in the situation itself. Because you are now about to return to your own provinces to take final and necessary resolutions, I have felt it my duty, so as not to fall short in anything that I think can serve the public, to recall to you briefly what I have often discussed with you before this at greater length. What I seek is that you point out to your masters the necessities of our situation as I reveal them to you and that, after hearing you, they will join you in adopting resolutions to repair the defects in our organization. Then, together, we may save the country and defeat the designs of our enemies, who are neither feeble in their undertakings, nor easy to surprise, nor lacking in desire to hurt us.

In the first place, gentlemen, ruin cannot be avoided if we remain irresolute in our affairs, for even if we take all the decisions which in our judgment can serve the country, we can still have enough to do with foes who are so numerous and powerful and are not at all bad soldiers. Now we must first decide before anything else whether we want peace or war. When I speak of peace, I do not mean it in general terms. For who is so much his own enemy and his wife's, his children's and, more, his country's, that he does not desire peace with all his heart, a peace which alone can enable him to pass his life pleasantly in his own home in the enjoyment of the goods which God has given him and in the service of God according to his conscience? The particular peace I have in mind is the one that is actually offered to us, for nothing is gained by talking of peace in general if we do not also consider the specific provisions of the treaties by which it is proposed to achieve it. . . .

But by some mishap or other it so happens that although in general we are convinced that we must use arms to defend the freedom of our country, our goods, our honor, our wives, and our children, when it comes to taking a specific decision, we ourselves spoil by unwise counsels and amendments on special points what we have decided upon in general terms as necessary. This makes our pains and labors useless and brings the country and ourselves to ruin.

The first and foremost fault is that you and your masters have not yet established any body or board, not even within the States, which has any power to take useful decisions in the general defense of this state; but each of you in his own province or city does what he pleases in his own interests, not considering that to give one city or province an advantage for a time means in the end to endanger the province or even the whole country.

The result is that we are compelled to wage war, not where it is most favorable for us and where the interests of the country require but often where the enemy want us to. He attacks first here and then there, while we for our part go where he goes, as if it were up to him to determine the place and time to fight. We shall always have to stay on the defensive as long as we can assemble only the forces of a single province at one time. These are not enough to stand up to the enemy forces, which he brings together into whole armies while our forces are dispersed and scattered in many places.

This malady arises from the cause I have mentioned, to wit: that you have not established a superior body or board to which the individual provinces pay obedience and which can meet dangers as they occur, which are sometimes absent in some places and very great in others. This is caused by the circumstance I have described, that is, that a province which comes under pressure suddenly cries out for help to me, and often in vain; the others, which do not feel the danger so close, want to get rid of the soldiers in their pay, either by discharging them outright or by transferring them to the pay of other provinces which are already quite burdened. If later the danger comes close to them, then they call for help, as if soldiers who are not kept on the rolls can be brought up out of the ground just by stamping your foot. . . .

But the true cause of all these disorders is our own indecision. We meet often enough and talk a lot, but are as negligent in carrying out our decisions as we are slow and deliberate in debating them. For we must not think, gentlemen, that there is no longer any valor in the hearts of the good people of this country; it is a fire which smolders beneath the ashes, but blow on it and it will soon burn high again, but let it stay as it is and it will soon be dead.

On the other hand, you know, don't you, that the enemy has difficulties which are even greater than ours: a shortage of money, powder, and munitions of all kinds; divisions, factions, and plots; many cities and provinces which are weary of the insolence of the soldiers and ready to rebel? But, gentlemen, it is because of our own inability to take advantage of any of the enemy's difficulties that our own people are pushed toward wrongdoing by our long delays and indecision. This is especially true because it is natural for everyone to seek his own safety and he would rather trust it to a council of men with a small force but possessing determination, than to a large but irresolute force, and because he sees cities and whole provinces abandoned by their allies for hardly any reason, even after the last Union that we made. This makes them think that when they themselves are in greater trouble, they will not find much help, and they are readier therefore to take the side which they think shows more determination. . . .

It seems to me, gentlemen, that you can restore order in our affairs if you keep up the good will you have always shown for the public weal and accept this counsel, to wit: give power to persons whom you name to take measures on all necessary occasions, with a promise (which is to be enforced) to obey those who will be chosen. Let us no longer have to hear so often the reply, "We have no power from our masters," which throws even our best meetings into confusion. I am not advising you to give power to these deputies to raise new taxes at their own pleasure and to have absolute power to decide everything as they please, but only that they be able to give orders for the effective collection of the taxes which are granted and which you yourselves decide are necessary, and which I hope, gentlemen, your masters will approve, and that they have the right to spend these funds as they find expedient, to assemble forces of soldiers and distribute them into garrisons when they are needed, and to see to all political events and affairs for the good of the country.

18. The Proscription of William the Silent

So clearly was William of Orange the heart of the revolt against his authority that Philip II, at the suggestion of Cardinal Granvelle, finally decided to seek his elimination by the most direct means, assassination. The moral aspect of the ban against William which he issued on March 15, 1580, did not trouble him, nor his church advisors, nor his commander in the Low Countries, the personally honorable Parma; but Parma doubted the practical wisdom of giving the rebels so eminent a martyr. They all accepted the doctrine that the good end of destroying one whom the ban called "the plague of the Christian community" justified the evil means necessary to achieve it. (This Machiavellian doctrine was generally accepted, no less by those who denounced Machiavelli's work as "devilish" but saw themselves as doing God's work, than by those who considered that Machiavelli was merely approving what was commonly practiced.) The public issuance of the ban in August sharply increased the peril to William's life. He was the victim of two attacks. The first, by Jean Jaureguy in 1582, wounded him gravely, but he survived, although his wife, Charlotte of Bourbon-Montpensier, wore out her own health in nursing him. The second attack, by Balthazar Gérards on July 10, 1584, at Delft, succeeded.

Source: Gachard, *Correspondance de Guillaume le Taciturne,* Vol. VI, pp. xxxvii–xxxix. Translated from the French by Herbert H. Rowen.

FOR THESE most just, right, and legitimate reasons and making use of the authority which we have over the said Orange both by virtue of the oaths of fidelity and obedience which he has often made to us and because we are absolute prince and sovereign of the said Low Countries, for all his perverse and baneful acts and because he alone is chief author and promoter of the troubles there and the principal disturber of our state, in brief is the plague of the Christian community, we do declare him to be a wicked traitor and an enemy to ourselves and the country. As such we have proscribed and do proscribe him for all time from our said countries and from all our other states, kingdoms, and lordships, and we forbid and prevent all our subjects, of whatever status, condition, or quality, from frequenting, living, discoursing, speaking, or communicating with him openly or in secret, or receiving or lodging him in their houses, or providing him with food, drink, fuel, or other necessities of any kind, under penalty of incurring our wrath, as shall be hereafter described.

But we give permission to all persons, whether our subjects or others, to arrest, hold, and make sure of his person, employing force and violence if need be in the execution of this declaration, baring the said William of Nassau to the whole world as an enemy of the human race; and we give to whoever can take and occupy or conquer them all his properties, real or personal, wherever situated or located, with the exception of the goods which are at present in our own hands and possession.

So that this purpose may be achieved more promptly and our people may be delivered more quickly from this tyranny and oppression, and wishing to reward virtue and punish crime, we promise upon the word of a king and as a servant of God that if there be someone, either our subject or a foreigner, with such good will and so strong a desire for our service and the public good that he can enforce our said ordinance and rid us of this plague, delivering Orange to us dead or alive or even just killing him, we will give and furnish to him and to his heirs the sum of 25,000 gold crowns, in land or cash at his choice, immediately after the accomplishment of the deed. If he has committed any crime or breach of the law whatever, we promise to pardon him and do pardon him as of now. Further, if he is not a nobleman, we grant him nobility for his valor. And if the principal agent uses other persons to assist him in his enterprise or in the performance of his deed, we will reward them each according to his station and the service which he shall have rendered to us on this account, pardoning them too for whatever crimes they may have committed and likewise granting nobility to them. . . .

19. The Prince's Powers Extended and Continued

In the four years between the issuance of the ban against him by Philip II and its consummation by Gérards, William the Silent continued his work in leadership of the revolt. On June 10, 1580, before the publication of the ban, the States General had already granted the Prince the stadholdership of the province of Friesland [a.], paralleling that which he already held in Holland and Zeeland. Two years later, on May 3, 1582, they voted to maintain him in the office of lieutenant-general for the whole country by a decision to continue payment of his salary; significantly, however, a straightforward decision could not be taken to this effect because one province, Gelderland, withheld its assent [b.].

Source: Gachard, *Correspondance de Guillaume le Taciturne,* Vol. VI, pp. 322, 336. Translated from the French by Herbert H. Rowen.

a.

EXTRACT OF the register of the resolutions of my Lords, the States General of the Netherlands, of June 10, 1580.

The States General, having heard the report of my Lord van Metkercke, Councilor of State, have asked and do hereby ask His Highness to have sent to my worthy lord, my Lord the Prince of Orange, a commission to accept and assume the government of Friesland.

In my presence,

HOUFFLIN.

b.

THIS DAY [May 3, 1582] my Lords the States General deliberated upon the lieutenancy-general of the country previously held by my gracious Lord the Prince of Orange; but the deputies of the provinces were not in agreement, although they considered it desirable to continue the salary of 36,000 guilders annually for the foregoing services which His Excellency has given to the country and which he, with God's grace, will continue to give; and they place a paragraph in the recess [resolution of decisions] to this effect. But the deputies of Gelderland declared that they may not accept this resolution.

20. The Prince's Reply to the King: The Apology

With the publication of the ban, William felt the need to justify his cause before the people of his country and before mankind. He instructed his court chaplain, De Villiers, aided by two of his own friends, the French Huguenots Languet and Du Plessis-Mornay, to draw up an Apology. The document, written between mid-September and mid-October, was officially presented to the States General on December 13, 1580, and published the next February. The personal accusations against William in the ban were met by equally personal invective against the Spanish king, some of it groundless but all designed to reply *ad hominem* to an attack *ad hominem*. But there was more to the *Apology* than personal recriminations: it defended William's leadership of the revolt against Philip II and breathed the spirit of love of freedom and willingness for sacrifice. The *Apology* was written in French, but translations were at once prepared and published in Dutch, Latin, English, and German, and copies were sent to the rulers of Europe with an apology (in the now more usual sense of the term) for its tone. The contemporary English translation, recently republished in a scholarly edition,[3] is of historical interest, but its Elizabethan prose itself virtually requires a quasi translation for the general reader, so that it has seemed best to re-translate the sections of the Apology given below directly from the original into modern English.

Source: "Apologie de Guillaume IX, Prince d'Orange contre la Proscription de Philippe II, Roy d'Espagne," in du Mont, Vol. V, part i, pp. 384–385, 389–390, 392, 395–397, 401–402, 405–406. Translated from the French by Herbert H. Rowen.

MY LORDS, from the time that I first dedicated myself and all my worldly goods to the recovery of your liberty and the defense of your persons, estates, and consciences, I have always prayed with all my heart that God should grant me this, that if I should ever prefer my own personal interests to your general welfare, I should suffer the eternal punishment and ignominy which I would have brought upon myself by my own doing. On the other hand, I asked God that if what I have done until now was undertaken only for the preservation of your state and if I have borne so much of the responsibility for the conduct of this present war, I have done so only for the common safety of the fatherland. If all the hatred felt by wicked men against this country and against all persons of merit and honor, which they had falsely hidden in their hearts, is now let loose upon me rather than upon all these worthy people or even upon the Republic in general, and if these have been my intentions toward you, my Lords, and toward your children, your cities, and your communities, then I prayed that I might some day publish solemn testimony that this was so, as much for my conscience's repose as in defense of my honor before all the nations of the earth and before all posterity.

That God permits me to receive this rare, noble, and excellent mark of honor that a cruel, barbarous proscription is put out against me, which is utterly without precedent and beyond belief in this country, famed among all peoples and nations for its charac-

3. H. Wansink, ed., *The Apologie of Prince William of Orange against the Proclamation of the King of Spaine* (Leiden: E. J. Brill, 1969).

teristic loving-kindness, gives me great joy and reason to be greatly gladdened and satisfied, for which I render everlasting thanks to our good God. For, although a man can desire nothing more than that his life should run a happy, prosperous, and even course, without shocks or knocks, it is also true that if everything had gone as I wanted, and if I had not earned the hatred of the Spanish nation and its adherents, I would not have been rewarded by this testimony paid to me by my enemies; it is the finest garland of glory that I could desire before I die. What gives more pleasure in this world, especially to one who has undertaken the great and excellent task of defending the freedom of a good people against the oppression of wicked men, than to be the target of the mortal hatred of his enemies, who are also the enemies of the fatherland, and to receive from their own mouths such a telling tribute to one's loyalty to his own people and to his constancy in the face of tyrants and disturbers of the public peace? The Spaniards and their adherents imagined that they would hurt me with this infamous ban, but they have only given me greater joy and satisfaction. Not only have I gained this fruit from their labors, but they have opened up for me a field wider than I could have hoped for where I can defend myself and tell the world that what I undertook was fair and just. Thus I could leave to my posterity an example of virtue to be followed by all of them who do not wish to dishonor the nobility of the ancestors from whom we are descended, of whom not one ever upheld tyranny but all loved the liberty of the peoples over whom they held office and legitimate power.

I do not have any reason to complain that before this I lacked adequate grounds for speaking of myself or for accusing my enemies of great and grievous faults. But modesty kept me from singing my own praises, although this is hard to avoid on such an occasion, however modest one tries to be, and common courtesy forbade that I dilate upon my enemies' crimes, for I preferred to bury in silence some of the atrocious acts of which they were guilty rather than reveal them; I did so despite the fact that they were true, lest I run the danger of being taken for a slanderer. Since it is not only my person, my Lords, which is the target of this ban making me the prey of barbarians, but obviously in attacking me it is the Republic and the authority of this entire country which they seek to hurt; since what we see now are not just slanderous little pamphlets written by nobodies, whose defamations no more affected me than the bite of a little snake which one crushes under-foot rather than slay it with weapons, but falsehoods and calumnies by which men of great station reduce themselves to vile meanness —therefore I have deemed it utterly necessary to speak out. I do not want our common fatherland, for which I am ready to risk my life as I already have risked my estates, to suffer by my silence, and I want the eyes of those who judge the affairs of this world more by shadows and appearances than by the firmness and solidity of reason not to be dazzled by the illustrious titles[4] of so many king-doms and countries extending to Africa and Asia.

I am quite aware that he who has put me under the ban has a number of advantages over me. Of these, the two most important are his high rank, so far surpassing my own, and that he whom he praises is himself. My foe may have for his part whatever gives him pleasure in such advantages, and I will take what is hard and de-spised by the world for my own. But I hope, my Lords, that your accustomed favor and affection toward me will protect me from suffering by either of his advantages, for you have long since learned by experience that high and illustrious rank when stained by tyranny makes little impression upon the hearts of free and generous men.

On the other hand, you who know me in the ordinary course of my life are aware that I no more like to find fault in others than to praise myself. But if I must do one or the other, as it seems I must, then if, with all the modesty that I can muster, I still do something which is not wholly befitting, you should put the blame, my Lords, upon the compulsions which my enemies place me under and not upon my character, and therefore you should lay all guilt upon their impudence and contumely. You will recall, my Lords, that I am false accused of being "ungrateful, unfaithful, a hypocrite, the likes of Judas and Cain, a disturber of the country, a rebel, a for-eigner, an enemy of mankind, a pestilence upon all Christendom, a traitor, and a wicked person, that I may be slain like a wild beast and that a successful assassin or poisoner will be paid for his deed." It is for you to judge whether it is possible for me to clear myself of such calumnies without speaking of myself and others in a way that I am not wont to do. Nonetheless, I have such confidence in the justice of my cause, in my integrity and loyalty to you and in

4. Of Philip II.—*Ed.*

your fairness, frankness, and knowledge of what I have said and done, that I ask of you only that you hear and judge this case and command as the laws, franchises, liberties, and privileges of the country require and as the people expect from your wisdom and integrity. This I beseech you to do by all that is holy and sacred and by your oath and duty to the country. I am certain that although I may be less than my enemies in some things, in this I shall be so much their superior because they have sought to violate, break, and suppress your laws, your privileges, and liberties, while I, on the contrary, have worked with good heart and all fidelity to maintain and preserve them. . . .

You will see, my Lords, that my defense against this jumble of impudent and malign slanders, without which this ban would be only a whiff of smoke, is simple and plain. If the man you know me to be is the man described by my enemies, if I bear in either body or soul the colors in which the concoctor of this document paints me, then, my Lords, you who have known me since my youth and among whom I have spent all my years of manhood, close your ears at once and refuse to hear any word from my lips. But if on the contrary I have been more meritorious, more honest, more chaste, and less miserly than the authors of this infamous document or the persons who made it public, to wit, the Prince of Parma and his predecessors, whose deeds are only too well known to history, and if you know that I and my ancestors have been men of greater worth than they and their ancestors, then you will believe that they begin by maligning me and that the rest of their accusations are no more credible than the first. For, I ask you, what is the purpose of such a long recital of slanders but to show the whole world that they can vilify and disparage one whom, by God's mercy, they have not been able to slay by poison or sword, nor deceive by promises and fool by idle hopes, and that they are striving to destroy him with the venom of tongues which have been trained since their youth in this infamous trade? . . .

Not only have they addressed themselves to me personally, accusing me of ingratitude and infidelity, but in their rage and fury they have turned their attack equally upon all, making no distinction between the innocent and those who are presumed guilty. So great has been their effrontery that they have made my wife's honor their target by impugning the validity of my recent marriage. I do not know whether I find their impudence or their stupidity worse, for these learned men who boast of their skill with words forgot to listen to what young schoolboys chant all the time, "People who live in glass houses shouldn't throw stones." If they are aware of these faults and nevertheless try to pretend that thistles and thornbushes are really rosebushes, then they are stupid and insolent; but if they aren't, how stupid can they be not to see what everyone else has before his eyes all the time? Every day they see an incestuous king who differs only half a degree from Jupiter, who married Juno, his own sister,[5] and they dare reproach me with a marriage which is holy, honest, and lawful, in accordance with God's laws, and which was celebrated according to the ordinances of God's church! Now I must ask you, my Lords, to realize that I am doing something now which you never saw me do before. I am moved by slander to reveal these horrible ulcers and cut into them with the cautery for all the world to see: but I beg of you to put the blame for what I do upon the rage and desperate fury of men who are enemies of God and all Christendom, and especially of yourselves, men who have turned their wrath upon me only because they know how active, diligent, and loyal I have been in your defense. . . .

[The *Apology* continues with charges of bigamy and adultery against Philip II.]

The objection is raised that I am a foreigner in the Low Countries. As if the Prince of Parma, who was not born in this country, who owns not a shilling's worth of land here, and possesses not a single title here, but who commands some dunderheads with a rod of iron and makes those who obey him into slaves, were a great patriot. But what does the word "foreigner" mean? It means someone who was not born in the country. Then the king is as much a foreigner as I, for he was born in Spain, a country which is the natural enemy of the Netherlands, and I was born in Germany, a neighboring country which is its natural friend. They will reply that he is a king, and I will reply that here I do not know this title of "king." He may be a king in Castile, Aragon, Naples, the Indies and wherever he commands according to his own pleasure; if he wants, he can be a king in Jerusalem or even a peaceful ruler in Asia and Africa. But in this country I know only of a duke and a

5. A reference to the marriage between Philip II and Anna of Austria, daughter of Emperor Maximilian II.—*Ed.*

count whose power is limited by the privileges which he swore at his Joyous Entry. As for my position, it is well known. My predecessors, from whom I am descended in the direct masculine line, became the possessors of the counties and baronies of Luxemburg, Brabant, Flanders, and Holland. For about the year 1340 Count Otto, from whom I am descended in the seventh degree and whose eldest heir I am, married the Countess of Vianden, and ever since the county of Vianden remained in our house and we enjoyed peaceful possession of it until the king deprived me unjustly of it. Afterward Count Engelbert I, grandson of this Count Otto, married the Lady of Lek and Breda, and I am also descended from him in the direct masculine line in the fifth degree. Can I rightly be called a foreigner then? Nor need I mention at the moment my estates in Burgundy, of which I have a good share, thank God. I leave it to you, my Lords, who know our laws better than anyone else in the world, to judge whether, according to the usages of our ancestors from time immemorial, the Lords of Ravenstein, Luxemburg, St. Paul, Nevers, Étampes, and others who held counties and baronies in this country were considered to be foreigners, and whether even today you do not consider as natives all those who possess such lordships, providing that they are willing to take this country's side. Is this not even a specific law among us in Brabant, as well as elsewhere?

[Further arguments for the proprietary rights of the ancestors of the Prince of Orange over those of the House of Habsburg in the Low Countries.]

They say "that from the time the King left these Netherlands, I have tried by sinister practices, plots, and wiles to win the good will of the Malcontents, and of men who are in debt, those who hate justice, who seek after novelties and especially those who are suspected of being adherents of the [Reformed] Religion." As for those who profess the Protestant religion, I admit that I have never hated them. It was the religion I was brought up in from the cradle; my father lived and died in it after having expelled the abuses of the Church from his lands. Who then will find it strange that this doctrine is so engraved in my heart and that it put down such roots that in time it bore fruit? But I was brought up for many years in the Emperor's chamber, and then when I became old enough to bear arms, I was at once given high posts and my head was filled more with thoughts of weapons, hunting, and the other activities of young noblemen than with what concerned the salvation of my soul. Yet I have great reason to give thanks to God, who did not permit this holy seed which he himself planted in me to be choked. I can say too that the cruel execution of Protestants by fire, the sword, or drowning, which was then only too common, was never to my liking. The author or painter of this infamous ban calls the Protestants "persons of the Religion," and although everywhere else he flatters, lies, or slanders, he uses his words quite well when he calls them this, for Protestantism is the only religion which truly deserves the name; it is an admission which was torn from his lips by its great force and the efficacy of its truth.

When I was in France[6] I was told by King Henry that the Duke of Alva was negotiating about ways to exterminate all suspected Protestants in France, in this country, and throughout Christendom. When King Henry, who thought that because I was one of the commissioners for the peace treaty and was informed of important matters I was also a party to this affair, revealed to me the true intentions of the King of Spain and the Duke of Alva, I replied in such a way that the king would not lose his esteem for me as someone from whom things had been concealed, and in his trust of me he therefore continued to discourse at length so that I could grasp what the Inquisitors really had in mind. I admit that I was moved by pity and compassion for so many worthy persons doomed to slaughter, and for this country to which I owed so much, into which they planned to introduce the Inquisition in a form even worse and more cruel than it was in Spain, and I confess that when I saw the nets put out to trap both the nobles of the country as well as the common people, and that no escape was possible, since one had to do no more than look askance at an image to be sentenced to burn at the stake, I deliberately began my endeavor of helping to drive those Spanish vermin from the country. I have never regretted that I did so but consider that my companions and I, and all the others who supported this meritorious enterprise, performed an act worthy of immortal praise, and that we would have achieved our entire purpose and risen to the heights of honor if we had slammed the door shut upon them after

6. In July 1559, as a hostage on behalf of Philip II to Henry II after the conclusion of the Peace of Cateau-Cambrésis.—*Ed.*

their departure, if we had found the means to rid the country of them so that they would never have come back. . . .

[Description of his negotiations and their failures and successes, and of his defeats and victories. The illegal seizure of his eldest son, William Philip, a student at Leiden university who was taken to Spain; the violations of the privileges of the Order of the Golden Fleece.]

You know, my Lords, the duties to which the King is bound and that he cannot do whatever he pleases, as he can in the Indies. Under the privileges of Brabant, he cannot compel a single one of his subjects to do anything by means of force except in accordance with the usages of the court of justice which has jurisdiction over him. He cannot change the constitution of the country by ordinance or decree in any way. He must be satisfied with his ordinary revenues and may not establish or collect any taxes without the approval and the express consent of the country given in accordance with its privileges. He cannot bring soldiers into the country without its consent. He cannot change the value of money without the consent of the States assemblies of the country. He cannot order the arrest of any subject without a hearing by the local magistrate, nor can he have a prisoner sent out of the country. . . .

They add the charge "that I introduced freedom of conscience." If they mean that I permitted the kind of impieties which are habitual in the Prince of Parma's house, where atheism and other Roman virtues have free play, then I reply that is among the heirs of Lord Peter Lewis[7] that such freedom, or rather such unbridled license, is to be sought. But I do indeed confess that I have never liked to watch so many poor Christians tortured, although it gave delight to the Duke of Alva and the Spaniards, and that I favored halting persecution in the Low Countries. I will admit further, so that my foes may know that they have to do with one who speaks frankly and without pretense, that the King, as he was leaving for Zeeland, his last stop in this country, ordered me to put to death

7. Pier Luigi Farnese (1503–1547), created first Duke of Parma and Piacenza by his father, Pope Paul III, and murdered by noblemen after a cruel, tyrannical reign of only two years. The Prince of Parma of whom Orange writes was Alexander Farnese, the Spanish governor-general and commander in the Low Countries; he was the grandson of Pier Luigi Farnese.–Ed.

several worthy persons suspected of being Protestants, and that I
did not do it but instead sent warnings to them. I know that I could
not do what I had been commanded to do in good conscience and
that I had to obey God before men. Let the Spaniards say what
they will, I know that what I have done will be praised and approved by other peoples and nations as good as they, who have
learned that fire and sword bring little profit. But you, my Lords,
have since approved what I did, condemning, with the universal
consent of the people, the rigor of the ordinances and halting such
cruel executions, and therefore I care not one whit for the grum-
bling of the Spaniards and their adherents.

But I cannot but be astounded by their stupidity in shamelessly
blaming me for the massacre of Catholics. Not only are they
unaware that such violence is wholly foreign to my character, but
they do not know, as you and everyone else knows full well, that it
was by my command and decree that some who were guilty of
such excesses as they impute to me were put to death, and that
others, notable members of illustrious houses, were arrested by
persons in my own service and were later released from the long
imprisonment to which they had been sentenced for their crimes
only out of regard to the houses of which they had the honor to be
members. But what was done by my order is so well known to all
that they cannot disguise or conceal it; yet they have learned to
state the truth in ways useful to themselves and say that when I did
something virtuous, I was only pretending. Who told them that I
was pretending? Who revealed my secret purposes to them? They
have seen what I did but they cannot judge my heart, and there is
no man, however malicious, except the author of this document or
a Spaniard, who should not base his judgment upon what he sees
rather than upon what he maliciously suspects.

They heap a multitude of accusations upon our religion and call
us heretics, but they have been trying to prove this for a long time
and have got almost nowhere. Their slanders are like the words
which men speak in the heat of anger and which do not deserve a
reply. Of all their slanders, the one which least deserves an answer
is the stupid charge that I have not trusted any priest or monk
unless he married and that I even forced them to wed. Who does
not know that in their unbridled fury and passion they will pick up
anything they find in the roadway to throw at me? Yet, even if
these things were true (which they are not) and based on reason

(for we are taught by our religion that marriage should be free, neither forced nor forbidden), they would still not compare with that tyrannizing over conscience which forbids a part of Christendom to marry, against the resistance not only of the Eastern Churches but also the churches of Germany and France. . . .

They upbraid me because "I have great authority among the people." Far from being ashamed of it, I deeply regret that I did not have greater influence and that I was not always able to persuade them to do what I repeatedly proposed in speech and writing. If they had done what I proposed, I would have long since cleansed this country of the Spanish filth with God's help. But if the people are as they describe them and I am as they describe me (which I will assume, to make them happy), then they cannot help but admit that their tyrannies and cruelty must have been enormous in every way to have earned them the universal hatred of the whole people, who earlier had held them in such affection and had been so loyal to their predecessors and even to them before they committed these excesses. If, on the contrary, the people willingly chose me to be the defender of their freedom, what else can be said by foreign nations or posterity except that the people believed that there was something in me worthy of such hatred? I admit therefore that I am popular and will be for the rest of my life. I admit, that is, that I will seek, I will maintain, I will defend your freedom and your privileges. . . .

I am also flabbergasted that they forget to repeat the accusation of hating the nobility which so many little lying writers of clumsy slanders and libels have made against me. Do I begin by hating myself, my relatives, and my friends, who are, thank God, all of ancient, noble, and illustrious race and of such high rank and great wealth that I do not fear comparison with our enemies, few of whom can match us in eminence? But experience has shown whether or not I am doing everything in my power for the advancement of the nobles. If I foresaw long ago that certain ambitious persons, who have since departed from our midst, wished to seize the government and its offices in order to abandon the country and betray their oaths, if, knowing their frivolity, vanity, and inconstancy, and their fondness for tyranny, I did not support them and thus helped to preserve the best, largest, and healthiest part of our state, this did not mean that I hated or scorned the nobility but that I wished with their aid to prevent the ruin of the country which was so close upon us. Their fathers were wiser, braver, and more virtuous than my accusers and they were my good friends. If they were still alive, they would be mortified at the sight of a race which has abandoned the constancy and virtue of its ancestors, who lived honorably and without reproach; especially if they also saw that they were looked upon everywhere as vacillators and great bargainers, and that the Spaniards whom they serve and the Cardinal whom they flit around make child's play of them, leading them by the nose like animals, supporting them until it is time to return the statues, instruments, tapestry, and other furnishings which they have taken from them, and then the time comes to send them to the slaughterhouse. All this is proved by letters they have written in their own hands, which you have seen and recognized, my Lords. . . .

[The Apology ends with William's point-by-point defiance of threats against his person in the ban.]

Therefore, my Lords, if you believe that either my absence or my death can serve you, I am ready to obey. Here is my head, over which no prince or monarch has power: use it for your welfare, your safety, the defense of your republic. But if you consider that this modicum of experience and industry which I have acquired in long and arduous toil, and what remains of my estates or my life, can still serve you (for I dedicate them all to you and consecrate them to the country), then make your decisions upon the points I have proposed to you. If you believe that I bear some love to the fatherland, that I have some competence as a counselor, then you should believe that this is the only way to protect and save yourselves. When you have done these things, continue together with good heart and will, embrace together the defense of this good people who ask only good counsel and the opportunity to follow it. If, doing this, you still continue to show me the favor which you have given until now, I hope, with your aid and by God's grace (which I have so often felt in times of perplexity before this), that what you will decide will serve your welfare and the defense of yourselves, your wives and children, and all sacred and holy things.

JE LE MAINTIENDRAI.[8]

8. "I will uphold it," the motto of the house of Orange-Nassau.—*Ed.*

21. The Renunciation of the King's Sovereignty

For long years, since even before armed revolt began, the legal fiction had been employed that the rebels were acting on behalf of the King of Spain against his evil servants, who did not act either in his interests or those of his subjects in the Low Countries. The proclamation of the ban against William of Orange made that fiction more difficult to sustain, but it was not until Orange turned to France and the brother of the French king, the duke of Anjou, as a source of sorely needed assistance, that it became impossible to carry on the pretense. William the Silent arranged the grant by the States General in September, 1580, of the sovereignty of the Low Countries to Anjou under constitutional limitations as *landheer*, "lord of the country"; implicit in such a grant was the doctrine that the ultimate possessors of the sovereignty were the States assemblies of the provinces. The sovereignty, furthermore, which had been given to Anjou now had to be taken from Philip. On July 26, 1581, the States General therefore adopted a measure which had been considered ever since 1575—the "abjuration" of Philip II on the grounds that he had broken his contracts with them, such as the Joyous Entry of Brabant, and therefore his legitimate power had ceased to exist. On this principle, it was not they who were breaking their oath to their lord, thus committing the feudal crime of felony, but he who had broken his oath to them, and thus dissolved their obligation of allegiance. The Act of Abjuration therefore declared the independence of the Low Countries from Philip II and his successors, but did not establish the country as an independent state, because the States General recognized Anjou as its sovereign. To call it the "declaration of independence" of the Dutch Republic is a misnomer on several counts: it was not only the legal requirement for a shift of sovereigns, as we have just observed, but it was also an act by and for the whole of the Netherlands (except for the provinces joined in the Union of Arras) and not just for the northern provinces which would ultimately constitute the Dutch Republic. The Act is important in the history of political thought as the most explicit statement of the doctrine of the right of a people to throw off a tyrant and establish government by its own authority until the American Declaration of Independence of 1776.

Source: "Plakkaat van Verlatinghe," in du Mont, V, i, pp. 413–414, 419–421 (in the original Dutch and contemporary French translation). Translated from the Dutch by Herbert H. Rowen.

THE STATES GENERAL of the United Provinces of the Low Countries, to all who shall see or hear these presents, greeting. As it is common knowledge that the prince of a country is established by

God as his subjects' sovereign in order to defend and protect them against all injury, force, and violence, just as a shepherd's duty is to keep his sheep safe, and that subjects are not created by God for the sake of the prince to obey all his commands, whether godly or ungodly, reasonable or unreasonable, and to serve him as slaves, but rather that the prince is established for his subjects' sake (for without them he would not be a prince), to govern them according to law and reason and to protect and love them as a father does his children and a shepherd his sheep, risking his body and life to defend and protect them; and that if he does not do this but, instead of defending his subjects, he endeavors to oppress and harass them, to deprive them of their ancient freedom and privileges and their ancient customs, and to command them and use them like slaves, then he must be looked upon no longer as a prince but rather as a tyrant. And therefore his subjects, according to law and reason, are not obliged to recognize him as their prince; and, without falling into error (notably when this is done by decision of the States of the country), he may be renounced and another chosen in his stead for Head and Lord to defend them. This happens mainly when subjects, by humble prayers, requests, and complaints, have at no time been able to mollify their prince nor turn him away from his tyrannical enterprises and conceptions, so that no other way remains for them to keep and defend their ancient liberty and that of their wives, children, and posterity, for which they are bound by the law of nature to expose their lives and possessions. This has happened on various similar occasions in different countries and different times, as has been seen recently in well known instances. This is what should happen principally in those countries which from ancient times have been and are supposed to be governed according to the oath taken by their prince when he receives them, in conformity with their privileges and ancient customs, without any power to violate them. In addition, most of these provinces have always received and accepted their princes and lords under set conditions by sworn contracts and accords, and if the prince violated them, under the law he forfeited the sovereignty of the country. Now it has come to pass that the King of Spain, after the death of the Emperor Charles V, of exalted memory, his father from whom he received all these countries, forgot the services which both his father and he himself received from these countries and their inhabitants; which were the

principal means by which he, the King of Spain, won victories over
his enemies of such glory and fame that his name and might were
celebrated by them and held in awe by the whole world; he forgot
too the admonitions which his Imperial Majesty has already given
him, and on the contrary he gave hearing, faith, and credit to the
members of the Council of Spain who were close to him, and who
had conceived a secret hatred against these countries and their
liberty because they were not permitted to govern or hold office in
them, as they do in the kingdoms of Naples, Sicily, Milan, in the
Indies, and in other countries subject to the power of the king, and
because they were tempted by the wealth and might of these countries, which was well-known to most of these counselors. This
same council, or at least some of its principal members, upon
various occasions remonstrated with the king that for the sake of
his reputation and majesty, he should reconquer these Low Countries, so that he could command freely and absolutely in these lands
according to his pleasure (that is, to tyrannize over them at his
will), instead of governing them under the restrictions and conditions which he had sworn to observe when he accepted the sovereignty of these lands. Following this counsel, the King of Spain
thereupon sought by every means to deprive these countries of
their ancient liberty and to reduce them to servitude under the
government of Spaniards. First, under the pretext of religion, he
attempted to place new bishops in the principal and most powerful
cities, endowing them with the wealthiest abbeys and assigning
nine canons to each bishop to serve as his counselors, three with
special responsibility for the Inquisition. By the grant of the
abbeys, the bishops, who would be the king's creatures and at his
service and command, and who would be chosen from foreigners
as well as from natives of these countries, would have first place
and the first voice in the assemblies of the States of these countries.
The assignment of the canons would bring in the Inquisition of
Spain, which, as is well known, has always been held in as great
horror and hatred in these countries as the worst of slavery. Thus
it was that when his Imperial Majesty proposed to introduce the
Inquisition in these countries at an earlier time, he received such
complaints against it that he withdrew this proposal, by which
action he displayed the great affection which he bore to his subjects. But, in spite of the many complaints made to the King of
Spain by the individual cities and provinces as well as by several of

the principal noblemen of the country—notably the Lord of Montigny and the Count of Egmont, who were in succession sent to Spain with the consent of the Duchess of Parma,[9] who was then Regent of these countries, and by the advice of the Council of State and the States General, for this purpose. Although the king gave them verbal assurances that he would satisfy the country as they requested, yet he sent orders exactly to the contrary by letter. He commanded specifically and under pain of incurring his wrath that the new bishops be accepted at once and be given possession of their bishoprics and incorporated abbeys, that the Inquisition be enforced where it had already been introduced, and that the decrees and statutes of the Council of Trent (contrary in various points to the privileges of the country) be obeyed and observed. When the common people learned of this, disorders resulted among them, and the good affection which, as good subjects, they had always borne for the king and his predecessors was greatly diminished. They were justified in what they did, for what was most on their minds was that the king was trying not only to tyrannize over their persons and property but also over their consciences, for which they believed they were responsible and held accountable only to God. On this occasion, in the year 1566, out of their pity for the poor common folk, the principal nobles of the country presented a remonstrance in the form of a request, in which they beseeched His Majesty, in order to pacify the commoners and to avert all rioting and sedition, to moderate these points, particularly those which concerned the rigorous Inquisition and punishments in religious matters (thereby demonstrating the love and affection which as a mild and merciful king he bore for his subjects). In order to present the remonstrance to the king in a more personal and persuasive way and to inform him how necessary it was for the good and the prosperity of the country and the preservation of its repose and tranquility to remove the aforesaid innovations and to moderate the rigor of the edicts issued in the matter of religion, the Marquis of Bergen and the Lord of Montigny, at the request of the Regent, the Council of State and the States General of the entire country, traveled to Spain as ambassadors. When they arrived there, however, the king did not give them audience or act to remedy the disorders about which they

9. Margaret of Parma, who was also the mother of Alexander Farnese, the Prince of Parma.—*Ed.*

remonstrated (which disorders had in fact begun to make their appearance among the commoners almost everywhere in the country because they had not been corrected in time, as had been urgently required); instead, responding to his instincts and to the persuasions of the Council of Spain, he declared all those who had presented the said remonstrance to be rebels and guilty of the crime of high treason (*lèse majesté*), who therefore forfeited both life and property. In addition to this, believing that he had made completely sure of the Low Countries by the Duke of Alva's force and violence, and that they were under his full power and tyranny, he then had the said Lords Ambassadors imprisoned and killed and all their property confiscated, in complete violation of the law, which has always been observed inviolably even among the most barbarous and cruel nations and by the most tyrannical princes. Yet, although almost all the rioting which had occurred in the year 1566 on the occasion mentioned had been allayed by the Regent and her suite, and although most of those who had come before her on behalf of the country's freedom had fled or been driven out and the others subjugated, so that the king had no occasion to invade these countries with force of arms, nonetheless, not wishing to neglect the opportunity which the members of the Council of Spain had so long desired and awaited (as is openly admitted by the letters intercepted in the year 1566, written by the ambassador of Spain in France, Alana by name, to the Duchess of Parma), of a pretext for abolishing all the privileges of the country and putting it under tyrannical government by Spaniards as they had done in the Indies and other countries newly conquered by them, and responding to his instincts and the counsel of the said Spaniards, he sent into these countries the Duke of Alva, who was notorious for his rigor and extreme cruelty and was one of the principal enemies of these countries, accompanied by a council of persons of the same ilk and humor as he (by which the king showed how little affection he bore for his subjects in these countries, violating his obligations as their prince to be their protector and good shepherd). The Duke of Alva entered these countries with his army without any encounters or resistance and was received by the poor inhabitants with all reverence and honor, in the expectation only of kindness and clemency, for that was what the king had promised them so often in his letters, as if in good faith, as well as that he had considered coming in person to the country and settling everything there to the satisfaction of everyone. Furthermore, at the time of the departure of the Duke of Alva to these countries, the king fitted out a fleet on the coast of Spain to bring him here, and another in Zeeland to meet and receive him (as it was given out) at great cost and expense to the country, in order to deceive and delude his poor subjects and to catch them more easily in his nets. In spite of this the Duke of Alva, although he was a foreigner and not of the king's blood, immediately upon his arrival declared that he had a commission from the king as supreme captain and shortly afterward as governor-general of these countries. This was wholly contrary to the privileges and ancient usages here. Adequately revealing his purposes, the duke suddenly put garrisons into the principal cities and fortresses of the country, had castles built in the strongest and richest cities to keep them in subjugation, and by letter, or otherwise, commanded the principal noblemen of the country to appear before him, on the pretext of getting their advice and assistance for the welfare and service of the country, as the king commanded. He then imprisoned those who trusted his friendly letters, as he called them, and appeared before him, and had them taken outside the province of Brabant, where they had been seized, contrary to its privileges. He had them tried before himself and his council, although they were not their competent judges, and without investigation or hearing their full defense found them guilty of having committed the crime of treason and had them put to death publicly and ignominiously. The others, who, being more familiar with the wiles of the Spaniards, had left the country and remained away, were declared to be rebels guilty of the crime of high treason, who therefore forfeited their lives and goods, and their property in the Low Countries was confiscated. This was all done so that the poor inhabitants could not obtain their aid in the just defense of their freedom against the oppression of the Spaniards in their fortresses, nor the assistance of the said princes. In addition, the duke had a host of other noblemen and eminent burgesses put to death or driven into exile, so that he could confiscate their property, and he tormented the rest of the good inhabitants by lodging soldiers upon them, who committed outrages upon them, their wives, children, and goods. He also compelled them by various exactions and taxes to contribute to the construction of new castles and fortifications in the cities, from which they could be oppressed, and to pay taxes of one, five, and ten per cent for the support of the soldiers whom he had brought with him and those whom he recruited here to be used against their fellow-countrymen and whoever risked his life to defend the liberty of the country. The subjects would be so poverty-stricken that they would retain no means to prevent his designs and he would be able to carry out more effectively the instructions given to him in Spain, to wit, to treat these countries as if they had been conquered. With this end in mind, he changed the form of government and justice in many places and the principal cities, formed new councils organized in the Spanish manner in direct violation of the privileges of the country. When finally he felt that there was nothing left to fear, he attempted to introduce by force a tax of ten per cent upon the sale of commodities and manufactures of all kinds, despite a multitude of remonstrances to the contrary submitted by each of the provinces individually as well as by all of them together, because it threatened the complete ruin of the country, whose welfare and prosperity lay chiefly in trade and manufacture. It would have been put into practice by violent means if Holland and Zeeland had not revolted against the Duke of Alva soon afterwards, with the aid of my Lord the Prince of Orange and a large number of noblemen and other natives of these countries, who had been exiled by the Duke of Alva and had followed the Prince of Orange and were for the most part in his service, as well as with the aid of other inhabitants who loved their country's freedom. Against these two provinces, which put themselves under the protection of the Prince of Orange, the Duke of Alva during the period of his governorship, and after him the Grand Commander of Castile[10] (who was sent in his place by the king not in order to soften and relieve somewhat the tyranny of the Duke of Alva in this country, but to seek it with greater cunning and concealment than the latter had used), compelled the provinces brought under the Spanish yoke by the garrisons and the castles in their midst to employ their persons and all their power in helping to subjugate these other provinces, but gave them no relief for themselves. They were treated as enemies, and the Spanish soldiers, under the pretext of a mutiny but in the presence and view of the Grand Commander, were allowed to enter the city of Antwerp by force, to remain there for

10. Luis de Requesens y Zuñiga, governor-general in the Low Countries from 1573 to 1576.—*Ed.*

a period of six weeks living at the expense of the poor burghers who were at their mercy. Furthermore, these burghers, in order to be rid of the violence of these Spaniards, were compelled to furnish the sum of 400,000 florins for their wages. After this, these same Spanish soldiers, becoming bolder with the connivance of their chiefs, continued making armed attacks upon the country as a whole; they attempted first of all to take the city of Brussels by surprise, turning it from the ancient and ordinary seat of the princes of the country into the seat and nest of their depradations. When they failed in this design, they seized the city of Alost and then forced the city of Maastricht. They have since forced a violent entry into the city of Antwerp, sacking and pillaging, burning and slaying, doing as much harm as the most barbaric and cruel enemies of the country could have done, and causing undescribable damage not only to the poor residents but also to almost all the nations of the world who had their goods, credit obligations, and money there. Although these Spaniards were declared public enemies of the country in the presence of Hieronymo de Roda himself, by ordinance of the Council of State, upon which the king had conferred the general government of the country after the recent death of the Grand Commander, this Roda, by his private authority (and, it may be presumed, by virtue of secret instructions from Spain) undertook nevertheless to act as chief of these Spaniards and their adherents. Without respecting the authority of the Council of State, he usurped the king's name and authority, counterfeited his seal, and conducted himself as Governor and King's Lieutenant in these countries. This prompted the States to make an agreement with the Lord Prince of Orange and the States of Holland and Zeeland, which was approved and found valid by the Council of State as legitimate governors, to make joint and common war upon the Spaniards as the common enemies of the fatherland and to drive them out of the country. Meanwhile, as good subjects, they endeavored by numerous remonstrances and humble requests made with all diligence and in every proper and possible way to persuade the king to take the Spaniards out of these countries in view of the riots, disturbances, and troubles which had already occurred and apparently would continue, and to punish those who had been responsible for the sack and ruin of the principal cities of this country and innumerable other acts of force and violence against his poor subjects, as solace to those who had suffered and an example to all others. However, although the king pretended in words that what had happened was against his will and liking and that he intended to punish its chiefs and authors and wished to provide and give orders for the repose of the country with all clemency, as was proper for a kind prince, not only did he not try or punish any of the said chiefs and authors but on the contrary it became obvious that everything had been done with his consent and by prior decision of the Council of Spain. This is fully proved by some of his letters intercepted shortly afterwards in which the king wrote to Roda and the other captains who were the authors of these misdeeds that he not only did not censure what they had done but found it good and laudable and promised to recompense them, especially Roda, for their notable services; which he did for Roda and all other agents of his tyranny in this country when they returned to Spain. At the same time the king, hoping to overawe his subjects, sent Don Juan of Austria, his bastard brother and therefore of his own blood, to this country as Governor-General. Pretending to the States that he approved the Pacification of Ghent and giving feigned promises to send the Spaniards out of the country, to punish the authors of the violence and disorders which had occurred, and to provide for the general tranquility and re-establishment of the country's ancient freedom, he in fact sought to separate these States and to subjugate some provinces before the others. This was revealed not long after by the permission or the providence of God, who is the foe of all tyranny, when certain letters were intercepted which made it obvious that Don Juan had instructions from the king to follow the instructions which Roda would give him when he reached the country. But, to conceal this plan more effectively, the king forbade Don Juan and Roda to meet or speak to each other, and he ordered Don Juan to behave towards the principal great nobles with every sign of kindness and good will, so as to win their affection, until, with their assistance and participation, he would be able to reduce Holland and Zeeland under his power; then he could deal with the other provinces as he wished. In accordance with these instructions, Don Juan, although he had solemnly sworn in the presence of all the States of the country to observe the Pacification made at Ghent, therefore violated its terms and sought by every means to gain to his side the German soldiers who were then in garrison and on guard in the principal cities and fortresses of the country. He used their colonels as his instruments, as they were already committed to him. In this way he tried to make himself the master of these fortresses and cities, and in many places considered himself sure he had control of them because he had already won over most of the colonels. In this way he sought to compel some to join him in waging war upon the Prince of Orange and the Hollanders and Zeelanders, and thereby hoped to arouse a civil war which would be even more cruel and bloody than it had been until then. But since things which are done secretly and by deceit will not stay hidden very long, this mad plan of Don Juan's was discovered before he could do what he intended, and he was not able to achieve what he sought. Nevertheless, he stirred up a new war which is still being waged, instead of bringing to the country the tranquility and assured peace of which he had boasted on his arrival.

These events have given us sufficient reason to forsake the King of Spain and to seek another mighty and benevolent Lord to aid in the defense of these countries and take them under his protection. This is all the truer because these countries have already suffered such oppression and outrages and have themselves been forsaken and abandoned by their king. Indeed, for the space of more than twenty years he has treated their inhabitants not as subjects but as enemies, and it was their own Prince and Lord who tried to ruin and subjugate them by force of arms. Furthermore, after the death of Don Juan, he sent here the Baron de Selles, who, under the pretext of proposing various means of reaching a settlement, declared clearly that the king would not acknowledge the Pacification of Ghent, even though Don Juan had sworn in his name to maintain it, and every day he put forward harsher conditions for agreement. In spite of this, we nevertheless did not wish to fail in the performance of our duty and sent humble remonstrances in writing and employed the favor and intercession of the principal lords and princes of Christendom, by these means seeking continually a reconciliation and accord with the king. For this purpose we kept our deputies in Cologne for a long period, hoping to achieve an assured peace with some gracious and moderate freedom of religion (which principally concerns God and men's consciences), as the country then required, by the intercession of his Imperial Majesty and the Electors who had undertaken this mediation. But in the end we found by experience that we would not be able to obtain anything from the king by means of such remonstrances and meetings at Cologne, and that the only purpose and effect of this conference was to divide the provinces and sow discord among them. The king hoped that he would be able to conquer and subjugate them more easily one by one. He could then execute upon them all his first purpose, which has since become publicly apparent in an edict of proscription published by the king. In it all the officials and inhabitants of these United Provinces, and those who take our side, are declared to be rebels and as such forfeit of our lives and property. Furthermore, a great sum of money is promised to anyone who kills the Prince of Orange. The purpose of all of this is to render the poor inhabitants odious, to impede their trade and business, and to bring them into utter despair. Therefore, despairing utterly of any means of reconciliation and lacking any other remedy or means of relief, in accordance with the law of nature and in order to preserve and defend ourselves and our fellow-countrymen, our rights, the privileges and ancient customs and the freedom of the fatherland, and the life and honor of our wives, children, and posterity, so that we may not become the Spaniards' slaves, and foresaking the King of Spain with good right, we have been compelled to devise and practice other means which seem to provide better for the greater safety and preservation of our aforesaid rights, privileges, and liberties.

Know all men that, in consideration of the matters considered above and under the pressure of utmost necessity as has been said, we have declared and declare hereby by a common accord, decision, and consent the King of Spain, *ipso jure* [of his own right], forfeit of his lordship, principality, jurisdiction, and inheritance of these countries, and that we have determined not to recognize him hereafter in any matters concerning the principality, supremacy, jurisdiction, or domain of these Low Countries, nor to use or permit others to use his name as Sovereign Lord over them after this time. In accordance with this decision, we declare all officials, judges, individual lords, vassals, and all other inhabitants of these countries of all ranks and quality, to be henceforth discharged from any oaths to the said King of Spain as Lord of these countries, or from any other obligations which they may have to him. Since, for the aforesaid reasons, most of these United Provinces have placed themselves by a common agreement and consent of their members under the lordship and government of the Most

Serene Prince, the Duke of Anjou, etc., under certain conditions and articles set forth in a contract and agreement with His Highness, and since the Most Serene Archduke Matthias of Austria has resigned the post of Governor-General of these countries into our hands and we have accepted his resignation, we order and command all judges, officials, and others to whom this will appertain and whom it will affect, that henceforth they shall abandon and cease the use of the name and title, and the grand and little seals, counterseals and signets of the King of Spain, and that, for so long as My Lord the Duke of Anjou remains absent, for urgent matters concerning the welfare and prosperity of these countries, they shall use in their place for all matters concerning the provinces which have entered into a contract with His Highness the title and name of Chief and Councilors of the Country, and the other provinces shall do likewise on a provisional basis; but since the said Chief and Councilors will not in fact have been named, called, and actually established in the exercise of their posts and offices, they will use our name; except that in Holland they will continue as heretofore to use the name of My Lord the Prince of Orange and the States of these provinces until the said Council will have been effectively constituted, and then they will follow the instructions made for the Council and His Highness. In place of the seals of the king, they will henceforth use our great seal, counterseal, and signets in business concerning the General Governorship, which the Council of the Country will be authorized to conduct according to its instructions. And in business concerning the public order, the administration of justice, and other matters which belong to each province individually and separately, the Provincial Councils and others will respectively use the name and seal of the province where the case shall arise and no other name or seal, under penalty of nullification of letters, documents, or dispatches which may be so prepared or sealed. So that this may be better observed and practiced, we have ordered and commanded, and order and command by these presents, that all the seals of the King of Spain which are presently in these United Provinces be placed in the hands of the States or of such persons as shall be authorized or deputized to receive them by each of the said provinces respectively, under penalty of such punishment as they may decide. We further order and command that henceforward the arms or name of the King of Spain shall not be placed upon any monies of gold or silver which may be minted in these United Provinces, but such figure and form will be placed there as will be ordered for new coins of gold and silver, with their fractional pieces. We likewise order and command the president and lords of the Privy Council and all other chancellors, presidents, members and servants of provincial councils, and all presidents, first councilors and ordinary councilors in chambers of accounts in the various provinces, and also all other judges and officers of law, as being henceforth discharged from their oaths to the King of Spain under the terms of their commissions, that they shall be required to take a new oath to the States of the province which has jurisdiction over them, or to a person delegated for that purpose, by which they will swear to be faithful to us against the King of Spain and all his adherents, according to the formulary which we have prepared. There shall also be given to the councilors, masters of accounts, judges, and officers of law in the provinces which have made contracts with the Most Serene Duke of Anjou, an act continuing them in their offices, which will contain instead of a new commission a declaration abolishing their previous commission and granting a provisional commission until the arrival of His Highness. And there will be given to councilors, masters of accounts, judges, and officers of law under the jurisdiction of provinces which have not made contracts with His Highness, a new commission under our name and seal; provided, however, that the possessors of the original commissions shall not have been accused and convicted of having contravened the privileges of the country, of misdemeanors, or of similar abuses.

We further instruct the president and members of the Privy Council, the chancellor and members of the Council of Brabant, the governor, chancellor, and members of the Council in Gelderland, and the Count of Zutphen, the president and members of the Council in Flanders, the president and members of the Council in Holland, the governor, president, and members of the Council in Friesland, the president and members of the Council in Utrecht, the bailiff of Tournai and Tournaisis, the receivers and chief officers of law of Zeeland east and west of the Schelde, the auditor of Malines, and all other judges and officers of law to whom it appertains, their lieutenants, and to everyone to whom it will appertain, that they will immediately and without delay announce and make public this our present ordinance in all places under their jurisdiction, by the towncrier wherever it is customary or by posting, so that none may plead ignorance. And they shall have to maintain and observe this ordinance, and cause it to be maintained and observed strictly and without any violation, and to bring to trial and cause transgressors and violators thereof to be brought to trial, to be punished rigorously in the manner stated above, without any favor, escape, or dissimulation. For we have found this to be for the good of the country. We give to each and all of us full power, authority, and special instructions to do these things and what flows from them.

In witness whereof we have caused our seal to be attached hereto. Given at The Hague in our assembly, July 26, 1581.

By order of the States,
J. Van Asseliers.

22. Sovereignty of the Provinces

The sovereignty of Anjou was a farce that was marked by tragedy. After a first brief stay in 1578-1579, he returned to the Netherlands in 1582 at Orange's urging; but, dissatisfied with the absence of real power in his position—so unlike the sovereignty of his royal brother in France—he attempted to establish his own absolute authority by a military coup. The "French fury" of January 17, 1583, in which his troops attempted to take Antwerp by force, failed, but Orange, seeing no alternative, persuaded him to remain and the provinces to tolerate him. In 1584, however, Anjou returned to his native France to die the same year, while Orange was removed by Gérards' bullet. The episode followed of rule by the Earl of Leicester as governor-general on behalf of Elizabeth of England, after she refused the sovereignty proffered to her. Leicester, arriving with a small English auxiliary force, also tried to govern autocratically, basing himself upon the Council of State and the lesser provinces, notably Utrecht. In the bitter conflict with Holland which ensued, he attempted to seize Amsterdam and Leiden but failed and returned home. During the controversy, the States of Holland published a declaration, written by François Vranck, a deputy from Gouda, which denied that the central organs of government, the Council of State and the States General, were sovereign, as Leicester's adherents had asserted. Instead this *Brief Demonstration*, or *Deduction* as it was also called, located the supreme power in Holland in the hands of the nobles and towns as represented in the provincial States. It therefore became the first in a long line of affirmations of provincial sovereignty in the history of the Dutch Republic.

Source: François Vranck, *Korte verhooninghe van het Recht by den Ridderschap, Edelen ende Steden van Hollandt ende West-*

*Vrieslant, van allen ouden tijden in de voorschreven Lande
ghebruyckt, tot behoudenisse van de vryheden, gerechtighden,
Privilegien ende Loffelijcke gebruycken van den selven Lande.
Uytgegeven door haer Hooghmogentheden de Staten van Holland en West-Vrieslandt, Anno 1587, ten tijde van Lycesters
Gouvernement.* (Amsterdam: Franciscus vanden Enden, 1650),
not paginated. Translated from the Dutch by Herbert H. Rowen.

THE NOBILITY and cities of Holland and West Friesland,[11] representing the States of this country,[12] have given full and mature
consideration to the present state of the country, after informing
the members of the nobility and the towns, who have discussed the
situation among themselves and in the town councils and have
reported their judgments. In accordance with their oath and duty,
they have therefore considered it necessary to explain by this
present statement the legal status of the province of Holland and
West Friesland, in the firm confidence that everyone who shall see
it will pass judgment upon it in the impartial and peaceful way that
the sad state of this country makes necessary.

It is well known that the lands of Holland (with West Friesland) and Zeeland have been governed for a period of eight
hundred years by counts and countesses to whom the nobility and
cities, representing the States of this country, legally conferred and
granted the rule and sovereignty over it, and that they conducted
themselves in their governance with such discretion and moderation that they never failed to declare war or make peace, to raise
taxes or contributions from the country, or to take any other
measures concerning the state of the country (although they were
usually provided with the good counsel of the nobles and natives of
the country) without obtaining the judgment and consent of the
nobles and cities of the country, who were always convened and
assembled for this purpose; and besides receiving their counsel,
they at all times granted to the nobles and towns of the country

11. West Friesland was the part of ancient Friesland lying west of the
Zuider Zee, contiguous with Holland proper to the south and including such
cities as Alkmaar, Hoorn, Enkhuizen, and Medemblik. It formed the
"Northern Quarter" of the political entity usually called "Holland" for
short, but whose governing assembly was the "States of Holland and West
Friesland."—*Ed*.

12. *Land*, "land" or "country," meaning the province.—*Ed*.

favorable hearing, complete credence, and good decisions on all matters which they ever had to present to them concerning the state and the welfare of the country in any way. . . .

But we may still in truth say that the state of Holland and Zeeland[13] was never conquered by the sword or brought into subjugation as a result of foreign or domestic wars during the period of eight hundred years; we do not know if this can be said now of any other country, except perhaps the Republic of Venice. No other reason can be given for this except that there was always good union, love, and understanding between the princes and the States of this country, because the princes (who possessed no power in their own right) could do nothing whatever without the nobles and cities of the country, ordinarily having no means other than the revenues from the domains to meet the costs of their courts and the salaries of ordinary officials.

We observe also the authority which the States of this country possessed to bring the princes, if they were misled by bad counsel to act to the country's harm, to judgment and reason, not only by remonstrations and petitions, but also, if adequate measures were not taken, by action, including severe punishment of those who misled the prince, acted improperly or misused his authority: of which there are many examples. . . .

Although we are sure that all of this is beyond dispute, nonetheless we have considered it necessary to relate it here, since many persons have erroneous and divergent opinions and judge the assembly of the States only according to what they think the quality of the persons who appear as delegates merits and according to the matters which are discussed there; they judge apparently that the above-mentioned persons who are sent as delegates by the nobility and the cities to the assembly of the States conduct themselves as if they were the States, and as such have the sovereignty in the supreme power of the country and decide upon all matters affecting the country according to their pleasure, following their personal intentions, hatred, and jealousy. But those who have a better insight into these matters, and also in what has been accomplished by the princes of the country with the help of the States, especially what has occurred during the period of the last fifteen years in the provinces of Holland and Zeeland, can easily observe

13. Zeeland was originally part of Holland, and then after legal separation shared its count, until the Abjuration.—*Ed.*

that the authority of the States does not consist in the leadership, authority, or power of thirty or forty persons more or less who appear at their meetings, and even the agents of the King of Spain, who have always sought to undermine our affairs by such arguments and sought to bring the authority of the States into scorn, have found out how wrong and misled they were in this opinion. . . .

The inhabitants of this land are divided into two orders or States, to wit, the nobles and the cities. . . . Whence it should be properly understood that these boards of the magistrates and councilors of the cities, along with the assembly of the nobles, undoubtedly represent the entire state and the whole body of the inhabitants, and no form of government can be conceived which could take its decisions with more certain knowledge of the situation of the country, or carry out its resolutions with greater concord, authority, or effect. . . . The corporations of the nobles and cities cannot be brought into one assembly except by sending their delegates. Thus, when it is necessary to meet in order to deliberate upon various notable matters, the assembly is convoked with inclusion of the principal points to be discussed. When the corporations have debated and taken decisions upon these points, deputies are sent off in whom they have confidence, and with such instructions and decisions as they find to lie in the interest of the country. . . .

For what is the power of a Prince if he does not have good relations with his subjects? What kind of good relations can he have with them, and what kind of support can be obtained from them, if he allows himself to be persuaded to take sides against the States, which represent the commonalty, or, to speak more precisely, against his people itself? Also, how can the well-being of the country exist if it can happen that the commonalty can be brought in the same way to take sides against the States, that is, against the nobles, magistrates, and town councilors, who are their champions and lawful rulers, and who in acting on their behalf must often take upon themselves personally the ingratitude of the prince and governors?

Adopted at Haarlem, October 16, 1578.

By Order of the States of Holland.

C. DE RECHTERE.

23. Terms for Peace, if Only for a Time

Parma died in 1592, having failed to follow up the reconquest of the southern Netherlands by that of the northern provinces, now the Dutch Republic. The military laurels passed to the Dutch commander, Maurice of Nassau, who not only reconquered the eastern and north-eastern provinces from Spain, "rounding off the garden" of the United Provinces, as the Dutch put it; he also began to gnaw steadily away at the Spanish-held provinces south of the great rivers. When Archduke Albert of Habsburg became joint sovereign of the southern Netherlands in 1598, together with his wife, Philip II's daughter Isabella, he worked to persuade the Dutch to come back under his authority, on terms which granted them virtually total self-government but also required freedom for the public practice of the Roman Catholic faith. Albert was seconded in his efforts by a competent general, the Genoese Ambrogio Spinola. In the north, the approaches for peace or a truce were met favorably by the province of Holland and its political leader, the Land's Advocate John van Oldenbarnevelt. Although Maurice, a soldier to the core, was opposed to anything short of victory, he could not thwart the negotiations, which brought a delegation from Brussels to The Hague, led by Spinola. The course of those negotiations, which extended from February 1 to October 19, 1608, is here described by Oldenbarnevelt himself.

Source: A. J. Veenendaal, ed., *Johan van Oldenbarnevelt: Bescheiden betreffende zijn staatkundig beleid en zijn familie.* Vol. II (The Hague: Martinus Nijhoff, 1962), pp. 232–235. Translated from the Dutch by Herbert H. Rowen.

The Last of September

SPINOLA COMES HERE, with Richardot and Mancicidor. Richardot declares for them that after the resolution of the Lord States, they had been inclined to depart, but had not wished to do so without taking their leave of the assembly; that they were in great sorrow because they had come here in accordance with the instructions of the King [of Spain] and the Archdukes, their masters, who were sincerely resolved to change the prolonged war of forty years into a good peace. They even came here [The Hague] at the cost of the reputation of their king and princes, since it would have been reasonable that we [the Dutch] should have gone to them, but having come here they had negotiated in all friendliness with the commissioners of this side. They had accorded the first point concerning sovereignty and freedom; saying that in all other points they had compromised to the limits of what their powers permitted and their instructions tolerated. That when there had arisen a dispute over several points, they had agreed to send Father [Jan Neyen], the Commissioner-General, to Spain, where it was true, he had remained longer than they expected, which they regretted no less than my Lords the States. That under pressure they had finally proposed the point concerning the Roman religion, in accordance with the instructions which they had had from the beginning but which they had not thought wise to propose when they saw that it could not be stomached here, hoping that the King could be brought to change their instructions, or that a better basis could be found here for a fruitful proposal on the same matter; that in this matter nothing had been sought that would profit the King's purse a single penny but only what he owed to the Lord God in satisfaction of his conscience and for the relief of the Catholics in this country. That we [the Dutch] had at once cut off the entire negotiation without a single word concerning communication or relief; that they had been surprised and disappointed, especially because we did not want to listen to them any longer. That a proposal concerning a final truce had then been made to the ambassadors of the kings and princes; that they had declared that they could not accept it under the terms of their instructions and asked sufficient time to receive further instructions from Spain. That a resolution was then taken upon this matter so harsh and precise, ordering them so definitely to leave, that they believed that they had never heard its like, and that they had reason not to be satisfied with it but were ready to follow the orders.

They said further that they hoped that we would not return to the rigors of war and cause further spilling of blood, calamities and miseries of war, and wanted those who were inclined toward war to think over the matter and to examine in their consciences why they wished to expose the country and its good people to the miseries and calamities of war, and to consider too that they could easily come under accusation and rue a renewal of the war and having broken off this negotiation or caused it to run into difficulty in this way.

Our reply was that in so far as they were sorry that the conclusion of the negotiation did not correspond to its beginning, the sorrow of my Lords the States was no less than theirs, for they had hoped to change the war into a good peace and had acted in the negotiation with fear of God, and they too had always tried to achieve this, truly desiring that the spilling of blood and the calamities and miseries of war should cease to the extent that this was in their power; but it was their intention to have their freedom recognized by the king of Spain and Their Highnesses [the archdukes] in proper form, and that without this the whole negotiation would be rejected. That a clear declaration had been made to the commissioners, Pater Ney and Verreycken, that there was no hope of obtaining anything in the question of religion because it would conflict with the freedom of the country, and my Lords the States knew what their proper conduct was on behalf of their subjects; that they [the ambassadors] had been urged in the beginning of the negotiation to put this question aside if it was their intention to speak of it, so that there would be no useless quarreling; that this point was raised now, after such a long delay, in addition to the ban on negotiating regarding the Indies, and they persisted in so many other disagreements, that my Lords the States had legitimate reason to cut off the negotiation, especially since they observed that they were wrong in having believed that His Excellency and the other lords [ambassadors] would not let themselves be used in an affair where a good outcome was not to be expected. And although when this had been done the deputies of the Lords the States declared that they had completed their duties, the commissioners remained free to propose to my Lords the States whatever they might approve and that this has not been refused, so that there was no adequate reason for complaint in this regard.

As for the second point concerning the resolution on the truce, [the Dutch commissioners] said that my Lords the States had been here in large numbers for a long time and saw that the delays by Spain were endless, and therefore they preferred that the lords commissioners await their further instructions at Brussels rather than here, where they caused great inconvenience to themselves and to the Lords the States; and that the resolution had been put in precise form in order to bring the provinces to agreement. But when this was balanced against the delays on the other side, the punctiliousness of the resolution was mitigated, and for that reason they did not believe that the responsibility could rightly be placed upon them, and that no difficulty would have been made over a few days' further stay if the business could have been moved along. . . .

Spinola replied when they rose that his purpose when he came here was only to bring the negotiation to conclusion for the common welfare and that if this could not be done he would depart with thanks for the resolution of the Lords the States, but otherwise, in order to bring such a good work to a happy end, would gladly remain here for some time with increased inconvenience.

Nothing further was said except goodbyes. Spinola left for Brussels, leaving the ambassadors to continue the negotiation.

24. Twelve Years' Truce

The negotiations conducted at The Hague in 1608 led to the final conclusion of a truce for a period of twelve years. The final negotiations at Antwerp were conducted with the mediation of the French and English envoys to The Hague. It was significant that the signatories included not only the States General of the United Provinces, as the government of the Republic was formally called, and the Archdukes Albert and Isabella, the sovereigns in the South, but also King Philip III of Spain, as one of the belligerents. The truce was a compromise: the negotiators from Brussels failed to gain acceptance of the improvement of conditions for Catholics in the North which the archdukes sought at almost any price, but the Dutch did not gain either the right of commercial entry into the Spanish colonies which they so coveted. But the overriding factor was the concession by the archdukes and the Spanish king that the United Provinces were in fact free and independent, although they still declined to acknowledge this as legally permanent. The "as if" provision on independence reflected the continuing hope of the archdukes that somehow the Dutch provinces could still be persuaded to come under their sovereignty. The key clauses of the treaty of truce, signed at Antwerp on April 9, 1609, are given below.

Source: du Mont, Vol. V, part ii, p. 100. Translated from the French by Herbert H. Rowen.

FIRST. The archdukes declare in their own names and that of the king that they are content to negotiate with the Lords States General of the United Provinces in their character, and considering them as such, of free lands, provinces, and States, against whom they make no claims, and to make with them in their names and characters as stated, and they do by these presents make a treaty under the conditions as written and stated below.

II. To wit, that the said truce will be in force and observed strictly, faithfully, and inviolably for the time of twelve years, during which there will be a halt to all acts of enmity between the

said king, archdukes, and the States General, at sea and in other
waterways as well as on land in all their realms, provinces, lands,
and lordships, and between all their subjects and residents of all
conditions and qualities, with no exception of places or persons.

III. Each party will remain in occupation and effective possession of the lands, cities, places, lands and lordships which he holds
and possesses at present, without being disturbed or troubled
therein during this truce: and this is understood to include the
boroughs, villages, hamlets, and countryside dependent upon them.

IV. The subjects and inhabitants of the lands of the said king,
archdukes and States will keep on good terms of friendship and
understanding with each other during this truce, without resentment for offenses and damage already suffered; and they shall also
be able to travel and stay in each other's countries and conduct
their business and trade in them in full security, both at sea and on
land. However, the king understands these conditions to be restricted and limited to the realms, countries, lands, and lordships
which he holds and possesses in Europe and other places and seas
where the subjects of other princes who are his friends and allies
engage in such business by mutual agreement; and as for the places,
cities, ports, and harbors which he holds outside these limits,[14] the
aforesaid States and their subjects cannot engage in any business in
them without the express permission of the aforesaid king. But
they shall be able to conduct such business wherever they please in
the lands of all other princes, potentates, and peoples who shall be
willing to permit them to engage in it, even outside the limits of
Europe, without any interference by the king, his officers and subjects under his authority, with the said princes, potentates, and
peoples who have given such permission for doing so, or to them or
the individuals with whom they have done and will do such
business.

V. And because a quite long period of time is necessary to warn
those outside the limits of Europe with troops and ships that they
shall refrain from all acts of hostility, it is agreed that the truce will
begin there only one year from this day; but it is understood that if
the word of the truce can reach a place earlier, hostilities will then
cease at once. But if any hostile action occurs after this period of
one year, then reparation will be given for it without delay.

14. That is, outside Europe.—*Ed.*

VI A Test of Power, a Test of Faith

The conclusion of the Twelve Years' Truce gave the United Provinces an interlude of peace abroad, but at home it was followed by one of the most severe conflicts to afflict the Republic in its entire history. The struggle which marked the decade from 1609 to 1619 pitted the Arminians or Remonstrants against the Gomarians or Contra-Remonstrants, but there was more to the controversy than an admittedly important contest between Calvinists of stern dogmatic persuasions and those who had an Erasmian tolerance and breadth of views. The Arminians and Gomarians battled with sermons and tracts not only to prove the truth of their own views but to win the adoption of their own concept of the proper relation of church and state. The Gomarians maintained that the ultimate and primary function of the state was to defend and serve the church, as God's preeminent instrument on earth. This was, by one of history's ironies, a continuation of the doctrine of the medieval papacy, so loathed by these staunch Calvinists, in its controversies with emperors and French kings. But it was the task of the church itself—preachers, professors of theology, and lay elders in synods and "classes" taking the place of the pope—to define its doctrines and to lay down its disciplinary decisions; the task of the state was to repress contrary doctrines and support the discipline decreed by the church. The Gomarians aimed at a monopoly position for their church within the country but rejected any right of government to rule over it; the church would be over, not under or part of the state. The Arminians, on the other hand, seeking to loosen the bonds of orthodoxy within the church, turned to the state to defend their rights as an equal contender within the ecclesiastical order. They assumed, as did the Gomarians, that only the Reformed church of Calvinist principles would be treated by the government as the true church; but they drew the corollary, which the Gomarians rejected out of hand, that the state therefore had a right and duty to oversee the church (a principle equivalent to the *jus reformandi* of late medieval and Reformation princes, Catholic and Protestant alike).

The Arminians won the name Remonstrants when they presented a petition for the relief of grievances to the States of Holland in 1610. In it they submitted to the assembly, a political body, their explanation of the doctrine of predestination and asked it to enforce revision of the Reformed church's confession of faith, which they saw as too constricting. But in so doing, they gave to a body of laymen who had the power of the sword, in medieval terminology, the right of decision on theological principle, and so aroused fierce resistance from the Gomarians, now called Contra-Remonstrants, who denied that the state had any such right. This controversy was exacerbated when the Remonstrants and Contra-Remonstrants clashed over the possession of church buildings, which were effectively in the grant of town governments or local magnates in the villages. Each side in effect appealed to political power, the Remonstrants to the States of Holland where Oldenbarnevelt and his young adherent, the brilliant pensionary of Rotterdam, Hugo Grotius, supported the cause of toleration and the right of the States to determine the status of religion within the province as part of its sovereign authority, and the Contra-Remonstrants to Maurice of Nassau. He had turned away from the close alliance with Oldenbarnevelt which had been so fruitful in his early career to himself and to the cause of the war against Spain; he was offended by the truce which he had not been able to prevent and as a mature man resented the continued dominance of the Land's Advocate. Maurice was neither learned nor much interested in religion itself; his attitude on theological matters was indicated by the remark attributed to him that he did not know whether predestination was green or blue. He did know what it meant, however, when the States of Holland attempted to create a provincial army of militia paid by the towns (*waardgelders*) and then sought to persuade the army of the United Provinces, commanded by Maurice, not to move against a force of *waardgelders* in Utrecht, which was ordered to dissolve by the States General.

Maurice ordered the arrest and trial by a special court of Oldenbarnevelt, Grotius, and two other leaders of the resistance to him (August 29, 1618). One committed suicide in prison, but Oldenbarnevelt was found guilty of treason and beheaded (May 13, 1619), while Grotius and the remaining defendant were sentenced to life imprisonment. During the same months, a national synod of the Reformed church was held in Dordrecht on the authority of the States General to determine the theological matters in dispute, although Holland disputed the right of the central body to take over what it held to be the right of a sovereign province only. The

Remonstrants appeared at the synod, outnumbered and as defendants, not as participants, and were finally condemned as heretics and drummed out of the Reformed church. Some of the Remonstrants left the church to form their own sect, but others remained in the Reformed church. For, although the synod of Dordrecht had given the formal victory to the Contra-Remonstrants, the power of their protector, Maurice, soon waned, and both the municipal magistrates and Maurice's successor, Frederick Henry, warded off the harsh measures demanded by the strict Calvinists. Tension between precisians and latitudinarians continued within the Reformed church and continued too to have significant implications in political life, for the issue of the relation between church and state remained essentially open.

25. The Estrangement of Maurice and Oldenbarnevelt

During the spring just before his arrest in 1618, Oldenbarnevelt was urged by Louise de Coligny, the widow of William the Silent and Maurice of Nassau's stepmother, to attempt a reconciliation with the Prince of Orange. This he did in a letter which he sent to Maurice on April 24; it was an indication of the degree of estrangement between them that he did not present it to Maurice in person but conveyed it by his son-in-law, Van der Mijle.

Source: A. J. Veenendaal, ed., Johan van Oldenbarnevelt: Bescheiden, Vol. III (The Hague: Martinus Nijhoff, 1967), pp. 381–388. Translated from the Dutch by Herbert H. Rowen.

MOST Serene and High-Born Prince, Gracious Lord, Gracious Prince and Lord,

I observe with the most profound vexation that Your Excellency has become totally estranged from me. I fear that the things first said by some churchmen some six months ago and then repeated by several politicians, to the effect that Your Excellency had become angry with me, must be true, although I could not believe it until now. Nevertheless, in all sincerity and honesty, I affirm that I do not know when I gave reason for such a change of heart. I have always been and still am Your Excellency's most faithful servant, and with God's grace I hope to die as such. Ten years ago, when we were negotiating for a peace or a truce, I did indeed remark the beginnings of such a change. May Your Excellency be so kind as to recall, however, that I affirmed to you then that my honest and sincere purpose in these negotiations was to serve and protect the country, Your Excellency, and all its good people, and that nonetheless I offered Your Excellency not only to resign all my offices but even to leave the country rather than to remain in office and in the country with Your Excellency's displeasure. This truce [of 1609-1621], concluded with Your Excellency's approval, won his satisfaction because it enabled the affairs of Your Excellency, your notable house, and your beloved brothers and sisters to be put in order. During the time it has been in force, this truce has brought the country prosperity, increased revenues, and won for it a lofty and admirable reputation among the greatest potentates, republics, and cities not only throughout Christendom and even among this country's enemies, but also in other parts of the world as well. Your Excellency's most admirable reputation was enhanced and increased by the truce, as is well known and as has been irrefutably demonstrated by the excellent alliances made after the truce with various potentates and republics. These ties have in their turn brought the friendship, counsel, and assistance of other great potentates and republics to this country at various times. The truce also enabled us to slow and halt the accumulation of debts, which formed a heavy burden upon the country and the provinces; the admiralty boards have paid off debts of about 2,800,000 guilders which they owed in 1609, while before the truce these debts had to be increased every year by borrowing at interest. In addition, this country has paid off its great debts to its neighbors and has repossessed the cities and forts which had been given in pledge. It became very apparent, therefore, that this country would have a lasting, desirable, firm, and assured position. It would bring Your Excellency and every member of his most excellent house great praise, honor, reputation, and advantage, for they are the greatest possessors of high offices, dignities, honorable titles, rights, and property in the country.

Two problems have troubled the country, however. The first was the dispute raised by the States of Zeeland several years before the truce and continued for many years afterwards over paying its share of the national budget. At times it held back for entire years and has persistently raised objections and refused to give its approval until the desired reduction was granted on several occasions by decisions of Your Excellency and the Council of State.

The second problem was the disputes over doctrine and authority in religion. These already existed in the country when the war first began but they became more frequent a few years before the truce, involving Professors Gomarus and Arminius of the University of Leiden and their respective adherents. Before and after the conclusion of the truce, my Lords the States of Holland and West Friesland, and I as their servant, worked to bring these quarrels to an end by all proper means. However, as a result of the rigorous censorship and the suspension of various preachers from their religious duties, with consequent complaints, the difficulties came out into the public more and more. At first we had hoped that we could settle this conflict by means of a compromise to be arranged by a legal and impartial assembly of the province of Holland and West Friesland, but it could not be done because some of the churchmen exerted such influence upon the government in a few cities that these refused to permit the States of Holland and West Friesland, who are the lawful sovereigns of this province, either to convene or direct or approve the activities of such an assembly. Yet this is a right which was used by the first Christian emperors and during the last century has been and is being employed by all the kings, imperial electors and princes, counts, lords and all the governors of great and small republics and free cities who have reformed religion and purged it of the superstitions, heresies, and tyrannies of Popery.

For this reason the States were compelled to issue a provisional order that those who could not in good conscience teach, hold, or believe the doctrine of predestination or its corollaries, except as these were held by the Remonstrants, should no longer be molested, prevented from holding services, or interfered with in their performance, while those who wished to teach or hold a stricter and different position remained free to do so. Both sides were then heard at great length, and the provisional order was repeatedly reaffirmed. His Royal Majesty of Great Britain also repeatedly approved the order, confirming it with good, pertinent, and salutary arguments.

Similarly, many preachers of Contra-Remonstrant feelings also approved this provisional order, for they were well aware from the beginning of the war that this attitude existed; it was publicly tolerated in many teachers and members of the church, not only by the government but also by the churchmen who held other opinions. The States then gave repeated orders to practice mutual Christian tolerance, for these reasons and so that no split resulting from these differences of opinion would be permitted or tolerated. Your Excellency knows that I spoke of this to him many times, exhorting him that it was his duty to support my Lords the States in this matter, and that I had specific instructions and obligations to undertake these offices. Your Excellency, saying that he wished to remain neutral in this affair, thereupon called upon me to avoid having him subjected to public exhortations. I then considered that Your Excellency might have in mind the opinions of the States of other provinces of which he was governor, and also recalled that Your Excellency for many years had always listened, while these questions were in debate, to the sermons of Uytenbogaert and La Haye[1] and to no one else, and had always taken Holy Communion with them, and also that Your Excellency, many years after he had publicly declared that he held the opinions of the Remonstrants in the five points concerning the doctrine of predestination and its consequences, had of his own initiative employed Uytenbogaert in his armies before Jülich and Rees in the years 1610 and 1614, and in the year 1614 had written letters to the magistrates of the city of Utrecht, who had the right to call him back to their own service, strongly requesting that they permit him to remain here in the service of and to the satisfaction of Your Excellency and the churches. Therefore Your Excellency, unless I am mistaken, cannot find it strange that I could not believe that, in opposition to the resolution of the States, he wished to favor and advance this split, with the manifest detriment to the position of the country which would result from harmful divisions within the church, whose members form the best and most trustworthy party in the country, and from the dissatisfaction of many thousands of the oldest and most tested patriots as well as of most of the rulers in many very good towns.

But when all orders for the prevention of a split were rejected here and disruption took place, even in Your Excellency's presence, as he knows, I worked on measures to achieve orderly practices with the least harm to the country, and I therefore proposed that the church[2] be designated as a foreign church, as indeed is

---

1. Preachers in the Walloon (French-language) church in The Hague.—*Ed.*

2. The *Kloosterkerk* (Cloister Church).—*Ed.*

done in other countries, that is, in lands where Dutch, French, and Italian churches exist which maintain their special order. But I received no support, so that the assembly of the States of Holland and West Friesland met for more than five months in the hope of achieving a settlement, but every way was rejected, there was no willingness to take steps against seditious preaching, writing, and speech, or against violence employed against the government and council in Oudewater, which caused fears in other towns that they would be treated in the same way. Certain reports came in that Your Excellency had given orders to some captains that they should not trouble him or even approach him with matters arising out of the religious disputes. But, in accordance with all reason of state, it must be agreed that the States, having met and debated repeatedly on this matter and having come to a decision by a majority of votes, and not wishing to remain any longer in session, finally had to decree what it had already repeatedly approved by majority vote. Otherwise, as many deputies of the cities said and protested repeatedly, the assembly would have had to recess without being able to meet again so long as a few towns could delay or prevent a decision upon the resolutions.

When this resolution[3] was adopted and presented to Your Excellency by members from the nobles and the towns, Your Excellency was requested to inform them of any point to which he might have objections, and they would give a good explanation of it to him and every reasonable satisfaction. Your Excellency did display some displeasure, but it was considered to be directed at the stubbornness of the deputies of the towns which for five whole months had refused to concur with the proposal of the majority. I made strong efforts to keep the assembly in session, but the deputies of the towns, fatigued by what had happened, were not to be persuaded. It is true that three days after the assembly recessed, Your Excellency revealed to me what had been done in Den Briel by a committee of the States and the magistrates of the town, but I asked Your Excellency to wait for the return of the committee and to believe their report, for they were representatives of the public authority and very good patriots. At that time I also proposed to Your Excellency that he lend his hand to enforcement of the resolution which had been adopted with the greatest discretion and

3. The so-called Sharp Resolution of August 4, 1617.—*Ed.*

without any offense to Your Excellency's meritorious reputation, praying that we might go ahead in unity and good understanding.

I spoke to Your Excellency twice again before my departure, the last time on Saturday before I left for Vianen the next Monday (where I had already told Your Excellency that I was obliged to go). On that same day I suggested a compromise of the whole affair to Your Excellency and offered all my good offices. Your Excellency seemed favorable, asking if a proposal for a compromise would be acceptable. I replied that it was certain that it would be accepted. At the same time I offered, if Your Excellency considered that I was hostile to his good intentions, to resign all my offices and take up residence outside of Holland rather than remain here in office with the displeasure of Your Excellency, and asked that in such an event Your Excellency lend me his hand in obtaining an honorable release from My Lords the States. But Your Excellency declared that you could not at all approve it and gave me hope that some means of compromise would be proposed.

I then went to Vianen, being weak and in bad health. I remained there for twelve days, continuing in the same weakness; and therefore I went to Utrecht to consult Dr. Sael, my old friend. I hoped to recover and to spend my seventieth birthday, which was September 24 according to the new style, in my birthplace, the city of Amersfoort, but my continued illness prevented my departure. I remained therefore in Utrecht for some six weeks in the hands of this doctor without hearing the slightest word about any proposal for compromise, but instead that it had been decided by a majority vote, which had never been done before, and despite the resolutions of the States of Holland and West Friesland, the States of Utrecht and the States of Overijssel, to bring the religious disputes before the assembly of the States General, which was a direct infraction of the Union of Utrecht and various other treaties, and also before a synod, to which the name of national was given. I also heard that in the meanwhile every effort was being made to discredit and bring into the scorn and hatred of the common people all those who tried to speak on behalf of the rights of the provinces. Among these I especially was put forward; a hundred lies, falsehoods, and calumnies against me were spread by means of squibs, seditious libels, and otherwise. One pretext for them was my absence from The Hague, so that I was compelled to return here from Utrecht.

Since then I have made my greeting to Your Excellency several times to offer my services in promoting the necessary settlement of all the misunderstandings. I also asked Your Excellency and the high-born Count William Louis, count of Nassau, Governor of Friesland, Groningen and Ommelanden, etc., to make your proposals for some effective means to achieve this. I demonstrated that the pressure for holding a national synod was a violation of the rights of the provinces, of the Union of Utrecht, and of other treaties and of precedent, so that it would probably bring no advantage but rather great difficulties. I have not received any proposal whatsoever.

Meanwhile I made various proposals both in the assembly of the States of Holland and West Friesland and to Your Excellency and His Grace, for I was always quite certain, as I am now, that the nobles and the regents of the towns of Holland and West Friesland who are unable to accept what the others consider to be the highest and most necessary law of the country, confirmed by all treaties, are friends neither of Spain nor of Popery but sincere, trustworthy, and tried friends of the liberties and the laws of the fatherland as a whole and of the provinces and cities individually, that they hold in sincere affection the most laudable merits of Your Excellency's father of blessed memory and of Your Excellency himself and are greatly concerned to maintain and enhance his praiseworthy reputation and authority to the advantage of the state and himself; and that they are for the most part sincere adherents of the true and pure religion, reformed according to God's Holy Word, and of lawful regulations to maintain and protect it. I am quite certain, too, that the province of Holland and West Friesland, together with its cities and members, can be quite assured about them for reasons founded in nature, as they are men who were born and have prospered in this country, where their forefathers and they themselves did and suffered so much for the good cause, and where they have proved their unchangeable affection and constancy in all circumstances with words and deeds. Your Excellency himself knows these things best of all, for he has often declared that he began his career without specific promises of support from the States of Holland and West Friesland and yet he received from them without exception good and laudable support, which has resulted in the common advantage of the country as well as in high reputation for them and Your Excellency. I am just as certain that in the future Your Excellency will receive good and laudable support from them in all circumstances, if good confidence, understanding, and mutual accord are re-established and faithfully maintained as they were during the previous thirty-one years. This is the goal I always had in mind and for which I worked and will continue to work, with God's help.

But if Your Excellency wishes to follow the counsels of the authors of the *Necessary Discourse* and *The Spanish Counselor*[4] and similar seditious, slanderous, and lying pamphlets, which God forbid, then I must declare frankly and according to my own opinion, but respectfully and subject to correction, that the result cannot but be the total ruin and downfall of this country, of Your Excellency, of his esteemed House and its members, of all pious patriots, and of the true Christian religion.

The Spanish Counselor could dream up no better advice than that given by these fellows, that is, to sow, nourish, and maintain mistrust and misunderstanding between Your Excellency and the nobles and cities and their servants. He has produced high-flown and arrogant fantasies[5] easy to write down but difficult to put into practice, which might be attempted in a dangerous gamble and might even succeed, but which could not endure in view of the character and constitution of this country and would serve no one's interest but the Spaniard's. I therefore beg Your Excellency not to believe such fellows but to reject their advice.

It is true that there may be among them some good, simple men who are zealous in religious questions, but what has happened in the separated provinces of the Low Countries as well as the events of the years 1586, 1587, and 1588 in these provinces which we held, has taught a clear lesson that there are mingled among them malicious hypocrites, ambitious men who seek their own advantage in changes of government, many penniless and callow fellows as well as many flagrant traitors. Furthermore, there are many who came to these provinces from the provinces and towns which are now Spanish and Catholic territory who, it is to be feared, either out of natural affection to their native lands and cities or out of vindictiveness, cannot stand that our provinces and cities should have greater prosperity and freedom than theirs, and in general

4. Two pamphlets directed against Oldenbarnevelt.—*Ed.*
5. An apparent reference to suggestions that Maurice be made the sovereign ruler of the United Provinces.—*Ed.*

there are twenty to one among them who would prefer to live at public rather than at private cost.

I request most humbly that Your Excellency graciously give his wisest thoughts to these considerations, while time remains for a settlement of the whole affair to general satisfaction, and to believe firmly that if Your Excellency seeks anything within the government of the country or in other matters which concern our whole country and its interests, then a well reasoned proposal to those who have authority under the laws and usages of the provinces will prove more laudable, more honorable, and more advantageous both for the country and for Your Excellency than a hundred thousand of these libels which try to make the sickness incurable and to prevent any possibility of a compromise settlement. I have repeatedly said to Your Excellency that the experience of thirty-one years has taught me that these people will cause Your Excellency more troubles, difficulties, and vexations in a single year than he would have in ten years in the management of the affairs of the whole country. To expect from other provinces or from the purse of Holland and West Friesland if there is further division, what Your Excellency has obtained for thirty-one years from the States of Holland and West Friesland, and which he can, with God's help, continue to obtain from them, seems to me to be, subject to correction, the greatest absurdity that can be imagined.

I fear that I have been too long-winded for Your Excellency, but I have been unable to say these things more briefly and still meet my duty and relieve my conscience. I am very sorry that in recompense for my long and manifold services and tasks, I am attacked by so many slanderous, lying, seditious, and fraudulent libels, and that these vicious and absurd falsehoods derive their pretext and nourishment from the ill feeling which Your Excellency is supposed to bear toward me. And although for thirty-one years I have been able to get over such things with silence, good conduct, and truth, now, in my advanced old age and ill health, I find myself compelled to publish a statement in defense of myself and my family,[6] although most unhappily and against my heart and feeling. I have decided to send Your Excellency a copy of it, humbly asking that Your Excellency be so kind as to consider it only as something forced upon me in my defense, and that he will

6. A printed remonstrance to the States of Holland of April 20, 1618.—*Ed.*

believe that I am, and hope with God's help to remain to the end of my life, Your Excellency's most humble servant. Placing my hope in this, I pray God the Almighty Lord, to preserve you, most serene and high-born Prince, in prosperity and health and under his holy protection.

From my chamber, April 24, 1618.

Your Princely Grace's most humble servant,

JOHN VAN OLDENBARNEVELT.

26. Oldenbarnevelt, About to Die, to His Family

The appeal of Oldenbarnevelt to Prince Maurice in his letter of April 24 failed to bridge the gap between them, for neither the Prince nor the Land's Advocate was unwilling to abandon his principles. After the arrest of Oldenbarnevelt and his friends, Maurice was adamant that they go on trial for their lives. Oldenbarnevelt denied the legitimacy of a special court set up by the States General; he was under the jurisdiction either of Utrecht, his native province, or of Holland, whose sworn servant he was. To no avail: for what was at issue, ultimately, was whether provincial sovereignty was absolute or subordinated to that of the provinces united under the States General. If the States General had such higher authority, then, as has been argued by Oldenbarnevelt's latest biographer, Jan den Tex, the special court was not a legal monstrosity perpetrating a judicial murder, but a constitutionally defensible body exercising its judgment in exceptional circumstances, when any judgment would be inevitably political in character. In any case, the 71-year-old Oldenbarnevelt, with William the Silent probably the greatest statesman his country ever knew, never appeared in better light than after he was found guilty, in the last letters he wrote to his family the night before and then on the morning of his execution, May 12 and 13, 1619. Neither he nor his family would ask for mercy, which would be in their eyes an admission of guilt; while Maurice would not grant pardon except if asked. So the great sword of the executioner was not stayed, and Oldenbarnevelt died, like William of Orange, as a martyr for his cause.

Source: A. J. Veenendaal, ed., *Oldenbarnevelt: Bescheiden*, Vol. III, pp. 485–486. Translated from the Dutch by Herbert H. Rowen.

VERY DEARLY beloved wife, children, sons-in-law and grand-children.

I send most affectionate greetings to you, all together. At this hour I have received the very hard and sorrowful news that I, an old man, for all my good and faithful services to the fatherland during so many years, who has performed with sincere affection all possible good offices and humble services to His Excellency, the Prince, to the limit permitted by my offices, duties, and instructions, and who has given my friendship to many persons of all sorts and has done injustice to none so far as I know, must prepare myself to die tomorrow.

I console myself in God the Lord, who knows all hearts and will judge all men. I beg you, all of you, to do the same. I have honestly, piously, and faithfully served My Lords, the States of Holland and West Friesland and their nobles and cities. I have also given honest and faithful counsel to their Lords, the States of Utrecht, as the sovereigns of my own fatherland, at their request, in order to spare them from the tumults of the populace and the bloodshed with which they had long been threatened. These were the same aims I sought for the States of Holland, so that everyone would be safe and no one come to harm.

Live together in love and peace. Pray for me to God the Almighty Lord, who will graciously hold us in his holy protection.

From my chamber of sorrow, May 12, 1619.

Very dear wife and children,

My end is near. I am very tranquil, with God's grace. I hope that you are no less so and that you may help each other to overcome all things, by mutual love, unity, and peace, for which I make my last prayer to the All-Highest. Jan Vrancken has served me well and faithfully for many years, even during these afflictions, and will stay with me until the end. He deserves a recommendation to you to help find him a good job with you or with others. I ask that you do the same.

I have sent a request to His Excellency, the Prince, to keep you, my sons, and children, in his good favor, to which he has graciously replied that this will be done so long as you behave well. I urge this upon you in the best form and give you all into God's holy keeping. Kiss each other and all my grandchildren for the last time in my name, and farewell.

From my chamber of sorrow, May 13, 1619.

27. *An Apology of the Remonstrants*

Some time during December, 1618, a petition was written, probably by Gaspar Barlaeus of the Theological Faculty at Leiden, on behalf of all Remonstrants, and sent to Prince Maurice. Despite its formal humility, it was a proud document, and the fact that it was made public indicated that it was also a political tract. It expresses the Remonstrant aims and character with great vigor, but it was of no more avail than Oldenbarnevelt's letter to the Prince. It is also worthy of note that the Remonstrant love of toleration did not extend to the Jews who found refuge from persecution in the United Provinces, at least in this polemic; the Remonstrants' practice was actually as mild as their rhetoric was harsh on this occasion.

Source: G. Brandt, *History of the Reformation,* Vol. II, pp. 576–579. The text has been broken up by the editor into shorter paragraphs for easier reading.

Illustrious and High-born Prince,
    Many thousands of the Inhabitants of these *United Provinces,* all of them friends and professors of the Christian *Reformed* Religion, both of high and low condition, both learned and unlearned, both men and women, cast themselves at your Excellency's feet with this Petition, begging and conjuring your princely grace in the deepest humility, and with great emotion of heart, kindly to receive it from your faithful and submissive servants; and postponing for about an hour's time your great and various affairs, to hear these their complaints, which their sorrow and deplorable condition extort from them, with patience and compassion.

Most Gracious Prince,
    'Tis well known to your Excellency, that throughout the whole Country, sometimes in one place and sometimes in another, divers Ministers, men of probity, and very dear to their respective flocks, have been ill treated, from one severity to another, their doctrines being calumniated and condemned, their persons deposed from their Ministry, and forbidden the exercise of it either in publick or private, even on pain of corporal punishment. From hence it proceeds, that not only the Ministers themselves, but their Hearers too are exposed to the utmost hatred and contempt of their Fellow-Christians, and are in a manner become what the Apostle *Paul* says

of the Christians in his time, "an off-scouring of the earth." It is of this we bitterly complain; and complain to him who only can change our sorrow into joy, our reproach into honour, our sighs and tears into a chearful countenance; that is to say, to your Excellency, to that high-born Prince, whom God has set at the head of these Provinces for the protection of good men, and for the defence of the rights of the innocent. Look down, Great Prince, on the deplorable condition, and hearken to the groans of so many innocent and devout persons of this country, occasioned by the rigorous proceedings against their Pastors, and consequently against themselves. Regard the floods of tears which are daily poured forth in the churches by innumerable Members, when they hear the sad farewell sermons of their Teachers Be perswaded, most illustrious Prince, that such sighs, issuing from the bosoms of those who seek neither temporal honours nor worldly goods, being extorted from them only by their affection to the doctrine of *Christ,* which they have espoused and owned to be true, cannot but be very efficacious and powerful when they mount up to the throne of God. Alas! how have we moved the anger of your Excellency (pardon us, most illustrious Prince, for speaking thus, being as it were overwhelmed with grief) to the turning of your wonted goodness towards us and our Pastors into such an aversion, as causes you daily to employ your Princely authority to our prejudice; insomuch that our adversaries shamefully abuse your most noble name to our reproach and contempt in every ballad, print, and picture?

We speak out plainly, most gracious Lord, and take the liberty to say, that neither our Teachers nor we have deserved such treatment. Are the *Contraremonstrants* lovers of their Country? so are we; nor are we in the least behind hand with them in our inclinations of giving the utmost evidence of this, when necessary, both by offering up our prayers to God, by sacrificing our estates, and pouring out our blood for it. Are they friends to the person of your Excellency? wherein have we shown our selves otherwise? Are they lovers of the Protestant religion, and haters of Popery, of its idolatry, errors, and tyranny? So are we. Do we not daily hear our Ministers offering up their prayers, and calling down the blessings of Almighty God upon the present Government, and on the head of your Excellency? Do we not hear them as heartily refute the errors of that Religion as any others whatever? If any object that they teach, that man may be saved by his own strength, and without the grace of God, they do them great injustice, and the eye of the Lord, which watches over the righteous, sees that it is a slander, and a mere fiction raised against them. Is it said of them, that they place salvation out of *Christ* and his knowledge, or even seek it in their own merits? This is doing them great wrong, for they teach us the contrary. Are we reproached with betraying our Country? We appeal, Great Sir, to your own conscience, and beg to be informed, wherein, when, and to whom the conduct of the *Remonstrants* has made this appear. Do they say (as we are sure it is given out) that our Pastors have received money from the enemy, why don't they give some proof of it? Infamous are they, and deserve to be exposed to the world whoever they be, whether *Remonstrants* or *Contraremonstrants*, who are capable of such practices. But if there have been any transactions in the State that are disagreeable to your Princely Grace, must we suffer for it who have had no share in the guilt? Must we therefore be torn from the arms of our Ministers, and our Ministers from our arms?

And admitting that our Teachers differ from others in certain dark and perplexed controversies, must they for that reason be immediately condemned as unfit to preach *Christ* to us, or to be esteemed Christian Ministers? To what did the Apostolical men oblige all Christians, both Teachers and Hearers? Was it to the doctrine of Predestination? We trust not. To what then? To the Twelve Articles of the Apostolical Creed: Those we believe, those our Teachers intirely and unfeignedly profess. Has the Church made some further explanations of the doctrines of salvations in her General Councils, since the Apostles times, in order to restrain the Clergy? These are likewise embraced and professed by our Teachers. Do the Articles and Confessions of several churches agree in all points? By no means. Do therefore the Teachers of such Articles cease to be true Ministers of the Church of *Christ?* Surely, no. They that place the whole of Religion in Controversial Points, take the certain way of losing it. Would they have us be nothing but Philosophers, and teach us the art of wrangling about scholastick questions? That will render us worse than we are. We shall indeed be more learned, but not more good; if that may be called learning which does not improve the heart as well as the head. We esteem them good Teachers who explain to us the

Articles of our Faith in such a manner as to refer us to one God and *Christ*, and to them only, in whom alone we are to seek salvation: Those who teach us we are sinners, and cannot be saved without the mercies of God in *Christ;* and that we cannot partake of those mercies otherwise than by faith, which worketh by love: Teachers who preach such doctrines in the main, and at the same time lead an inoffensive and edifying life, we judge to be orthodox and sound enough to guide us in the way of salvation. These are the doctrines which the holy Scriptures press upon us; to these they join salvation, and these are such as may be understood by the meanest Christians; this is the food we all are able to digest. And O, that we knew no more! O, that all the preaching among us would turn upon these points! We should be wiser, better, and more agreeable to God.

Most illustrious Prince, believe your own senses, but take no man's word besides. God has endowed your Excellency with an understanding sufficient to enable you to distinguish between good and evil, beyond many other Princes. Your Excellency is not ignorant that those who complain against us are our most inveterate enemies, and that there are daily brought to your Excellency many stories in prejudice of us, which you in your great wisdom know to be false and without any foundation. Lend us then one ear, Sir, and believe not every thing they seem to insinuate to your Excellency. Consider, most gracious Prince, that the happiness of this Country consists chiefly in the free exercise of Religion according to every man's conscience; a privilege bought with the blood of the House of *Nassaw*, and of so many brave men. This liberty consists in this: *That we may serve, honor, and believe in God after our own way.* But how can we believe without hearing, and how can we hear without Preachers; or when we are deprived of those who have planted and watered us, that is to say, brought us up in the Christian Religion, whose voice we have been accustomed to, who have comforted us when sick, admonished us when fallen into sin, yea, who are even our spiritual Fathers, who have regenerated us through *Christ?* Their doctrine is edifying, their lives inoffensive. Why then are such shepherds smitten and their sheep scattered? Is it for the benefit of our Country, that multitudes of people are kept out of the churches, and that one man goes over to one sect, another to another, or else stays at home without worshipping God in either Church or Conventicle? Is this the way to make Christians, or to propagate the Reformation? Is this the way to seek the honour of God, and edification of the Community? Is this the peace which the *Contraremonstrants* follow? Is this a service to our Country, that willing Subjects who with joy would follow their respective trades and occupations under their Governours, are thus harassed, and almost compelled to quit their dwellings?

It is always better for Sovereigns to be loved than feared by their Subjects. Is it for the service of our Country, that we are necessitated to hold our Assemblies out of the publick churches, in order to serve our God, and to offer up our prayers together; or that the boats on *Sundays* are seen laden with Burghers, who are forced to go five or six miles from their own homes to hear a sermon? If they don't care we should frequent the publick churches, let us be allowed the free exercise of our Religion in private places. What is there to be feared from us who are true to the Government, who freely contribute to its support and defence as well as others; who pray for our Sovereigns, and take the Oath of Allegiance to them?

The Priests and Monks were used to insinuate to the Council of the King of *Spain, That the Reform'd must be expelled; that the land could not bear two Religions; that the* Geuses[7] *must be so effectually extirpated, as that the very remembrance of them might perish.* But how have they been extirpated? For one that was cut off are there not ten new ones sprung up? Is this preserving a Country, to render it a mere wilderness? Our adversaries are walking in the same path. They cry, the *Remonstrants* must be suppressed, so as their name may no more be heard, and boast they will do it so effectually, that a reward shall be given to any who can show an *Arminian*, as they are pleased to call us. The land cannot bear both parties, say they, *ergo*, the weakest must be trampled under foot. But they will find quite the contrary. The more truth is suppressed, the more strongly it breaks forth and diffuses itself. Nay, some scarce esteem truth to be such, unless it be persecuted.

If the land can bear *Lutherans* and other Christians, who have separated from us, why may not we be tolerated? Are we too strong? The more it will be for the service of the State, that such a number of men should have satisfaction given them in the business

7. The *Gueux* or "Beggars," as the first rebels against the King of Spain were called.—*Tr.*

of Religion. Judge yourself, Illustrious Prince, if it be not a deplorable and unaccountable manner of proceeding, that the *Jews*, open enemies and blasphemers of our Saviour, are permitted to enjoy the free exercise of their Religion in the most powerful City in *Holland*, whereas we, who are Christians, and of the *Reformed* Religion too, cannot be tolerated either there or elsewhere? Shall it be accounted for the advantage of our Country, that such may hold religious assemblies, who teach their people that our Lord was a Seducer; and will any one pretend, that it would be prejudicial to the State, that we who acknowledge *Christ Jesus* for our Redeemer, should enjoy Liberty of Conscience?

If it be objected, that our Ministers do not preach the truth, we answer, that we believe your Excellency is well satisfied and convinced, *that our Ministers teach what is at least sufficient to salvation;* and as for the points in controversy, we think our Pastors in the right, and theirs in the wrong. If it should be attempted to make us believe otherwise by human authority, and by the power of a Synod, we appeal from thence to the Word of God. Why should not the judgment or opinion of such Christians who fear God, and daily pray for his Spirit, be as worthy of belief as that of a Synod? Do we not pray to God for understanding as well as the Clergy? Have they greater promises of being heard than we? Does not God frequently baffle, and render their speculations vain? We must either take for truth all that the Synod says, or else we must judge for our selves: Are we to believe implicitly every thing they say? Then do we fall again into the old way of Popery. But if our judgments be left us free, and if we judge that our Pastors teach us the *Truth*, and accordingly receive it as such, why then will they not suffer us to retain those Pastors. The rather, because there is no contest between us and them, about the fundamentals of the *Christian* faith. If it be objected that our doctrines are new, we answer, that novelty is not prejudicial, provided it be truth: And we say further, that what our Pastors teach us, is not *new*, but *old*. . . .

Your Excellency, in your great wisdom, can judge what mischiefs will proceed from our being oppressed. The present state of the Towns of the *Brill, Schoonhoven, Rotterdam, Horn, Utrecht, Nimeguen, Tiel, Bommel,* and *Woerden*, makes it evident enough. Is it not much better that the Burghers enjoying their liberty of consciences, should chearfully and unanimously defend their Towns against foreign enemies, than that the Government should be obliged to make use of its Troops, to keep the Burghers themselves in awe? Trade must necessarily decay in a country full of troubles: Where Soldiers enter, the Merchants will retire. All business is at a stand; the rents of houses and lands are fallen; nor will things easily mend, but rather the contrary, if they thus proceed to deprive us of our Pulpits, our Churches, and the worship of God. But if we may be supported in the free exercise of our religion as well as others, then like the grass which raises up its head in the morning, Commerce and Arts will revive and flourish again: the Churches of the *Reformed* will increase, the feuds and animosities of our Citizens wear off, our disturbances will be composed, our unanimity will strike a terror into the hearts of our enemies, and both parties, as well *Contraremonstrants* as *Remonstrants*, will have cause to applaud your Excellency's goodness and clemency.

To conclude, We humbly beseech your Princely Excellency to be perswaded, that we are sincere lovers of our country, and will never be wanting, every one of us personally, to contribute our utmost out of our estates, for the support of the Government, and what we are most cordially affected to, the Reform'd religion. We further beg your Excellency, to give the necessary orders, that those scandalous Books, Ballads, and Cuts, by which we and our Printers are represented as traytors to our country, and persons not fit to live in this Republick, may be supprest; as also that our Ministers may not be deprived on account of the articles of *Predestination*, and their dependencies. Or in case this cannot be obtained, let us at least be permitted to hold our meetings out of the publick churches, under the protection of the State against all force and insolencies, on condition of continuing always like good Burghers and Inhabitants, true and faithful to the higher powers.

May God, the Father of Mercies, who holds the hearts of Kings and Princes in his hand, incline your Excellency's heart and spirit, to the end, that attending to the complaints and prayers of so many thousands, you may please to exert your self in granting them some relief! May the same God preserve the person of your Excellency from all misfortunes, and bless your counsels, for the defence of truth, for the good of our country, and his own glory!

28. The Contra-Remonstrant Program of Action

Toward the end of its sessions, on April 27, 1619, the Synod of Dordrecht sent four of its leading members to the States General with an address of thanks. In thanking Their High Mightinesses the States

General for their graciousness in having called a national synod, they did not admit that the assembly had power over them but only the authority to put the synod's decisions into effect. What the synod wanted is made explicit in the address.

Source: G. Brandt, *History of the Reformation*, Vol. III, pp. 324–327.

To the High and Mighty Lords, the Lords the States General of the free United Netherlands, *our Sovereign Lords.*

With all due reverence and humble submission, the National Synod of the *Reformed* churches in the *United Netherlands,* assembled by the authority of your High Mightinesses in the Town of *Dort,* do represent, That pursuant to your Lordships' laudable commands, and the usage of all National Synods, they have taken into their consideration not only in general the Doctrine and Discipline of the Church, but likewise in particular the *Gravamina* and complaints which the several Churches of these Provinces have transmitted to the Synod; and they have made several Ecclesiastical Statutes and Laws about the same; all which shall shortly be laid before your Lordships.

But forasmuch as the said Statutes cannot, as indeed they ought not, to be put in execution in the respective churches of these Provinces, without the consent and concurrence of your High Mightinesses, our lawful Sovereigns; this Synod does most humbly pray and beseech you, that your High Mightinesses would vouchsafe, after having read and examined the proceedings of this Synod, to corroborate them by your christian approbation and concurrence; and to use your authority, in causing the same to be every where observed for the peace and edification of these churches.

And especially since the doctrine of these churches, which is contained and professed in their *Confession,* and in the *Heidelberg Catechism,* which is received by us, has been pursuant to the express commands of your Lordships again maturely examined according to the Word of God by this Synod; and since it has been determined by the unanimous voice, not only of all the Foreign Divines, but also of the Deputies of the *Low-Country* Churches assembled by order of your High Mightinesses, that the said Doctrine is very conformable to Scripture, and to the Confessions of all the Reformed churches, as will more fully appear by the

Explanations hereunto annexed: This Synod does therefore pray with all humility, that your High Mightinesses would graciously vouchsafe henceforwards more and more to protect and defend, to strengthen and support the said Doctrine of the churches of this land; as also the full and comprehensive Explanation made and agreed upon by this Synod, by order of your Lordships, according to the Word of God, with respect to the *Five Points;* together with the condemnation of those errors, which have been broached by some persons in these Provinces against the aforesaid pure Doctrine.

And likewise, that your High Mightinesses would vouchsafe to approve of the *Ecclesiastical Constitution,* as it has been examined by this Synod, and enlarged in some of its Articles, for the more effectual promoting of peace and edification; and to order that the said Constitution be uniformly observed throughout all the churches of these Provinces, as far as possible.

And forasmuch as the Synod has thought proper, that the churches of these Provinces, according to the example of all the *Reformed* churches of other nations and languages, should likewise have an accurate and faithful Version of the Old and New Testament in the *Low-Dutch* tongue, as has been frequently resolved in former National Synods; which work, by your Lordships' order, was committed first to the care of that worthy Gentleman, the Heer *Philip Marnix* of *St. Aldegonde,* of blessed memory; and after him to Dr. *Wernerus Helmichius* and *Arnoldus Cornelius,* who accordingly made a beginning of the same: therefore the Synod has now appointed three Ministers (if it might be done with your High Mightinesses' approbation) to translate the Old Testament, and three others to translate the New, together with the Apocryphal books; who, to the end they may make the greater dispatch, and finish that work the sooner, are in the mean time exempted from all other Ecclesiastical functions, and are to meet together and communicate their thoughts to each other. And forasmuch as according to this scheme the said work will be very expensive, the Synod does likewise beseech your Lordships to approve this Resolution, and to allow such a sum of money as may be sufficient to answer the charges of the work; and besides, to send letters to those churches, whose Ministers are appointed to carry it on, to the end that the said churches may not make any difficulty of their long absence.

And since your Lordships are not ignorant how much it concerns the churches of this land, that both the high and low, or inferiour Schools, should be well regulated; and since experience itself has taught us what great inconveniences have happend both in the Church and State, for want of a due regulation and management of the said Schools, it is desired that your High Mightinesses would likewise take such care in that matter, as thereby to prevent and obviate all the abuses arising from thence, that the proper fruits thereof may be produced and enjoyed.

For which purpose, so far as it may concern the *Universities*, and the *Gymnasia* or High-Schools; the Synod humbly intreats your Lordships to attend to those Articles which were presented last year to the Lords the States of *Holland* and *West-Freesland* on the same account, by the Synod of *South-Holland;* copies of which are hereunto annext, to the end that they may be recommended to the States of the respective Provinces, where there are any such Universities or Schools.

But as for the trivial or inferiour Schools, the Synod likewise most humbly prays your High Mightinesses, that you would be pleased to order, that some general rules for the Government of such Schools be drawn up and prepared, by and with the advice of such learned men who understand best what relates to the instruction of Youth; whereby those defects, which are so frequently observed in Schools, may be amended; and as far as possible, a uniform method of teaching be established, especially in the principles of *Grammar*, *Logic*, and *Rhetoric*.

And whereas it appears that the abuses in Matrimonial cases more and more increase, and that the Churches of these Provinces meet with many difficulties in relation thereto; and besides, that there is no uniform method observed about Marriages, your Lordships will be pleased, after having consulted with the Divines, to appoint some general form of Marriages, such as may be observed by all the Churches of these Provinces, as far as is practicable.

'Tis likewise their humble request that, besides the present commendable Laws relating to the printing and selling of all kinds of books, some more effectual Orders may be made about visiting or inspecting books already printed, and also about the whole affair of printing, in order to prevent the publication of all sorts of pernicious and scandalous books, with which these Countries have been infected, to the very great hurt of the Church, and visible offence of the Community.

And since all good Christians, on account of that zeal and charity with which they are commanded to promote the honour of God, and their neighbours' salvation, are obliged to use all the means proper for those ends; since also God has been pleased to open a way for us of these Provinces to very remote and distant countries in the *Indies*, and elsewhere, which are intirely destitute of the knowledge of the true God; the said Synod humbly prays, that your Lordships would be pleased to lay this holy case to heart, with a Christian zeal, earnestly to take it into consideration, and to make use of such methods as may be most proper and expedient for *the propagation of the Gospel* in those countries.

Moreover, that your High Mightinesses would graciously be pleased to have an eye upon those good Christians and Churches, which are now groaning under the Cross in the neighbouring oppressed Provinces of the *Netherlands*, so as to find out and apply some means for their service, and for the strengthening them in the true religion; for which purposes your Lordships may be pleased to recommend it to the respective Provinces, to maintain some fit persons to serve the said churches, as the Lords the States of *Holland* and *West-Freesland*, and also those of *Zeland* have long maintained, and still do maintain two Ministers on that account.

That at a proper season some care may likewise be taken about the Popish Priests, who still publickly officiate within the bounds of the *United Provinces*, and particularly in the Barony of *Breda*, and the Marquisate of *Bergen op Zoom*; to the end that said Priests be driven out of these places, and *Reformed* Ministers settled in their stead, as we see has been done in other parts of your Dominions.

Also, that your Laws and Placards against the creeping in, and stroling about of the aforesaid *Popish Priests* and *Jesuits*, may be put in execution, many simple souls being seduced by their means; and that some more effectual Laws be made against the exercise of Popish Idolatry; it being found by experience, that these abuses increase more and more every day. And that at the same time some way be thought on to restrain the blasphemies of those *Jews* who dwell in the midst of us, and to prevent them likewise from perverting any of our Christians to their religion.

Moreover, that the abominable and manifold profanations of the *Sabbath*, which daily happen by means of *Markets*, *Fairs*, and *Feastings of Companies; by keeping Watch and Ward, by merry Meetings and Weddings;* by the *Exercises* of the *Militia;* by *Fish-*

ing, Fowling, Stool-ball play; by *Comedies, Dancing, frequenting of disordery Houses and Clubs;* or by any kind of unnecessary servile works, and many other irregular customs, which are daily increasing in this land, to the great reproach and dishonour of the *Reformed* religion, and to the great obstruction of piety, may be forbidden and hindred.

And that those numerous and glaring abuses, by which the people are seduced from true holiness, to the pomps and vanities of the world; such as *Carnivals, Comedies, Farces* of *stroling Comedians* and *Mountebanks, Hocus-pocus tricks, drunken Clubs, Dancing-Schools,* and many other things of the like nature, may be prohibited and banished out of these Provinces: And above all, that some good Laws be made and executed by the Civil Magistrate against that dreadful *Cursing* and *Swearing,* which is daily heard among us, to the utmost dishonour of God's holy name.

And since it appears that in some places such forms of *Oaths* are used, which border upon Popish idolatry, we pray that there may be established one uniform manner of taking Oaths, and that the like abuses may cease.

Finally, since it appears that the maintenance of Ministers, and the pensions allowed to their Widows, are very mean in several Provinces, notwithstanding that the Church-lands, in the places to which such Ministers belong, would be sufficient for that purpose; the Synod does likewise beseech your High Mightinesses earnestly to recommend this matter to the respective Provinces, to the end that the wants of the Clergy may be obviated, and they sufficiently provided for, as the dignity of their office requires.

29. The Remonstrant Doctrine Denounced

The theological position adopted by the synod of Dordrecht was summarized in its sentence of April 24, 1619, condemning the doctrine of the Remonstrants. It was presented to the Remonstrant representatives, who were no longer given the opportunity even to attempt to debate these principles.

Source: G. Brandt, *History of the Reformation,* Vol. III, pp. 301–303.

THE TRUTH being thus far, thro' the Mercy of God, explained and established, Error rejected and condemned, and all unjust Calumnies wiped off; there remains nothing more to be done by this Synod of *Dort*, than most seriously and conformably to that right and authority which, according to the Word of God, belongs to them over all the Members of their churches, to beseech, to warn, exhort, and charge, in the name of *Christ*, all and singular the Ministers of the churches throughout the *United Netherlands*, all Doctors, Rectors, and Governours in the Universities and Schools, and in general, all those to whom either the Care of Souls, or the instruction of Youth is committed: *That they forsake and abandon the well-known* Five Articles *of the* Remonstrants, *as being false, and no other than secret magazines of Errors*, and preserve this sound doctrine of saving Truth, drawn from the pure foundation of Holy Writ, unmixed and inviolate to the utmost of their power, according to the duty of their office; that they faithfully and prudently instil the same into the minds of all people, both young and old; that they diligently explain *the most comfortable and beneficial use thereof, both in life and death;* that they gently instruct, by the bright rays of Truth, those which wander from the flock, which are of different opinions, being seduced by the *Novelty of Doctrines*, in hopes that God may one day give them repentance to the acknowledgment of the Truth; to the end, that they being come to a better mind, may return to the Church of God, and the Communion of Saints, in one spirit, with one mouth, and with the same Faith and Charity; and that thus the wounds of the Church may at last be healed, and all the Members thereof become one heart and one soul in the Lord.

But whereas some, *who are gone out from among us*, calling themselves *Remonstrants* (which word, as well as that of *Contra-remonstrants*, the Synod wills and requires to be buried in perpetual oblivion) have, *out of private views and ends*, unlawfully violated the discipline and government of the Church, and despised the exhortations and opinions of their Brethren, have presumed, in a violent and dangerous manner, to disturb the churches of these Provinces, which were formerly so flourishing and so strictly united in peace and love, by venting the above-mentioned doctrines; have not only *trumped up old Errors, but hammered out new ones* too, and have zealously promoted the same among the people both publickly and privately, both by word of mouth and in writing, have blackened and rendered odious *the Established Doctrine of the Church*, with impudent slanders and calumnies, without end or measure; have filled all places with scandal, discord, scruples and troubles of conscience; all which heinous offences committed against the Faith, against Charity, against Good manners, against the Unity and Peace of the Church, as they ought by no means to be endured in any persons whatever, *so ought they to be restrained and punished in Clergymen with severest censures,* as has likewise been the practice of the Church in all ages: THEREFORE this National Synod, after having invoked the most holy name of God, being assured of its own authority, as grounded in his word, treading in the footsteps of all the ancient and modern lawful Synods, and lastly, being *supported by the authority of the High and Mighty Lords the States-General,* does hereby declare and determine, *that those Ministers who have acted in the churches as Heads of Factions and Teachers of Errors, are guilty and convicted of having violated our holy Religion, of having made a rent in the Unity of the Church, and given very great scandal; and as for those who were cited before this Synod, that they are besides guilty of intolerable disobedience to the commands of the supreme Powers promulgated in this Synod, and to those of the venerable Synod itself:* For all which reasons the Synod does, in the first place, *discharge the aforesaid cited persons from all Ecclesiastical Administration, and deprives them of their Offices; judging* them likewise unworthy of any Academical employment, till such time as they shall have given full satisfaction to the Church by their *sincere repentance, appearing by contrary words, actions, and endeavours; as when being really and fully reconciled to the Church, they shall be re-admitted to her Communion.* All which we heartily wish for their good, and for the joy of the whole Church, thro' our Lord *Jesus Christ.* And as for the rest of the *Remonstrant* Clergy, whose case has not come under the cognizance of this National Synod, they are hereby recommended to the Provincial Synods, Classes, and Consistories, conformably to the established Order; *who are to take the utmost care, that the Church suffer no prejudice either now or hereafter; that the Patrons of Error be prudently discovered; that all obstinate, clamorous, and factious Disturbers of the Church under their jurisdiction be forthwith deprived of their Ecclesiastical and Academical offices;* and that they the said Provincial Synods, &c. are therefore exhorted, as soon as they shall have received the Sentence of this National Synod, and obtained leave from the Civil Magistrate, to meet together without delay, least the evil gather strength by missing this opportunity. They are further exhorted to endeavour to bring back to a true and entire Unity with the Church, in all meekness, gentleness, and charity, all such who thro' weakness, or the wickedness of the times, are fallen and seduced, or who doubt, and perhaps differ in some small matters, and yet are men of quiet, peaceable, and unblameable lives, and ready to be better informed; *yet so as to take a particular care, that they admit none into the Ministry who shall refuse to subscribe, or promise to preach the Doctrine asserted in these Synodical Decrees; and that they suffer none to continue in the Ministry, by whose publick dissent the Doctrine which has been so unanimously approved by all the Members of this Synod, the Harmony of the Clergy, and the Peace of the Church, may be again disturbed.* This venerable Synod does further most earnestly exhort all Ecclesiastical Assemblies diligently to watch over the Flocks committed to their charge, and *timely to oppose all innovations endeavoured to be introduced into the Church, and to extirpate them as tares and weeds out of the Lord's Field;* to keep a watchful eye over the Schools and their Masters or Regents, to the end that the Youth be not infected with strange notions and opinions, which may hereafter become dangerous and destructive to the Church and Commonwealth. Finally, this Synod returns thanks in the most respectful manner to their High Mightinesses the States-General of the *United Netherlands* for their so seasonable and necessary assistance, graciously afforded to the Church in her deplorable and sinking condition, by the remedy of a Synod, and *for taking into their protection the faithful Ministers of the Lord,* and for the holy and solemn Resolutions by them taken of preserving the sacred Pledge of the Divine Presence, and all other heavenly blessings, that is to say, the Truth of God's Word in these Provinces, and for having spared no pains nor costs for promoting and perfecting so great a work; for all which favours this Synod does most heartily wish their High Mightinesses an abundant recompense from the Lord, both publick and private, both spiritual and temporal. And they most earnestly and humbly beseech the same gracious God, *that their High Mightinesses may suffer and ordain this wholsome doctrine, which the Synod has faithfully expressed according to the Word of God, and the Harmony of the* Reformed *churches, to be maintained alone and in its purity within their Provinces,* that they may oppose growing heresies, and *restrain turbulent and unruly spirits;* that they may henceforwards shew themselves true and beneficent Foster-fathers and Defenders of the Church; and *that they may likewise put into execution the Sentence pronounced against the above-mentioned persons, conformably to the authority and rights of the Church established by the laws of the Land, and ratify and confirm the Decrees of the Synod by their authority,* &c.

VII A Land of Traders

If ever an historical cliché was true, it is that trade was the life-blood of the Dutch Republic. The tiny country on the North Sea achieved its astounding prosperity and strength because during most of the seventeenth century it dominated the shipping and commerce of Europe. Almost every other kind of economic activity was ultimately dependent upon trade: farmers who grew crops to feed an urban population or to make products for sale abroad; financiers who served the credit needs of traders; the providers of goods and services in the cities who catered to their physical needs and their conveniences; and even the governing class, or "regents," who became more and more separated from the commercial classes but nonetheless knew full well that their function was to protect and advance the interests of merchants and shippers. The "mother trade," as the Dutch called it, was commerce and shipping to the Baltic, in which the Hollanders had almost completely replaced the once-mighty Hanseatic towns of Germany. From the Baltic the Dutch brought cereal grains to supply their own needs for bread-stuffs which the local countryside could not provide adequately, and also to supply the needs of other lands where local supplies were in chronic shortage, as in Spain, or of other countries struck by bad harvests. Next in importance, and virtually as vital to a country which built more ships than all the rest of Europe while it possessed virtually no forest lands of its own, were the timber and naval stores of the Scandinavian lands. The Dutch also carried the high quality iron and steel produced in Sweden. To the Baltic the Dutch brought the goods of their own and other countries' manufacture and the desirable food products of southern lands, notably wine and brandy. This two-way trade, in which the Dutch alone of European shipping nations were able to sail in and out with cargoes instead of carrying ballast at least one way, was typical of the fundamental position of the United Provinces—the warehouse of the Western world, through which passed most of the goods in European interregional trade, especially along the main North-South and East-West routes. It was a position which was reinforced by the wealth of the Dutch in capital, which enabled them to finance credit in trading transactions for longer terms and at lower rates than any other nation.

Trade across the oceans to Asia and the Americas was an important although auxiliary part of the Dutch economic position. Trade to the East Indies was in the hands of the extraordinarily successful East India Company, which held a charter from the States General granting it a monopoly in Eastern commerce. To the West Indies—which in the seventeenth century meant not only the Caribbean, but Brazil and North America as well—the West Indies Company attempted to conduct a parallel trade, with considerably less success. Profitable although the East Indies trade became, its earnings never compared in volume with those of Dutch commerce within the bounds of Europe, although the rate of profit was significantly higher. But the overseas trade was of the greatest political significance, especially after the middle of the seventeenth century, when England and then France became formidable competitors, ready to put power at the service of profits no less than subjects' wealth at the service of the state.

30. Foundation of the Dutch East India Company

Although not the most important branch of Holland's trade, none gripped the envious admiration of other countries as much as the commerce to the East Indies, the achievement of the famed Dutch East India Company. The General Dutch Chartered East India Company, to give it its full title, or the United East India Company (V.O.C., *Verenigde Oost-Indische Compagnie*) as it was usually called, was established in 1602 with a charter from the States General. The personality behind the ticklish enterprise of compelling the various competing "Companies for Far Journeys," each representing the interests of a different port and group of investors, was Oldenbarnevelt, then at the height of his influence. The motives for the Dutch endeavors to establish their own routes to the far-away East and the principal steps in the creation of the East India Company are described in the present selection by Pieter van Dam (1621–1706). The advocate (chief legal officer) of the company from 1652 until his death, Van Dam undertook the task of writing a *Description of the East India Company* at the direction of its administrators, the "Lords XVII."

Source: Pieter van Dam, *Beschryvinge van de Oostindische Compagnie*, ed. F. W. Stapel, Vol. I (The Hague: Martinus Nijhoff, 1927), pp. 7–9, 78–79, 138–139. Translated from the Dutch by Herbert H. Rowen.

IF PHILIP II, king of Spain, had been capable of winking at the shipping and trade of the inhabitants of these provinces with Spain and Portugal and had permitted it to go on, it is very probable that they would never have attempted to extend it any further, for it was only when he began to interfere with it that they started to look beyond, even to the East Indies.

So long as these lands remained under the dominion of Spain, even during the government of Emperor Charles V, Netherlanders were not permitted to voyage either to the West Indies or the East Indies, lands belonging for form's sake to the first discoverers or to those who made the first journey to them in the East Indies, and hence assigned by the decree of Pope Alexander VI[1] to the kingdoms of Spain and Portugal, each receiving for its share lands and realms to possess, travel, and trade in, with all other nations excluded. Therefore those who lived in these provinces at that time had to be satisfied to send their trading ships only to Spain and Portugal and no further.

Besides, a very large trade to the Baltic and the adjacent lands had long been in existence, principally in grain and naval stores and timber, most of which was then re-exported from here to Spain and Portugal for the construction and repair of ships, especially the heavy carracks and galleons of a burden of a thousand, twelve hundred, and even more tons; for warships and merchantmen needed cables and cordage, masts, anchors, sails, and sailcloth, as well as pitch, tar, and other naval stores which all had to be imported from abroad, in exchange for which they brought back silver, spices, and other wares which came from the East and West Indies. This trade continued for many years, even after this country declared its independence from the king of Spain, under the name of various Baltic merchants and others with whom the Dutch formed companies.

Although this situation came to the attention of Philip II a number of times, he permitted it to continue unnoticed for some years in view of his own shortages and necessities, especially of naval stores, but also because it increased his revenues from customs tolls. It is also possible that he was afraid that if he interfered with this trade, the people of this country, who cannot survive

1. The decree confirming the treaty of Tordesillas made by Spain and Portugal in 1494.—*Ed.*

without trade, industry, and shipping, would attempt to discover other distant lands and thereby cause him great harm and loss. But when various persons caused him to change his mind, he began, despite these considerations, to subject our shippers and crews to all kinds of vexations, which became more frequent and troublesome; ships were seized and detained under the pretext that the king needed their crews for his own service at very low pay. Then, declaring that they were rebels and heretics, he threw them into jail, where they perished from hunger and other hardships; he confiscated their goods, turned some of them over to the Inquisition; then finally he ordered a general seizure of all ships and goods belonging to Dutchmen to be found in his kingdoms of Spain and Portugal and had the rudders and sails removed. The Dutch began to abandon this trade, at least for a time, although the Council of Portugal let it be known that if the Dutch refrained from aiding France and England with warships, the king would continue to allow their shipping and trade. A short time later their ships were released, supposedly at the request of Archduke Albert, who had been named Governor General of the [southern] Netherlands and wished to make the United Provinces more friendly to him. But we could not put any trust whatever in Spain, where, after the death of King Philip II in the year 1598, his son who succeeded him did not merely continue the cruel conduct of his father but treated our people even more harshly, throwing them into foul, stinking jails, putting some to death and sending others to the galleys, confiscating their ships and goods, and the like. Furthermore, because of the loss or obstruction of this trade it became necessary to find work and employment for the seamen, of whom there was now a large number. It became necessary therefore to seek out new trading routes to places as far as the East Indies, in order to buy and bring back the spices and other wares which otherwise we would have had to go to get from the Spaniards and the Portuguese, often at high prices, and then bring here for resale by our merchants in other countries. As a result, the first efforts were made to find a shorter route to these lands in the East Indies, to wit: China, Japan and others, by the northeastern route along Tartary, although it had been investigated by other nations, especially the English, for many years and found unprofitable (about which we shall say more later.) Others chose the route around the Cape of Good Hope because, although it was estimated to be a good 2,000 miles longer than the other, it was safer. Those who favored this route were nine in number, eminent merchants in Amsterdam, among them Hendrik Hudde, Reynier Pauw, and Pieter Dircksz Hasselaer, who were also members of the municipal government. They took the risk of sending out four ships on this voyage, including a yacht, all well-provided with cannon and ammunition for vigorous self-defense, as well as with the money and trading goods most wanted in those regions. This society was named the Company for Far Journeys. These ships met a Spanish ship between Africa and America which was returning to Europe with a valuable cargo and had become separated from the other ships of its fleet; they allowed it to sail on because they were instructed to act only on the defensive, not offensively, which the Spaniards, who had considered themselves doomed to defeat, reported on their arrival at Lisbon. This brought great renown to the Dutch. . . .

After various private merchants joined with others in the 1590s and after the turn of the century to form companies, first in Amsterdam and then in other cities of Holland and Zeeland, to open up and undertake travel and trade with the East Indies, and from time to time equipped and sent out many ships, which returned, on the average, with no small success, the States General came to the conclusion that it would be more useful and profitable not only for the country as a whole but also for its inhabitants individually, especially all those who had undertaken and shared in navigation and trade, that these companies should be combined and this navigation and trade be placed and maintained on a firm footing, with order and political guidance. After much argument and persuasion, this union was worked out by Their High Mightinesses, in their own words, to advance the prosperity of the United Netherlands, to conserve and increase its industry and to bring profit to the Company and to the people of the country.[2]

Their High Mightinesses later, by an edict of Sepember 19, 1606, acceded to vigorous requests of the Company and granted to it a charter for a period of twenty-one years, permitting it to voyage east of the Cape of Good Hope or through the Straits of Magellan and excluding all others, under penalty not only of confiscation of ships and cargo but also of fines and imprisonment.

2. The words, that is, of the charter of the United East India Company of 1602.—*Ed.*

By another edict,[3] Their High Mightinesses declared that terms, franchises, and advantages already accorded were to be maintained and continued, without any direct or indirect infringement within this country or abroad in any matter, personally or through intermediaries, under penalty of imprisonment and fines and with the distribution of said fines.

Furthermore, the Company's charter authorized it to make alliances with princes and potentates east of the Cape of Good Hope and beyond the Straits of Magellan, to make contracts, build fortresses and strongholds, name governors, raise troops, appoint officers of justice, and perform other necessary services for the advancement of trade; to dismiss the said governors and officers of justice if their conduct was found to be harmful and disloyal, provided that these governors or officers could not be prevented from returning here to present such grievances or complaints as they think they might have to Their High Mightinesses. This was further confirmed by the eighth article of the instructions of the year 1617, approved and ratified by Their High Mightinesses, which established and regulated the government in the Indies in such a way that, as is easily seen, the Company after the date of this charter has made great progress in the Indies. It has captured a number of fortresses from the Spaniards and the Portuguese, its enemies, and has established trading posts at several places. It was decided as a consequence that it was desirable to establish a formal government in the Indies, with a Governor General and a Council, and to provide it with proper instructions, and this was done by the assembly of the XVII[4] and by Their High Mightinesses. . . .

The inhabitants of this country were permitted to invest as much or as little as they pleased in shares of the Company.

The subscription had to be made before September 1, 1602; the first part of the price had to be paid before October 1, with interest of 8 percent until the next April; the second third before October 1, 1603, and the remaining third before October 1, 1604, at the same rate of interest.

It was further agreed that a full third of the capital would be

3. Of July 1, 1606.—*Ed*.

4. The administrators, or board of directors, of the United East India Company.—*Ed*.

furnished for the equipment of the first fleet, the original paid-up capital amounting in all to 6,424,588 guilders 8 stivers, as follows:

in the Chamber of Amsterdam	3,674,915: —: —	guilders
in the Chamber of Zeeland	1,300,405:4 : —	„
in the Chamber of Delft	469,400: —: —	„
in the Chamber of Rotterdam	173,000: —: —	„
in the Chamber of Hoorn	266,868: —: —	„
in the Chamber of Enkhuizen	540,000: —: —	„
	6,424,588:4 : —	guilders,

in which connection it is to be noted that according to the resolution of the assembly of August 12, 1603, the subscribed capital then amounted to 6,459,840 guilders.

When the time for this investment or subscription had expired, various competent persons in different places presented requests in person or by sealed letter to the assembly of the XVII, asking that they be permitted to join the Company with the investment of certain sums of money; it was decided that no one else should be permitted to join in violation of the charter and to the detriment of the shareholders who had paid in their subscriptions before the expiration of the date fixed, and that the subscribed capital should be neither increased nor reduced, and it was further resolved that the sum presented by the Chamber of Enkhuizen after the fixed date should not be accepted.

31. Freedom of the Seas for People Who Trade

The Dutch, in seeking to create their own trading routes to the East, came at once into conflict with the Portuguese (which meant, as Van Dam observed, the king of Spain, who was also king of Portugal from 1580 until the revolt of 1640). The Portuguese claim for a monopoly of European trade to the East Indies rested not only on the partition of the world between Spain and Portugal in the treaty of Tordesillas of 1494, but also on a variety of other claims of exclusive right. The classic Dutch rejoinder came from the pen of Hugo Grotius (1583–1645), the great jurist and follower of Oldenbarnevelt. In 1609 Grotius published his first major work, *Mare Liberum* ("The Free Sea") to uphold the thesis that the sea belonged to no one, that it was, in political terms, under no state's sovereignty. In this work, of which the key passages are given here, Grotius drew upon the works of classical antiquity, both political and literary, as well as upon the legists and

philosophers of medieval and Renaissance Europe, including the great
Spanish jurists of the sixteenth century like Vittoria, despite their
Catholicism. His treatise, so theoretical in the form of its exposition,
was of course eminently practical in its purpose, and its arguments was
enforced in the waters of the East Indies by the superior naval and
military power of the Dutch East India Company. Its application to
European powers would come under fire from the English, notably
John Selden, probably as great a scholar if a lesser thinker than
Grotius, who contributed the classical defense of British sovereignty
over the "narrow seas" around England in his *Mare Clausum* ("The
Closed Sea") of 1635.

Source: Hugo Grotius, *The Freedom of the Seas, or The Right
which belongs to the Dutch to Take Part in the East India Trade*,
trans. Ralph Van Deman Magoffin, ed. James Brown Scott
(New York: Oxford University Press, 1916), pp. 7–10, 61–64,
72–76. Reprinted by permission of Carnegie Endowment for International Peace.

By the Law of Nations navigation is free to all persons whatsoever

My intention is to demonstrate briefly and clearly that the
Dutch—that is to say, the subjects of the United Netherlands—
have the right to sail to the East Indies, as they are now doing, and
to engage in trade with the people there. I shall base my argument
on the following most specific and unimpeachable axiom of the
Law of Nations, called a primary rule or first principle, the spirit
of which is self-evident and immutable, to wit: Every nation is free
to travel to every other nation, and to trade with it.

God Himself says this speaking through the voice of nature; and
inasmuch as it is not His will to have Nature supply every place
with all the necessaries of life, He ordains that some nations excel in
one art and others in another. Why is this His will, except it be that
He wished human friendships to be engendered by mutual needs
and resources, lest individuals deeming themselves entirely sufficient unto themselves should for that very reason be rendered
unsociable? So by the decree of divine justice it was brought about
that one people should supply the needs of another, in order, as
Pliny the Roman writer says, that in this way, whatever has been
produced anywhere should seem to have been destined for all.
Vergil also sings in this wise:

Not every plant on every soil will grow,

and in another place:

Let others better mould the running mass
Of metals, etc.

Those therefore who deny this law, destroy this most praise-worthy bond of human fellowship, remove the opportunities for doing mutual service, in a word do violence to Nature herself. For do not the ocean, navigable in every direction, with which God has encompassed all the earth, and the regular and the occasional winds which blow now from one quarter and now from another, offer sufficient proof that Nature has given to all peoples a right of access to all other peoples? Seneca thinks this is Nature's greatest service, that by the wind she united the widely scattered peoples, and yet did so distribute all her products over the earth that commercial intercourse was a necessity to mankind. Therefore this right belongs equally to all nations. Indeed the most famous jurists extend its application so far as to deny that any state or any ruler can debar foreigners from having access to their subjects and trading with them. Hence is derived that law of hospitality which is of the highest sanctity; hence the complaint of the poet Vergil:

What men, what monsters, what inhuman race,
What laws, what barbarous customs of the place,
Shut up a desert shore to drowning men,
And drive us to the cruel seas again.

And:

To beg what you without your want may spare—
The common water, and the common air.

We know that certain wars have arisen over this very matter; such for example as the war of the Megarians against the Athenians, and that of the Bolognese against the Venetians. Again, Victoria holds that the Spaniards could have shown just reasons for making war upon the Aztecs and the Indians in America, more plausible reasons certainly than were alleged, if they really were prevented from traveling or sojourning among those peoples, and were denied the right to share in those things which by the Law of Nations or by Custom are common to all, and finally if they were debarred from trade.

We read of a similar case in the history of Moses, which we find mentioned also in the writings of Augustine, where the Israelites justly smote with the edge of the sword the Amorites because they had denied the Israelites an innocent passage through their territory, a right which according to the Law of Human Society ought in all justice to have been allowed. In defense of this principle Hercules attacked the king of Orchomenus in Boeotia; and the Greeks under their leader Agamemnon waged war against the king of Mysia on the ground that, as Baldus has said, high roads were free by nature. Again, as we read in Tacitus, the Germans accused the Romans of "preventing all intercourse between them and of closing up to them the rivers and roads, and almost the very air of heaven." When in days gone by the Christians made crusades against the Saracens, no other pretext was so welcome or so plausible as that they were denied by the infidels free access to the Holy Land.

It follows therefore that the Portuguese, even if they had been sovereigns in those parts to which the Dutch make voyages, would nevertheless be doing them an injury if they should forbid them access to those places and from trading there.

Is it not then an incalculably greater injury for nations which desire reciprocal commercial relations to be debarred therefrom by the acts of those who are sovereigns neither of the nations interested, nor of the element over which their connecting high road runs? Is not that the very cause which for the most part prompts us to execrate robbers and pirates, namely, that they beset and infest our trade routes?

By the Law of Nations trade is free to all persons whatsoever

If however the Portuguese claim that they have an exclusive right to trade with the East Indies, their claim will be refuted by practically all the same arguments which already have been brought forward. Nevertheless I shall repeat them briefly, and apply them to this particular claim.

By the law of nations the principle was introduced that the opportunity to engage in trade, of which no one can be deprived, should be free to all men. This principle, inasmuch as its application was straightway necessary after the distinctions of private owner-ships were made, can therefore be seen to have had a very remote origin. Aristotle, in a very clever phrase, in his work entitled the *Politics*, has said that the art of exchange is a completion of the independence which Nature requires. Therefore trade ought to be common to all according to the law of nations, not only in a negative but also in a positive, or as the jurists say, affirmative sense. The things that come under the former category are subject to change, those of the latter category are not. This statement is to be explained in the following way.

Nature had given all things to all men. But since men were prevented from using many things which were desirable in every day life because they lived so far apart, and because, as we have said above, everything was not found everywhere, it was necessary to transport things from one place to another; not that there was yet an interchange of commodities, but that people were accus-tomed to make reciprocal use of things found in one another's territory according to their own judgment. They say that trade arose among the Chinese in about this way. Things were deposited at places out in the desert and left to the good faith and conscience of those who exchanged things of their own for what they took.

But when movables passed into private ownership (a change brought about by necessity, as has been explained above), straight-way there arose a method of exchange by which the lack of one person was supplemented by that of which another person had an over supply. Hence commerce was born out of necessity for the commodities of life, as Pliny shows by a citation from Homer. But after immovables also began to be recognized as private property, the consequent annihilation of universal community of use made commerce a necessity not only between men whose habitations were far apart but even between men who were neighbors; and in order that trade might be carried on more easily, somewhat later they invented money, which, as the derivation of the word shows, is a civic institution.

Therefore the universal basis of all contracts, namely exchange, is derived from nature; but some particular kinds of exchange, and the money payment itself, are derived from law; although the older commentators on the law have not made this distinction sufficiently clear. Nevertheless all authorities agree that the ownership of things, particularly of movables, arises out of the primary law of nations, and that all contracts in which a price is not mentioned, are derived from the same source. The philosophers distinguish two kinds of exchange using Greek words which we shall take the liberty to translate as "wholesale" and "retail" trade. The former, as the Greek word shows, signifies trade or exchange between widely separated nations, and it ranks first in the order of Nature, as is shown in Plato's *Republic*. The latter seems to be the same kind of exchange that Aristotle calls by another Greek word which means a retail or shop trade between citizens. Aristotle makes a further division of wholesale trade into overland and overseas trade. But of the two, retail trade is the more petty and sordid, and wholesale the more honorable; but most honorable of all is the wholesale overseas trade, because it makes so many people sharers in so many things.

Hence Ulpian says that the maintenance of ships is the highest duty of a state, because it is an absolutely natural necessity, but that the maintenance of hucksters has not the same value. In another place Aristotle says: "For the art of exchange extends to all possessions, and it arises at first in a natural manner from the circumstance that some have too little, others too much." And Seneca is also to be cited in this connection for he has said that buying and selling is the law of nations.

Therefore freedom of trade is based on a primitive right of nations which has a natural and permanent cause; and so that right cannot be destroyed, or at all events it may not be destroyed except by the consent of all nations. For surely no one nation may justly oppose in any way two nations that desire to enter into a contract with each other.

*The Dutch must maintain their right of trade with the East
Indies by peace, by treaty, or by war*

Wherefore since both law and equity demand that trade with the East Indies be as free to us as to any one else, it follows that we are to maintain at all hazards that freedom which is ours by nature, either by coming to a peace agreement with the Spaniards, or by concluding a treaty, or by continuing the war. So far as peace is concerned, it is well known that there are two kinds of peace, one made on terms of equality, the other on unequal terms. The Greeks call the former kind a compact between equals, the latter an enjoined truce; the former is meant for high souled men, the latter for servile spirits. Demosthenes in his speech on the liberty of the Rhodians says that it was necessary for those who wished to be free to keep away from treaties which were imposed upon them, because such treaties were almost the same as slavery. Such conditions are all those by which one party is lessened in its own right, according to the definition of Isocrates. For if, as Cicero says, wars must be undertaken in order that people may live in peace unharmed, it follows that peace ought to mean not an agreement which entails slavery, but an undisturbed liberty, especially as peace and justice according to the opinion of many philosophers and theologians differ more in name than in fact, and as peace is a harmonious agreement based not on individual whim, but on well ordered regulations.

If however a truce is arranged for, it is quite clear from the very nature of a truce, that during its continuance no one's condition ought to change for the worse, inasmuch as both parties stand on the equivalent of a *uti possidetis*.

But if we are driven into war by the injustice of our enemies, the justice of our cause ought to bring hope and confidence in a happy outcome. "For," as Demosthenes has said, "every one fights his hardest to recover what he has lost; but when men endeavor to gain at the expense of others it is not so." The Emperor Alexander has expressed his idea in this way: "Those who begin unjust deeds, must bear the greatest blame; but those who repel aggressors are twice armed, both with courage because of their just cause, and with the highest hope because they are not doing a wrong, but are warding off a wrong."

Therefore, if it be necessary, arise, O nation unconquered on the sea, and fight boldly, not only for your own liberty, but for that of the human race. "Nor let it fright thee that their fleet is winged, each ship, with an hundred oars. The sea whereon it sails will have none of it. And though the prows bear figures threatening to cast rocks such as Centaurs throw, thou shalt find them but hollow planks and painted terrors. 'Tis his cause that makes or mars a soldier's strength. If the cause be not just, shame strikes the weapon from his hands."

If many writers, Augustine himself among them, believed it was right to take up arms because innocent passage was refused across foreign territory, how much more justly will arms be taken up against those from whom the demand is made of the common and innocent use of the sea, which by the law of nature is common to all? If those nations which interdicted others from trade on their own soil are justly attacked, what of those nations which separate by force and interrupt the mutual intercourse of peoples over whom they have no rights at all? If this case should be taken into court, there can be no doubt what opinion ought to be anticipated from a just judge. The praetor's law says: "I forbid force to be used in preventing any one from sailing a ship or a boat on a public river, or from unloading his cargo on the bank." The commentators say that the injunction must be applied in the same manner to the sea and to the seashore. Labeo, for example, in commenting on the praetor's edict, "Let nothing be done in a public river or on its bank, by which a landing or a channel for shipping be obstructed," said there was a similar interdict which applied to the sea, namely, "Let nothing be done on the sea or on the seashore by which a harbor, a landing, or a channel for shipping be obstructed."

Nay more, after such a prohibition, if, namely, a man be prevented from navigating the sea, or not allowed to sell or to make use of his own wares and products, Ulpian says that he can bring an action for damages on that ground. Also the theologians and the casuists agree that he who prevents another from buying or selling, or who puts his private interests before the public and common interests, or who in any way hinders another in the use of something which is his by common right, is held in damages to complete restitution in an amount fixed by an honorable arbitrator.

Following these principles a good judge would award to the Dutch the freedom of trade, and would forbid the Portuguese and others from using force to hinder that freedom, and would order the payment of just damages. But when a judgment which would be rendered in a court cannot be obtained, it should with justice be demanded in a war. Augustine acknowledges this when he says: "The injustice of an adversary brings a just war." Cicero also says: "There are two ways of settling a dispute; first, by discussion; second, by physical force; we must resort to force only in case we may not avail ourselves of discussion." And King Theodoric says: "Recourse must then be had to arms when justice can find no lodgment in an adversary's heart." Pomponius, however, has handed down a decision which has more bearing on our argument than any of the citations already made. He declared that the man who seized a thing common to all to the prejudice of every one else must be forcibly prevented from so doing. The theologians also say that just as war is righteously undertaken in defense of individual property, so no less righteously is it undertaken in behalf of the use of those things which by natural law ought to be common property. Therefore he who closes up roads and hinders the export of merchandise ought to be prevented from so doing *via facti*, even without waiting for any public authority.

Since these things are so, there need not be the slightest fear that God will prosper the efforts of those who violate that most stable law of nature which He himself has instituted, or that even men will allow those to go unpunished who for the sake alone of private gain oppose a common benefit of the human race.

32. French Merchants Complain against Dutch Usurpation

The skill and diligence of Dutch traders often won them the collaboration, if not the friendship, of those who had goods to ship but few ships to send them in; but they also met fierce resentment from native merchants who saw their business taken away by the more efficient Dutch. The arguments against allowing the Dutch (or the English) a free hand in trading were stated with vigor, if with more than a little confusion of language, in a plea sent by French merchants at Nantes to Louis XIV and the King's Council in 1645, to bar Dutchmen from settling in France to do business. Against the various advantages of the Dutch they sought the political protection of their monarch, for their sake and for his. But such pleas as this would fail to sway the French government as long as France was the ally of the Dutch in the war against Spain (since 1635); it would not be until the Dutch had made a separate peace in 1648 that the rulers of France would move effectively to reduce or even eliminate Dutch merchants from their soil and from their trade.

Source: "Moyens d'intervention que mettent et baillent par devers le Roy et Monseigneurs [!] de son Conseil la communauté des Merchands Bourgeois de la ville et faubourgs de Nantes, demandeurs et reçus parties intervenantes en l'instance pendante au Conseil entre les nommés, ci-après, suivant l'ordonnance par eux présentée audit Conseil du 24 d'Avril 1645, pour qu'il soit défendu aux étrangers de tenir boutique en France," ed. Henri

Sée, in *Economisch-Historisch Jaarboek*, XII (1926), pp. 126–130, 133–134. Translated from the French by Herbert H. Rowen.

. . . . Despite all these excellent ordinances[5] and the efforts which have been made to re-establish commerce in France and restore it to its original luster, we cannot help but see that it grows weaker every day. The best seaports do not have the large number of ships which ought to be in them, and most French sailors, pilots, and bargemen, for lack of employment, are compelled, either to quit the sea and take jobs on land or to work for foreigners to earn their bread. What we see in France today in the best ports and havens are only foreign ships and foreign factors. Good, true-born Frenchmen can suffer such a sight only with great shame and distress.

The main cause of France's weakness in commerce is that it is held in scorn, so that those who are in a position to engage in trade take very little interest in it while foreigners freely violate the ordinances of the realm and the privileges of the cities in which they reside.

Among the cities of this kingdom, Nantes has always had a reputation as one of the most eminent and best fitted to engage in commerce and shipping because of its location near the sea upon one of the finest rivers in France, so that it can easily export and import commodities of all kinds from and into the realm. This is why it was given for its coat of arms a ship under full sail running before the wind, in recognition of the importance always placed by its inhabitants upon commerce and shipping. By skillful practice, they had made these into the main source of their wealth and their city's honor and greatness. Until recently navigation was widely engaged in here with its inhabitants owning more than one hundred and fifty ships. But now it is hard to find even ten or a dozen, so low and shameful is the state to which it has fallen. Our ships no longer sail because foreigners have run them aground and wrecked them, leaving them without sails or rigging. Merchants and sailors no longer sail the sea routes because they have no employment. We no longer see any ships or faces but those of foreigners, mainly Dutch, English, Scots, Irish, and Portuguese; families, factors, and

5. Especially that of January 15, 1629, articles 414, 415, 428, 429.—Note by Henri Sée.

agents from these nations have now resided here as long as fifteen or twenty years, and new ones arrive every day. They have taken away all the business, the agencies, and dealings which the natives had had with the foreigners who came frequently to our ports to purchase our fruits and goods and to sell us their merchandise.

Formerly everything ran in the good order that honest merchants desire, for there was abundance in the country and the merchants were prosperous. But since these factors and agents set themselves up here, they have drawn all business to themselves. By a sworn league among themselves they have tied the hands of our merchants and plotted the ruin of our country. They have brought all business into their own hands and revealed to their fellow-countrymen when we were in difficulties, because they could see what we did with their own eyes. They take advantage of the weather to delay or advance the price and sale of our fruits and goods as they please, in this way causing substantial damage to the interests of every Frenchman, particularly to the Nantese who used to carry on this trade.

These usurpations have come about because most of those who come from Holland to France, especially to the city of Nantes, are factors. On their arrival they enter into a league with their fellow-countrymen which has the force of national law among them; by it they promise to help each other and to permit no Frenchman to share in the profits which can be made in business. It has now come to the point where all profitable business will pass through their hands, thanks to their league and secret understandings, while the scraps they leave will be the most honorable employment that the native residents will be able to find. They will use this power in order to make their fortunes, not directly as did some of their countrymen, notably Bonnaventure Bron, Henry Rammelman, Reynier, Alexander Velters, Lambert de Grutter, William van Houtte, Anthony Casteleyn and several others who returned to their country with more than one hundred fifty thousand livres each in wealth; but indirectly, by means of big bankruptcies, such as happened during the past twelve or fifteen years to Jacob van Rinsen, Adrian Poupe, Michael van Lamsuerst, Charles and John de Langhe, George Hontorst, Paul Traudeny, Adrian Michiels, Jacob van Ravestein, John Vermasen, Giles van Lussel, Tilman Gorris, Peter Francis Bave, Nicholas Slingerland, Henry Bucenet, Melchior Staers, Peter van Lusset, Gerard van Rossen, Jacob le

Bleu, Fop Adrians, John Tap, William Vrouling, Joris Ravestein, Peter van de Velde, Gerard Noe, and several others. Frenchmen lost more than eight or nine thousand livres in these bankruptcies so that it is we who run the risks for their fortunes. They pay us if they prosper, and if it is not to their advantage to pay they take off with our wealth, knowing full well that we will not dare to sue them in the courts of their own country because they carry their appeals to their Provincial courts, where cases involving foreigners last forever and not a single Frenchman has won a case because they stick so closely together.

In order to maintain this league they meet in clubs and assemblies twice a week, conferring over their orders and noting the quantity and quality of the merchandise which they need according to their inclinations and the orders of their principals. They can, therefore, set whatever price they want upon our fruits, goods, and products, knowing full well that the French will not dare to pursue and track down these meetings, for fear that they will cause their own ruin rather than gain any advantage. This has happened several times. Thus, they make themselves the masters of the revenues and commerce of France by this dangerous conspiracy.

But in order to avoid being caught in these monopolistic practices and to pass as people necessary to the public welfare, they have agreed among themselves to pay more for their fruits and goods to a few influential persons in order to gain their support and backing, and they treat with great contempt the others who come to them to ask that they buy their wares which they find they can no longer afford to hold in their own hands. But when the Dutch see themselves courted in this way, they put up a cold front, pretending that they have no use for these wares until they have brought them down to the price agreed upon in their assemblies and arguing that they are under strict obligations in their purchases. Not satisfied with tricking us and taking advantage of us by force, they invite other foreigners to form similar leagues. What is worst of all is they laugh at us among themselves. *"De Grieken en verstaen de negotie niet"* (The Greeks do not understand business), they say, meaning us Frenchmen, for "Greek" is used among them as a kind of code name and so they pass us off as ignorant, with little knowledge of business, people who let themselves be fleeced easily.

Furthermore, they have become so greedy that they engage the poor artisans and craftsmen of the city of Nantes to make brandy and vinegar for them, which they supply and sell to foreigners and their own countrymen. When these poor folk, finding themselves oppressed and deprived of their bread and with their privileges infringed, took their case to court, the Chamber of the Edict in the Parliament of Paris, to which they had had recourse, found their complaint so justified that they were given an injunction as they requested.

The Dutch also have barrel-makers of their own nation who work for them in their houses and shops. Although they do a large business in wine, brandy, and vinegar, they very seldom give jobs to French coopers and these poor workmen are reduced to utter and pitiable poverty. Besides the fact that this is very detrimental to the country since they are at present the most important exporters of wine, they compel the landowners to buy the casks which they have had made at a high price, often as much as half the value of the wine; if this privilege were taken away from them and permitted only to Frenchmen, as is done in all the other big cities of this realm, French winegrowers and coopers would earn what the Dutchmen now get.

They act in the same way toward the keepers of the inns and taverns where most of them take their board and lodging in Nantes. They are so numerous and so watchful lest the natives make any profit from them, that if anyone shows the least sign of resisting their oppression, they meet him with threats. They assert that they have the same privileges as the native residents of the city and that if anyone puts a hand on them, they will complain to their own States and will call the public powers to their assistance. They lodge their appeals directly with the Council and call upon their agents and ambassadors to intercede for them on every occasion. Their envoys are themselves all merchants and make the least quarrel into matters of state, and in order to maintain themselves more effectively impose a levy of several pennies upon the fruits and wares which we sell them, on the pretext that this goes to support the poor of their own nation, but they sometimes use this money themselves and thus oppress poor Frenchmen. . . .

They make an absolute mockery of France when they say that they permit us to trade and do business freely in Holland and Zeeland. It is a small and infertile country which produces no goods of its own and consumes only a little, but which, by the practices and policies of their trade aimed at their own subsistence, is made to serve as a way station and storehouse for the goods and merchandise which they bring from outside to distribute and sell to other nations. Add to this that they are all merchants who have the powers of the courts and government in their hands, and that they do not allow foreigners to do anything except what is useful and profitable to themselves, and that they always act both as judges and parties in cases before the courts and it will be seen why it is impossible for Frenchmen to live and make a profit there.

Furthermore, they are not satisfied to deceive us and mistreat us on the land. They do so at sea as well. Their ingratitude toward Frenchmen is so great that after having permitted them to extract whale oil on Greenland, as they still permit the English to do, they now compel the poor Frenchmen to do this on the high seas, at the peril of fire or death in the ice.

These are the tricks and deceits which the Dutch play on Frenchmen on every occasion. They offer us their own country to do business in when they know that there is nothing that we can do there, and prevent us from making a profit wherever they themselves have a chance to get rich. Yet they are now so presumptuous that they claim that they are dispensed from the laws and ordinances of the French state and may infringe the statutes and privileges of the cities in which they reside, and that their usurpations may not be repressed, on the pretext that they must be treated more favorably in this kingdom than any other nation, as appears in this case which we plead before the Council, as disinterested parties, as shall be shown hereafter.

33. A Defense of Dutch Traders Abroad

By no means all foreign businessmen resented the presence of Dutch traders and sought to drive them out. In many places, and notably in France where the primary economic activities of agriculture and industry continued to be more important than commerce, producers were glad to sell to the Dutch, who paid with ready cash, were regular and generally honest in their dealings, and had at their disposal a network of shipping and trading which enabled them to use almost all products. In 1661, just about the time that the great French exponent of mercantilism, Jean-Baptiste Colbert, was assuming an important role in the government of Louis XIV, the Dutch special ambassador in Paris, Coenraad van Beuningen, was able to submit to the French government a declaration of Paris businessmen in support of the maintenance of mutual trade with the Dutch and the English. This

hitherto unpublished document has been translated from the copy in
the Dutch archives at The Hague.

Source: "Advis que donnent les Marchands et Négocians de Paris,
  qui trafiquent dans les Païs d'Angleterre et Hollande; pour faire
  voir, qu'il est très important de maintenir et conserver la Négo-
  ciation réciproque," in Algemeen Rijksarchief, The Hague,
  Staten van Holland, box D214. Translated from the French by
  Herbert H. Rowen.

IT SHOULD be observed that there is a very substantial difference in
the kind, quantity, and cost of all the commodities which are
exported from France to England and Holland. They are manufactured in various towns and provinces of this kingdom, including
Lyons, Tours, Forez, Auvergne, Brittany, Normandy, Picardy,
Champagne, and others, as is shown in detail below. This memoir
has been drawn up to demonstrate that the maintenance of this
trade with our neighbors is not only important to the State but is
also very useful to the King's subjects, for there are employed in
the manufacture and preparation of these wares and articles an
almost infinite number of handicraftsmen, laborers, and others.
They earn a livelihood in this work and are able as a result to pay
the *taille* and other taxes to the State; but they would never be able
to do so if this trade were not maintained and protected, for then
they would be reduced to the shameful necessity of begging for
their bread. There is reason to fear that this would happen if the
English and the Dutch forbade the importation of the goods and
merchandise from France. They pay an enormous sum for these
imports for they are not satisfied to meet their own country's needs
but transship large quantities to distant lands, including the Indies
and other foreign parts. There can be no doubt that such a ban
upon trade would be imposed if they were prevented from selling
the cloth and other wares which the French import from England
and Holland, yet these are not large in quantity and cannot be
compared with what we send to the English and Dutch. A few
days ago a memoir was published by persons whose private interests were clearly visible in their attempt to show that the importation of foreign cloth was harmful to France, but we shall not linger
over it because it contains more assertion than fact. The truth, as
can be shown, is that the entire supply of cloth imported from
England and Holland amounts to no more than 2,500,000 livres, or

at the most 3,000,000 livres a year, while the imports of these countries from France amount to more than ten times as much, as can be seen in the articles below. Furthermore, not one louis d'or or écu[6] is shipped out for the payment of these commodities, because, besides the explicit ban on export of coin in the ordinances, which provide a penalty of imprisonment and confiscation of property, the louis d'or is worth only seven pounds four shillings in England and eight guilders ten stivers in Holland. Payment is therefore made by letters of exchange or is covered by the goods which the English and Dutch import from France. This is justification for making mutual trade possible and convenient. There is no point in saying that even if foreign cloth is barred from France, the foreigners will nonetheless continue to buy the goods they are in the habit of importing from France because these are absolutely necessary to them and they cannot do without them. This is especially untrue because everyone knows that these foreigners are able to attract French workers and artisans to their countries and in that way establish in their country the manufacture of these goods, cloths, and products which they import from France; this has already happened with a number of articles. If this happens, there cannot help but result great harm to France and all the subjects of the King, and a great decline in the revenues from customs duties, which are very large. To these we can add that if the import of these goods from England and Holland is forbidden, the English and the Dutch will forbid the use of their ports as *entrepôts* for goods shipped to Spain, as is now done, and trade between France and Spain would therefore collapse completely, for the goods which go to Spain can be sent only by way of these ports in England and Holland. This ban would also be very harmful to France, for in return for the goods which are going to Spain a large quantity of golden and silver reals[7] as well as silver in barrels come in as can be proved.

[Seventeen articles indicate the kinds and worth of the various exports, including the place of manufacture.]

34. Trading in the Wind: The Tulip Speculation

The immense expansion of commerce in the United Provinces, by separating the various phases of trade from each other, encouraged

6. French coins.—*Tr.*
7. Spanish coins.—*Tr.*

gambling upon profits to be made from speculation in all kinds of products. It was the price that had to be paid for the increased efficiency of a complex system of business. But now and again speculation intensified into a frenzy of what the Dutch called *windhandel*, literally "trading in the wind," that is, buying or selling in futures, without actual possession of goods. The most famous example of such gambling was the tulip mania of 1636–1637, involving the bulbs of tulips and hyacinths, which had become the modish flower of the day in their myriad new varieties. Rapidly escalating prices spurred the gambling instinct of all sorts of people, especially in the district around Haarlem, to this day the bulb-growing center of Holland. Measures of Haarlem's town government to dampen the madness were slow to work at first, but suddenly in 1637, after prices had soared to fantastic heights based far more on what other speculators would pay than what consumers would, the speculative castle in the sky collapsed. For those who lost— or did not make—fortunes, there was tragedy, but some observers saw the entire episode as a ludicrous instance of human greed paid off as it deserved. One of the wittiest of such comments appeared in a pamphlet published in Haarlem in 1637, after the collapse of prices, under the title, *A Conversation between Waermondt and Gaergoedt about the Rise and Decline of Flora*. The names are indicative of character: "*Waermondt*" means "true mouth," and "*Gaergoedt*" something like "ready goods."

Source: "Samen-spraeck tusschen Waermondt ende Gaergoedt nopende de Opkomste ende Ondergangh van Flora," reprinted in *Economisch-Historisch Jaarboek*, XII (1926), pp. 21–24, 32–35. Translated from the Dutch by Herbert H. Rowen.

WAERMONDT: God grant you a fine day, Gaergoedt, my special friend. How are things with you?

GAERGOEDT; Everything is fine for me and the Florists. Our lives are a joy and we are quite satisfied. But come in, we'll talk a bit together by the fire.

WAERMONDT: Thank you, I'm on my way to someone else's.

GAERGOEDT: Oh no, you're not in that much of a hurry. I have something I must tell you, and I'll let you go when you want.

WAERMONDT: Well, if you want me to, I will.

GAERGOEDT: Sit down there, my friend. Come, Anneken, bring wood and turf, I must talk a little with my old friend. Where have you been all this time? Give me the bottle of brandy, or do you want Spanish wine, or a good French wine to drink, or a draught of good beer?

WAERMONDT: You're offering so many things that I don't know how to choose among them.

GAERGOEDT: We Florists have everything we need now, for a little flower pays for it all.

WAERMONDT: If you are paid as well as you hope, that's fine, but many a plowman has high hopes when he sows his grain and all he reaps is stubble.

GAERGOEDT: No, this is too sure a business for that. Come now, have a drink, here's one for you.

WAERMONDT: Thank you, I'll repay you in kind. But what expensive bottle is this?

GAERGOEDT: Everything comes from noble Flora. I was at the brandy distiller's just now; I offered him a little flower and took this full bottle for it. That is what I usually do; I get my meat, my bacon, my wine, for nothing, as much as I need for this whole year.

WAERMONDT: If you can earn a profit so easily, that is a good business. The storekeepers and workpeople are all complaining about high costs and little work. The merchants complain about the great damage they suffer from pirates at sea and from the great storms which ruin their cargoes or cause their total loss.

GAERGOEDT: I could talk about such things too, but now that I have gone into the flower business, I have only made profits, and let me tell you, I have made more than sixty thousand guilders in a space of four months—but don't tell anyone.

WAERMONDT: Well, that's a big profit. Have you received it all?

GAERGOEDT: Oh no, but I have letters from the buyers in their own hand.

WAERMONDT: That's enough. You almost make me ready to invest a little too.

GAERGOEDT: If you've a mind to, I'll sell you a small shipment, and since you're a good man and my special old friend, the price will be fifty guilders less than for anybody else, and let me add that if you don't make a hundred imperial dollars[8] on it within a month, I'll make up the difference myself.

WAERMONDT: What kind of sales talk are you giving me? If I owned this supply, how would I get rid of it? Would people come to me or would I have to go to them?

GAERGOEDT: I'll tell you. You have to go to a tavern. I'll name a

8. 250 guilders.—*Ed.*

few, for I know hardly any without a "club." Go in and ask if
there are any florists. When you go to their room, some will quack
like a duck because you're a newcomer, and some will say,
"There's a new whore in the brothel," and such things. But you
mustn't let it disturb you, they'll stop. They put your name on a
slate and then the board goes around. That is, everyone in the club
must send the board to anyone whose name is on the slate, and he
asks for an offer. You must not put up your own goods for
auction, even if you have a bit more than you're able to carry. But
if you drop a word that you have something, someone will want
them and drag them away from you; otherwise you'll receive the
board. When the boards are given out, each seller and buyer picks
a "man." The seller goes to his "man" first and if his wares are
worth, say, a hundred, he demands two hundred; then the buyer
comes to the "man" and when he hears the asking price, he be-
comes angry and offers as much less as you demanded more. The
"men" establish the price; everyone receives a figure on his board.
The men announce the price, and if you are satisfied with it, you
leave your figure on the board and if the buyer and the seller both
leave their figures, then a sale has been made. But on the other
hand, if the figures are erased, the sale is off. And if a person leaves
his figure on his board only the other party who has erased his is
written down for a payment to the club. In some places it's two
pennies, in others three, or five, or even six. And if a sale is made,
then the seller gives a half penny for each guilder, but only three
guilders if the sale is 120 guilders or more, not even if it is over a
thousand guilders.

WAERMONDT: What do they do with this money?

GAERGOEDT: They have to drink, don't they? They pay for
tobacco, beer, wine, fuel, light, and make contributions to the poor
and to the girls too.

WAERMONDT: Enough is gotten for all that?

GAERGOEDT: Yes, often the sales of wine bring in even more than
that. Several times I brought more money home than I took to the
tavern, and I had eaten and drunk wine, beer, tobacco, all kinds of
fine foods, fish, meat, even poultry and rabbits, and sweet pastries
too, from morning until three or four o'clock in the night.

WAERMONDT: It's smart to be that kind of a guest.

GAERGOEDT: Well, I made a good profit too; I took in some six or
seven "triplets," for I did twelve thousand guilders' worth of

business and the "triplets" kept falling like drops of water off a thatched roof after it has rained.

WAERMONDT: I've never heard stories the likes of this. But will it go on?

GAERGOEDT: If it lasts a year or two or three, that's enough for me.

WAERMONDT: I'm afraid that the Florists will find that in the end, Flora, whose name they bear and was a whore in Rome, will deceive them. You must have read her story.

GAERGOEDT: No, I haven't! Please tell me about it.

WAERMONDT: In the time of the Romans this Flora was a harlot whose beauty and pleasant talk, proud looks and graceful manner won her many lovers including such important men as Roman senators, who came to visit her. Her great conquests and the gifts they brought made her proud and haughty.

GAERGOEDT: Well, what you tell me is to the advantage of the Florists, for Flora became rich and so will the Florists. . . .

WAERMONDT: You don't understand what I mean. Flora made out well, but not the Florists who followed her, although they all lived on hope. And I fear that the same will happen with you and that you will lose in this business of yours the fine piece of property which your fathers earned by so many hours of long work and anxiety. Would it not have been better for you to have stuck to your own trade? . . .

WAERMONDT: It's almost noon, I'd better go home and see what I've got to do there. I'll take your books with me.

GAERGOEDT: Come, sit a little while and be my guest. My wife should be back from market soon with some fish. What can be keeping her so long? She must be doing business again. When I am out, she often buys and sells more than four or five thousand guilders's worth. Sit, maybe she'll bring us some news.

WAERMONDT: I'm sorry, my friend, I cannot stay now. I must go home; I left some people there waiting for me. Good day, my friend.

GAERGOEDT: When shall I expect you again, so that I can go over the books?

WAERMONDT: At exactly two o'clock.

GAERGOEDT: That's fine, I'll wait. Goodbye. I wonder where my wife has been for so long? She knows that I'm home. Doesn't she like me any more? I don't know what to think. Isn't that she coming there? Yes, it is. I'll wait for her inside. Well, my little Christina, how are things? Where have you been so long? You could have sent the fish home as soon as the fishwife cleaned it. I had hoped to have a guest dine with us.

CHRISTINA: Darling, I have no fish. I heard the quail sing such a wonderful song that I had no taste for fish. Come inside, I have something to tell you.

GAERGOEDT: I still think that your sister is not with child. She has run around so much with that fellow that either one of their friends has died or they are through. You know what I mean. I don't know what to think.

CHRISTINA: That's not what I'm talking about. I was visiting our niece Anneken, who told me that the Florists are in a panic. Some goods are going for less than half that what they brought the same evening.

GAERGOEDT: Oh, I hope not.

CHRISTINA: The time for hoping is past. Everything I've told you is true. . . .

GAERGOEDT: Well, wife, don't be too worried, for it isn't as bad as you say. I've got a chance. Someone is coming this afternoon to whom I hope to make a good sale. I must get rid of some of my stock, for too much is on hand. But he won't know that. Of course, he is a good, special old acquaintance, but everyone must look for himself, for in business it is better to see a brother in trouble, not to speak of an acquaintance, than oneself. . . .

ANNEKEN: Madame, the clock has struck two.

CHRISTINA: I'll stay a quarter of an hour for your sake, my dear, but I really cannot stay after that, for my heart aches with what I've just told you. I must go out and find out what is happening.

GAERGOEDT: That's not worth the trouble to go out for. I'll hear soon enough when I go to the club in the evening, for everything that happens in the city is talked over. Anneken, Anneken, someone is knocking. Let him in.

ANNEKEN: It is the man who was here this morning.

GAERGOEDT: Let him in.

WAERMONDT: Good day, my friend Gaergoedt, and you too, Christijntje.

CHRISTINA: Come and sit here by my husband. I have to go out.

Anneken, it's cold outside, bring some wood and open a small jug of wine.

WAERMONDT: There's no need to do that, I won't be long.

GAERGOEDT: Stay as long as you'd like. Come and sit down.

CHRISTINA: Goodbye, husband, goodbye, friend Waermondt. Have a good chat.

WAERMONDT: Goodbye. I went over your books for the flower business quickly and went to my cousin to discuss what it would be best for me to do. He advised me to wait a few days and see how things come out. There is no buying now, so that I am afraid I cannot take anything on now.

35. A Tragic Business: The Slave Trade

Dutch commercial and shipping prowess was applied not only to the ordinary goods of trade—the products of the soil and man's industry—but also to man himself. During the seventeenth century, despite the war with Spain, Dutchmen, as well as Englishmen, began to supply slaves from Africa to the plantations of America. The slave trade became the principal source of the profits of the Dutch West India Company, and after Spain made a formal peace with the United Provinces in 1648, the Dutch predominance in the supply of black human merchandise to the Americas lasted half a century. The Dutch sold ten times as many slaves as the English in this period, but lost the *asiento* (contract for slave deliveries) to the English during the War of the Spanish Succession. The Dutch applied to this dismal trade, in which the overcrowded slave-ships lost on the average fifteen to twenty-five percent of their human cargoes in the "middle passage" from Africa to the Caribbean, the same meticulous business methods that they used in the purchase or sale of grain or guns. This is illustrated by the following contract of the West India Company to deliver 2,000 slaves to Curaçao, the principal supply depôt in the Caribbean.

Source: S. van Brakel, "Bescheiden over den Slavenhandel der West-Indische Compagnie," *Economisch-Historisch Jaarboek*, IV (1918), pp. 61–66. Translated from the Dutch by Herbert H. Rowen.

AGREEMENT to Deliver two thousand or More Slaves to Curaçao, dated 15 September 1662.

This day, September 15, 1662, there appeared before me, Pieter Padthuysen, notary public admitted to practice before the Court of

Holland and resident in Amsterdam, in the presence of the witnesses named hereafter, Messrs. the Honorable Abraham Wiemer-
doncx and Jacob Pergens, administrators of the chamber of the
chartered West India Company in this city, with special commissions, on the one side, and Mr. Alexandro Bosco, having powers of
attorney and instructions from Messrs. Domingo Grillo and
Ambrosio Lomelino, resident in Madrid, Spain, in accordance with
their powers of attorney given at Madrid on July 5 of this present
year before Geronimo Muuos, a notary there, on the other side,
and declared that they had reached a mutual agreement and
promise, which they, the parties in presence, do hereby agree and
promise as follows.

The aforesaid administrators will without delay fit out one, two,
or more ships, as they shall decide, and must have them ready in the
Texel[9] one month after the signing of these presents, provided with
cargoes, all necessary stores, and orders which shall be required for
the voyage to be undertaken, so that they can sail with the first
good wind.

Secondly, eight months after the sailing of the said ships, the
above-named administrators shall deliver to the above-named Alexandro Bosco in his aforesaid quality or upon his orders, at the island
of Curaçao, 1,000 Negroes, under the conditions stipulated hereafter, but with the proviso that if the administrators are unable to
purchase 1,000 Negroes and therefore bring a smaller number to
Curaçao, but at least 700, that this number shall suffice, and likewise that they may deliver as many as 1,400 slaves to the aforesaid
Alexandro Bosco if they possess them, and these may not be sold
by the aforesaid administrators to others; with the further proviso,
however, that if the aforesaid administrators deliver to the above-
named Bosco 1,000 slaves of the stated quality, they may keep 100
of any remainder for their own use to be sent to their colonies in
New Netherlands, Cayenne, etc.

On the other hand, the above-named Alexandro Bosco, *qualitate
qua*, must be ready upon the expiration of the aforesaid eight
months, and while the conditions relating to the ninth month
remain in full force, to receive and to disembark upon the said
island not only the aforesaid 1,000 Negroes but also such number

9. The passage between the Zuider Zee and the North Sea just north of
Holland.—*Tr.*

as the aforesaid administrators may bring, to a total of 1,400, at the price established hereinafter, without any exceptions; but if the aforesaid administrators, upon the expiration of the aforesaid eight months, the conditions relating to the ninth month remaining in full force, bring and deliver to Curaçao a total of less than 700 slaves, then the above-named Bosco, *qualitate ut supra*, shall also be obligated to receive the number brought in, but he may subtract from the monies to be paid for the Negroes delivered the sum of 20 pieces of eight for each slave less than the figure of 700.

And in the event that the above-named ships of the administrators are ready in the Texel within one month but weather and wind do not permit their departure, compelling them to wait until the month of December or longer, the respective parties to this contract shall discuss extension of the above established time of eight months, and not less than one month beyond the above-mentioned eight months shall be given to the aforesaid administrators; but if within one month the wind turns fair and permits departure and the ship or ships of the above-mentioned administrators do not sail, then they shall be held to deliver in Curaçao in eight months the slaves contracted for, the conditions relating to the ninth month remaining in full force, and all other conditions also remaining in full force.

In the event that the above-mentioned ships depart at the proper time so that no extension is given and the aforesaid Alexandro Bosco, *qualitate ut supra*, is ready to receive the Negroes contracted for at the expiration of the above-mentioned eight months, and that the aforesaid administrators do not make delivery by that time, then the above-mentioned Alexandro Bosco *in qualitate* as above, shall have to wait for one additional month at his own cost, without the right to make any claim upon the said administrators; but if the administrators are not ready to make delivery after the expiration of the said ninth month, they shall permit the said Alexandro Bosco *in qualitate* above-mentioned, to subtract for each day that he shall have waited after the expiration of the said ninth month the sum of 40 pieces of eight from the purchase price of each slave that he shall receive after that time.

If, on the other hand, the above-mentioned administrators are ready to make delivery of the said slaves in Curaçao on the expiration of the aforesaid eight months and the said Alexandro Bosco *in qualitate* as above is not yet ready to receive them, the aforesaid administrators shall have to wait for one month at their own expense.

But if the aforesaid Alexandro Bosco, *dicta qualitate*, is not yet ready after the expiration of the said ninth month to receive the aforesaid slaves, these shall be maintained there at his costs and risks from the last day of the ninth month, so that he shall have to pay four stivers per day more than the agreed price for each slave and in addition assume the costs of any such slaves who die and make good to the Company the number that it had ready and fit for delivery upon the expiration of the ninth month.

All the aforesaid slaves shall be aged from 15 to 36 years, in good health, not blind or crippled, but able to board ship without help, and each shall be calculated as one piece fit for delivery; but all who are older than 36 and less than 45 years of age, or less than 15 years and more than 8 years, shall be counted at the rate of 3 to 2; those between 8 and 4 years, 2 for 1; and those below 4 years of age shall follow the mother; provided, however, that the second party to this contract shall not be held to accept Negroes older than 45 years of age except at his own discretion and after agreement on price with the clerk of the aforesaid administrators. With regard to their sex, two-thirds of the slaves must be men and one-third women, but in the event that the discrepancy amounts to ten to twelve percent, then the respective contractors shall make a mutual settlement.

All these slaves being delivered in this condition, the second party to this contract must pay in his aforesaid quality at Curaçao 107 1/2 pieces of eight of full value for each slave fit for delivery who is actually delivered to him there. Furthermore, the aforesaid Alexandro Bosco, *qualitate qua*, shall be obliged to pay a sum of 50,000 guilders (at the rate of 50 stivers to each piece of eight) as security as soon as the said ships to be fitted out in the Texel shall be ready to sail, so that the aforesaid second party may subtract for these 50,000 guilders the sum of 20,000 pieces of eight in Curaçao from the purchase price of the slaves who will be delivered in Curaçao.

If any ships of the aforesaid administrators should happen to meet any accident on their voyage to the Guinea coast or from there to Curaçao (which God forbid), or be taken by enemies or pirates, then a third shall be subtracted from the figure of 700 slaves if one ships fails to arrive and two-thirds if two ships out of three; and if all the slaves to be delivered are carried in two ships, then, if one ship fails to appear, the aforesaid administrators may complete their contract with half of the said 700, without any penalty for delivery of a lesser number or longer wait as stated above. But if (God forbid) all the ships should fail to arrive, or the ships of the party of the second part meet the same difficulties, both parties to this contract shall be released from the performance thereof for this period but shall also be held to repeat the voyage upon the same conditions as before.

The aforesaid Alexandro Bosco shall in the aforesaid quality name and maintain in Curaçao a clerk to correspond with the director [of the West India Company] there and to receive the aforesaid slaves, and the director of that place shall provide him with every help and assistance without payment, and furnish him with wagons or ships to go any place he wishes to, provided that they reach agreement beforehand.

Finally, the aforesaid administrators shall fit out other ships six months after the departure of the first ships mentioned above, to deliver a number of slaves as above to Curaçao, except that the aforesaid administrators agree to deliver half of the aforesaid 700 slaves five months after the delivery of the first number, and the other half three months later; and the party of the second part agrees in the aforesaid quality to take off the aforesaid first and second halves at the proper time and to accommodate the said administrators if they arrive there at different times with 200, 300, or more slaves, leaving the said first half and all the other slaves who may be delivered to be subtracted from this last figure of 700 slaves which must be delivered after eight months in conformity with the foregoing by the second expedition upon the conditions and prices as above, all other conditions respecting delays, the delivery of a greater or lesser number and the quality of slaves, the payment of cash, and the like, remaining as stipulated, but with the provision that the parties of both sides are not required to accept a contract for a third voyage after the second, unless they come to a further agreement.

To assure the performance of this contract, the above-mentioned administrators first obligate themselves in their aforesaid character to make available all the property, real and otherwise, of the Company, and especially all the slaves which the aforesaid administrators shall have brought to Curaçao as security for nondelivery at the prices established above, and also as security for the 50,000 guilders to be paid in cash, but not further, do pledge their own persons and property real and personal, present and future; and the said Alexandro Bosco in the said quality, places at the disposal of all courts the said sum of 50,000 guilders in particular and in addition the persons and property, real and personal without exception. Done in good faith in this city of Amsterdam in the presence of Mr. Jeuriaen Baechaet and the Honorable Jeuriaen Baeck, castellan of the Company's lodgings here, as witnesses thereto.

VIII The House of Orange and Dutch Republicanism

The signature of a treaty of peace with Spain at Münster in 1648 was an acknowledgement by the one-time master that the republic of the United Provinces was now, legally as well as in fact, a free and independent state. The Eighty Years War was at an end. The victory was an extraordinary achievement, to which two forces—the province of Holland and the House of Orange—had contributed most. But the treaty was made against the will of Prince William II, who had larger ambitions that required continuation of the war, and tension between the Princes of Orange and the province of Holland became the primary fact of Dutch political life until the republic of the United Provinces ceased to exist a century and a half later. It was a contest for leadership of what continued to be for the rest of the seventeenth century one of the great powers of Europe.

The strength of the States party, or, as it is sometimes called, the republican party, rested primarily upon the merchant and patrician classes of the province of Holland. They needed peace again, as they had at the time of the conclusion of the Twelve Years' Truce in 1609, to recuperate from the tremendous burden of debt accumulated by the Dutch state during the Eighty Years War, by paying off principal and reducing both the absolute amount of interest as well as its rate; and to trade in peace, safely and profitably, bringing in the revenues by which the Dutch people lived. The Holland "regents" (the Dutch name for members of ruling bodies in the towns) were not alone in this policy, however. They gained support in the other provinces from a smallish group of principled and dedicated republicans, titled noblemen as well as men of business, but also from other groups that needed Holland's favor. These included landowning noblemen who could not live off the fairly meager income from their estates in the poorer inland provinces but needed remunerative posts in the army, more than half of which were on Holland's payroll, or one of the sides vying for dominance of the provincial States assemblies.

The House of Orange, on the other hand, had a variety of forces behind it, none quite equal under ordinary circumstances to the wealthy merchants of the principal province but still, taken together, a force that could not be disregarded. There was the common people, at least its intensely Calvinist portion (for Catholics, other Protestants, and Jews generally looked for security to the more tolerant States party), led by its preachers and moved by a simple love of the House of Orange, to whom it gave all credit for the defeat of Spain; the army and navy, which saw in the princes their traditional commanders-in-chief and in war their opportunity for profit and glory; and the lesser provinces, jealous of Holland which was so rich, strong, and arrogant in its preponderance within the Union. The struggle between the Orangists and the States party was complicated by the dynastic connection established between the House of Orange and the English royal family by the marriage of Frederick Henry's son, the later William II, to Princess Mary Stuart in 1641. For England, for a quarter century after the conclusion of the Münster peace in 1648, was to be the principal rival of the Dutch in trade, in competition for colonies, and for maritime supremacy; and, after the countries were driven into alliance against Louis XIV, it was England which snatched trading and naval domination from the United Provinces. Yet the House of Orange was led by its royal connection not only to swell its own ambitions within the Dutch republic, but also to put Dutch power at the service of English interests.

Under these conditions, the ideological stances adopted by both parties were off balance, for their theory seldom corresponded neatly with their practice. The States party is usually considered to be the advocate of republicanism, but the target of its anti-monarchism (the essential trait of traditional republicanism) was directed against a prince of Orange who was in law a servant of the republic which he led. Republican doctrine did not deny absolutism, but attributed absolute power to the provincial States assemblies and opposed either the continuation of the position of stadholder or, when it could not be suppressed, permitting the stadholder to be captain-general at the same time. Orangist doctrine did not flaunt monarchist principles and seek a royal crown for the stadholder (at least in the Netherlands); but it vaunted the superiority of the single authority of an "eminent head," which was after all part of the general argument in favor of the superiority of monarchy as a form of government. Such discrepancy between political institutions and practice, on the one hand, and theories on the other, gave to Dutch political life some of its individuality, which often puzzled foreign observers.

36. The Peace of Münster: Capstone of Independence

The treaty concluded at Münster on January 30, 1648, was a triumphant conclusion of the Eighty Years War but it came about, like the Twelve Years Truce four decades earlier, only after a struggle within the Dutch Republic. To its advocates it was peace with victory, to its opponents a cowardly and selfish betrayal. The Hollanders, in the years of the negotiation at Münster (1646–1648), thought it obvious that once the Spaniards were willing to grant the United Provinces legal recognition of their independence and sovereignty, even abandoning efforts to obtain safeguards in the peace treaty for Dutch Catholics, there was nothing left to fight for. But this was not how their adversaries, grouped around the House of Orange, saw it. The stadholders—Frederick Henry until his death in 1647, and then his son, William II—saw their influence diminishing with peace, and they retained some lingering bits of William the Silent's dream of a truly united Netherlands, not just the rump republic of the North but both parts of the divided country reunited (although, if need be, with cessions of territory to an allied France). The Calvinist dominees could not forget that Spain was the historic enemy, the defender of the interests of the "Papists" within the republic who did not cease their "audacities," that is, the exercise of their religion. Zeeland had its principal interests in the West India Company, which wanted to carry on its depredations and its smuggling in Spanish and Portuguese territories under the legitimizing cloak of war. The influential nobility in the landward provinces looked to war as the state of affairs which gave them posts in the army. But Frederick Henry was too weak of body and spirit in his last years, and his son too new in power upon his accession to the stadholdership and captaincy-general in 1647, to hold off the stubborn insistence of Holland. After the treaty was signed in Münster, Holland compelled the States General to conclude in favor of ratification on April 4 by a thin majority, although such measures ordinarily required unanimity. After the peace was proclaimed publicly on June 5, the last recalcitrant province, Zeeland, had to accept what had been done. Peace had come, but it was a peace with much bitterness at home—a sign of peril to those who remembered what had followed the disputed conclusion of the Twelve Years Truce. But among the states of Europe, the treaty, whose principal clauses are given below, was proof that the United Provinces had become one of the great powers, a small but mighty state.

Source: C. Smit, *Het Vredesverdrag van Münster, 30 Januari 1648* (Leiden: E. J. Brill, 1949), pp. 30–60. Translated from the Dutch by Herbert H. Rowen.

TREATY OF PEACE,

concluded on January 30th of this present year 1648 in the city of Münster in Westphalia, between his Most Serene and Mighty Prince, PHILIP, fourth of the name, King of Spain, etc., on the one side, and the High, Mighty Lords States General of the United Netherlands, on the other.

In the name of God and in His honor. Let all persons know that, after a long succession of bloody wars which for many years have oppressed the peoples, subjects, kingdoms and lands which are under the obedience of the Lords, King of Spain, and States General of the United Netherlands, the aforesaid Lords, the king and the States, moved by Christian pity, desire to end the general misery and prevent the dreadful consequences, calamity, harm, and danger which the further continuation of the aforesaid wars in the Low Countries would bring in their train, even spreading to other cities and regions and remote lands and seas, and to put in the place of such baleful effects on both sides a pleasing, good, and sincere peace, with the fruit of complete and firm peace for the solace of the aforesaid peoples and provinces under their obedience, and for the repair of the harm which has been suffered, with the aim of the general welfare not only of the Low Countries but also of the whole of Christendom. They invite and call upon other princes and potentates to allow themselves to be moved by the same pity and to avert the mishaps, destruction, and disorders which the heavy plague of war has made men suffer for so long and so heavily. In order to achieve this good and much desired purpose, the aforesaid Lords *Don Philip the Fourth*, king of Spain, and the *States General* of the United Netherlands, have appointed and delegated the following persons: The aforesaid Lord King, Don *Gaspar de Braccamonte y Guzman, Count of Peñeranda, Lord* of *Alea Seca de la Frontera*, Knight of the Order *Alcantara*, permanent administrator of the commandery of *El Daymiel* of the Order of *Calatrava*, nobleman of the chamber of his Majesty in his councils and chambers, extraordinary ambassador to his Imperial Majesty, the first plenipotentiary to the general peace negotiation; my Lord *Antony Brun*, knight, councilor of his Catholic Majesty in his councils of state and of the Superior Council for the affairs of the Low Countries and Burgundy, in attendance upon his person, and his plenipotentiary for the treaties of general peace. And the aforesaid Lords States General of the United Netherlands, my Lords *Bartolt van Gent*, Lord of *Loenen* and *Meynerswyck*, etc., bailiff and dikegrave of *Bommel, Tielreweerden,* and *Bommel- weerden*, deputy to the Assembly of the Lords States General from the Order of Knighthood and nobles of the province of Gelder- land; my Lord *Johan van Matenesse*, Lord of *Matenesse, Riviere, Opmeer, Zouteveen*, etc., delegated councilor and deputy to the Assembly of the Lords States General from the Order of the Knighthood and nobility of Holland and West Friesland, superior councilor in the Polder Board of Schieland; my Lord *Adriaan Pauw*, knight, Lord of *Heemstede, Hogersmilde*, etc., first presi- dent of the Council of Accounts of the county of Holland and West Friesland, and deputy of the province to the Assembly of the Lords States General; my Lord *Johan de Knuyt*, knight, Lord of *Old* and *New Vosmar*, first member and representative of the nobility in the States and the council of the county of Zeeland and in its admiralty, first councilor of *his Highness the Lord Prince of Orange*, ordinary deputy to the Assembly of the Lords States General; my Lord *Godart van Reede*, Lord of *Nederhorst, Vrede- land, Cortehoef, Overmeer, Horstwaart*, etc., president of the Lords, the nobility, and knighthood of the land of Utrecht, and a deputy in their name to the Assembly of the Lords States General; my Lord *François van Donia*, Lord of *Hinnema in Hielsum*, etc., deputy to the Assembly of the Lords States General for the province of Friesland; my Lord *Willem Ripperda*, Lord of *Hengelo, Boxbergen, Boculoo,* and *Russenborg*, etc., deputy to the Assembly of the Lords States General from the knighthood and nobility of the province of Overijssel; my Lord *Adriaan Clant tot Stedum*, Lord of *Nittersum*, etc., ordinary deputy to the Assembly of the Lords States General for the province of Groningen and surrounding lands [*Ommelanden*]; all extraordinary ambassadors in Germany and plenipotentiaries of the aforementioned Lords States General to the general peace negotiation; all provided with a complete procuration, appended at the end of this document; Who, assembled in the city of Münster in Westphalia, accepted by general consent for negotiation of general peace in Christendom, have, by virtue of their aforesaid procurations, made, concluded, and accorded the following Articles for and in the name of the aforesaid Lords King and States.

I.

Firstly, the aforesaid Lord King declares and recognizes that the aforesaid Lords States General of the United Netherlands and the respective provinces thereof, with all their associated districts, cities, and dependent lands, are free and sovereign states, provinces, and lands, upon which, together with their associated districts, cities, and lands aforesaid, he, the Lord King, does not now make any claim, and he himself and his successors descendants will in the future never make any claim; and therefore is satisfied to negotiate with these Lords States, as he does by these presents, *a perpetual peace*, on the conditions hereinafter described and confirmed.

II.

To wit, that the aforesaid peace shall be good, firm, faithful, and unbreakable, and that there shall be therefore cessation of all acts of hostility of any character whatever between the aforesaid Lord King and the States General, upon the sea and other waters, as upon the land, in all their respective kingdoms, districts, lands, and lordships, and for all their subjects and residents, of all ranks and conditions, without exception of places or persons.

III.

Each shall keep and make actual use of the districts, cities, places, lands, and lordships which he at present holds and possesses, without being troubled or molested in them, directly or indirectly, in any manner whatever; it is understood these include the market-places, villages, hamlets, and countrysides which are their dependencies: And therefore the entire bailiwick of 's-Hertogenbosch, together with all the lordships, cities, castles, marketplaces, villages, hamlets, and countryside depending upon the said city and baili-wick of 's-Hertogenbosch, the city and marquisate of Bergen-op-Zoom, the city and barony of Breda, the city of Maastricht and its jurisdiction, as well as the county of Vroenhoef, the city of Grave and the land of Kuyk, Hulst and the bailiwick of Hulst and Hulster-Ambacht, as well as Axele-Ambacht, located to the south and north of the Geule, together with the forts which the aforementioned Lords States have at present in the land of Waas, and all other cities and places which the said Lords States hold in Brabant, Flanders, and elsewhere, shall remain under the aforesaid Lords States with all and like rights and parts of sovereignty and supremacy without exception, in the same way as they hold the provinces of the United Netherlands; it being clearly understood that all the remainder of the land of Waas, with the exception of the aforesaid forts, shall remain to the King of Spain. As for the three quarters beyond the Maas, to wit, Valkenburg, Daalhem, and 's-Hertogenrade, these shall continue in the same state in which they now find themselves: And in the event of dispute and controversy, these shall be referred to the *Chambre mi-partie* [Bipartite Chamber], of which there will be mention later, for its decision.

IV.

The subjects and residents of the lands of the aforesaid Lords King and States shall maintain all good understanding and friendship with each other, without consideration of the offenses and hurt which they have suffered before this. They shall also be permitted to enter and remain in each other's lands and there conduct their business and trade in full security, on the sea, in other waters, as well as on land.

V.

Shipping and trade to the East and West Indies shall be maintained in conformity with the charters already granted or to be granted, the security of which shall be given: And this aforenamed treaty shall include all potentates, nations, and peoples with whom the aforenamed Lords States are allied, or which are allies and friends of the East and West India Companies within the regions of their charters. And the abovementioned Lords King and States shall continue to possess and enjoy those lordships, cities, castles, fortresses, trades, and lands in the East and West Indies, and in Brazil, as well upon the coasts of Asia, Africa, and America respectively, as each respectively now have and possess, with special inclusion of the places seized from the Lords States and occupied by the Portuguese since the year 1641, or the places which they shall hereafter come to obtain and possess without violation of this present treaty. And the administrators of the East and West India Companies of the United Provinces, as well as the ministers, officers of high and low rank, soldiers and sailors in the present service, or one or the other of the aforesaid two companies, or formerly in such service, as well as those who shall continue in or hereafter come into their respective services upon the European mainland as well as in the district of the aforementioned companies, shall be as free and unmolested in all the lands under the obedience of the King of Spain in Europe, and shall be permitted to travel, trade, and journey in the same way as all other inhabitants of the lands of the aforenamed Lords States. It is further promised and stipulated that the Spaniards shall continue their navigation to the East Indies in its present form, without permission to extend it further; just as the inhabitants of the United Netherlands shall refrain from visiting the Castilian places in the East Indies.

VI.

And for what concerns the West Indies, the subjects and inhabitants of the kingdoms, provinces, and Lands of the aforesaid Lords King and States respectively, shall refrain from journeying to and trading in all harbors and places held and possessed by either party with fortresses, residences, castles, or otherwise; to wit, the subjects of the aforesaid Lord King shall not journey to and trade in the harbors and places which are held by the aforesaid Lords States, nor the subjects of the aforesaid Lords States in those which are held by the aforementioned Lord King; and among the places which are included in the possession of the aforesaid Lords States shall be the places which the Portuguese have taken from the aforenamed Lords States in Brazil since the year 1641, as well as all other places which they possess so long as these are under the Portuguese; but the preceding article shall not derogate from the content of this present article.

VII.

And since a considerable length of time is necessary to inform those who are beyond the aforesaid limits with forces and ships that they shall desist from all acts of hostility, it is granted that the peace conferred upon the East India Company of the United Netherlands within the limits of its charter already granted or hereafter continued, shall not begin before one year after the date of the conclusion of the present peace, and as concerns the limits of the charter heretofore granted by the Lords States General, or accorded in continuation, to the West India Company, that the peace in that region shall not begin before one half year after said date; it being clearly understood that if the news of the aforesaid peace shall reach the aforesaid respective regions within these Limits by public announcement at an earlier date, the hostilities shall cease at that time; but if there are any acts of hostility within the aforesaid Limits of the aforesaid Charters after the prescribed time of one year and one-half year respectively, then the damage shall be made good without delay.

VIII.

The Subjects and Inhabitants of the Lands of the aforenamed Lords King and States, trading in each other's Lands, shall not be required to pay more duties and imposts than the other side's own Subjects, so that the Inhabitants and Subjects of the united Provinces shall continue to remain exempted from a certain tax of twenty per cent, or similar tax of lesser or greater amount, or any other Imposition which the King of Spain raised during the Twelve Years' Truce, or shall desire to place directly or indirectly upon the aforenamed Inhabitants and Subjects of the united Provinces, or at their expense, above or in larger amount than upon his own Subjects.

IX.

The aforenamed Lords King and States shall not be allowed to collect any taxation upon entry or exit, or otherwise, upon goods passing by water or land outside their respective Limits.

X.

The Subjects of the aforenamed Lords King and States shall mutually enjoy in each other's Lands the former freedom from tolls which they peacefully possessed before the beginning of the war.

XI.

Visits, travel and commerce among the respective Subjects shall not be interfered with, and if any such interference occurs, it shall be removed in fact and deed.

XII.

From the day of the conclusion and ratification of this peace, the King shall cease to collect all tolls upon the Rhine and Maas which before the war were under the jurisdiction of and in the Territory of the united Netherlands, notably the Zeeland Toll, so that this toll shall not be collected by his aforesaid Majesty, either within the City of Antwerp or elsewhere: It being well understood that from the aforesaid day the States of Zeeland shall mutually accept as its responsibility and pay the annual interest upon bonds for which the aforesaid Toll was pledged before the year 1572, but only from the aforesaid day, which bonds were in the possession of their owners and receivers of interest before the beginning of the said war. This shall also be done for the owners of the other aforesaid Tolls.

XIII.

Refined white salt coming from the united Provinces into the lands of his aforenamed Majesty shall be received and admitted without paying a higher tax than crude salt. At the same time, salt coming from the lands of his aforenamed Majesty into the united Provinces shall be admitted and consumed without having to pay any higher tax than the salt of the aforenamed Lords States.

XIV.

The River Scheldt, together with the canals of Sas, Zwyn, and other connecting channels, shall be kept closed on the side of the Lords States.

XV.

Ships and goods entering and leaving the harbors of Flanders shall be required by the aforenamed Lord King to pay and to continue to pay all such imposts and other charges as are placed upon the goods moving upon the Scheldt and other canals included in the prior article upon entry and exit; and a mutual agreement shall be made hereafter among the parties upon the footing of the aforesaid equal charges.

[Article XVI provides equal treatment of Dutch and Hanseatic merchants and sailors. Article XVII accords Dutch subjects equal treatment with subjects of the King of Great Britain. Article XVIII provides that the King of Spain shall make arrangements for burial of Dutchmen dying in his territories, i.e., that their corpses shall not be thrown upon dungheaps because burial in Catholic cemeteries was forbidden.]

XIX.

The subjects and inhabitants of the lands of the aforementioned Lord King entering the lands of the aforenamed Lords States shall be required to conduct themselves in the matter of public exercise of religion with all piety, giving no scandal by word or deed and speaking no slander. And the same shall be observed by the subjects and inhabitants of the lands of the aforenamed Lords States entering the lands of his Majesty.

[Subsequent articles provide for various legal relations, rights, and procedures between the subjects of the two states, with special provision for the interests of the Prince of Orange in properties in the Spanish Netherlands (Articles XLIV–XLV, XLIX).]

LIII.

The aforesaid Lord King obligates himself to labor effectively for the continuation and observance of neutrality, friendship, and good-neighborly relations on the part of his Imperial Majesty and the Empire with the aforesaid Lords States; and the aforesaid Lords States similarly obligate themselves reciprocally to do the same, and this shall be followed by his Imperial Majesty's confirmation within a period of two months and by that of the Empire within a year after the conclusion and ratification of the present treaty.

LVIII.

No new fortresses may be constructed in the Netherlands on either side, nor new canals dug which may interfere with or cause damage to the other side.

LXIII.

All prisoners of war shall be released by both sides without payment of any ransom and without distinction or reservation concerning prisoners who served outside the Netherlands and under other standards and flags than those of the Lords States.

LXXV.

And to the end that the present treaty be better maintained, the aforesaid Lords King and States promise mutually to assist each other and employ their might and means within their own territories to keep passage free and the seas and rivers navigable and safe against the incursions of mutineers, sea pirates, corsairs, and marauders, and if they catch them, to punish them rigorously.

[After the signatures of the plenipotentiaries of both sides, the treaty includes a special article on trade and shipping between the two countries, as affected by the continuing war between Spain and France.]

37. The Saucy Servant a New Master?

When peace was made in 1648, William II publicly seemed to bow to the accomplished fact, although he denounced its makers as "scoundrels"; but secretly he intrigued with France to resume the war with Spain at the same time as another war would be begun against Cromwellian England, where his father-in-law, King Charles I, had just been put to death. The Prince's conflict with Holland was sharpened when the province, which sought to stay on terms of peace with the new rulers in England, insisted on a reduction of the Dutch army. The Prince and the province each held fast at first, then gradually edged toward a compromise—but in the end neither would take the last step of concession to the other. In the Spring of 1650 William obtained from the States General a decision to send him with a delegation to the towns of Holland to urge them to change their vote in their provincial assembly. The Hollanders denounced the delegation as an unprece- dented, unconstitutional measure, for an appeal of the States General directly to the towns over the head of the States of Holland was a violation of the province's sovereignty. William and his fellow- delegates were met coldly in most of the towns and in a few, notably Amsterdam, he was even refused entry except if he came in as stadholder. Unable to change the minds of the Hollanders, and angry at their intolerable insults, William decided upon a coup d'état, by which he would break the province's resistance and clear the way for his political purposes.

On July 30, six deputies of the States of Holland, representing the towns where he had been rebuffed, were arrested by surprise in the government buildings at The Hague; at the same time, a military assault designed to capture the great city was launched against Amster- dam. The arrested deputies were sent to Loevestein castle, where Grotius had once been held prisoner; but the attack on Amsterdam failed because the troops strayed in fog en route, a passing post courier warned the burgomaster, and measures of defense, including prepara- tions for flooding the besiegers, were taken hastily. William settled for a compromise: the faction in Amsterdam's government which had opposed him was replaced by new magistrates, and the prisoners at Loevestein were released after some weeks when they agreed to resign their offices and quit political activity. The Prince had removed some obstacles to his power, but at the same time he had frightened not only the regents of Holland's town but also many of the deputies to the States General, who also feared a military takeover of the government. Before the Prince acted on any of his plans, however, he fell victim to smallpox early in November.

The following selections from newsletters sent by an English repub- lican spy in the entourage of the exiled King Charles II to the govern- ment at Whitehall not only give a picture of the events of 1650, but also reveal the concern of the English revolutionaries lest William II use his magnified power in an effort to restore the Stuarts, and their readiness to strike against Dutch trade and fishing to dissuade the Dutch from allowing him to go with such a policy. The reports were published at the time as part of a series called "brief relations," and were republished in this century by the distinguished historian, Pieter Geyl.

Source: P. Geyl, "Een Engelsch Republikein over Willem II's Staatsgreep in 1650," *Bijdragen en Medeeelingen van het Histor- isch Genootschap*, XLV (1924), pp. 78–81.

Leyden, 4 August, 1650. Stilo novo.

Sir,

This week hath happened in these parts a very strange attempt of the Prince of Orange, which in all probability will produce a very great revolution and catastrophe of affairs in these countreys; if the Provinces be not blinded, but that they take the advantages that God hath hereby put into their hands, for the recovery of their true Liberty, of which for a long time they have enjoyed onely a shadow, and have pleased themselves with an empty name, which they may now make real, if they please, and cast off the yoke of their servant. He hath handsomly trodden in his Father in Law's steps, and it is not hard to see his end is beginning. I will onely give you what has passed here at the Hague, and for that at Amsterdam, leave you to the Relations that I doubt not you will have thence from many hands.

Here the business passed in this maner: Upon Saterday the 30 of July, new stile, at six of the clock, in the morning, the company of the Guard of the Prince of Orange were commanded by beat of drum to take Arms and march into the fields about Scheveling,[1] where three Butts were set up, as if they should there shoot for a wager: This only served to put off suspition. About nine of the clock six Lords and Members of the States of Holland, were severally sent for by Messengers, to come to the court to speak with the Prince, not one of them knowing of the other; being come, they were arrested by the Lieutenant of his Guards, and conducted each to a several [separate] chamber; all which was done very privately, and was so kept till eleven of the clock. When the Guard came back—having not been in exercise—and was placed in the yard of the court, they disbanded not as is usual at other times, but remained in three Squadrons at the three Gates: About twelve of the clock came two other companies from Delph [Delft], two from Rotterdam, and one from Schedam [Schiedam]. The other States of Holland being in the mean time assembled, expecting each one of his colleague(!), and thought they had been with the Prince onely about some business as they had been informed. By this time the fact was discovered, and a very great concourse of people in the streets and all places about the court. But by reason of those five companies placed round about, that

1. Scheveningen, the fishing village west of The Hague.—*Ed.*

none could stir, though there was much murmuring and discontent appeared. The night following a Troop of 100 Horse came into the Park here at the Hague, by whom, and by fifty Muskettiers of the Guard, those six seized Members were conveyed, being carried in two coaches of the Prince of Orange, to the castle of Lovenstein, which stands at the confluence of the Maes and the Wahl neer to Gorcum. This being done, the Prince certified the States General of it, who did nothing thereupon, but the Courts of Justice were otherwise affected with it: It is said they went to the Prince, and remonstrated the foulness and danger of the fact, and commanding their release, as I was told by some that know it.

But that afternoon the Prince went towards Amsterdam with a great train of Courtiers, whither he had before sent Grave [Count] William of Nassaw, Governor of Friezland with eight or nine thousand Horse and Foot, and all was done with such speed and secrecy, that he had without question surprized the Town, had not the Providence of God, by sending a great Rain and Darkness, so retarded the Soldier's march, that they could not get thither so soon as they had appointed, which was to have been just at the opening of the Gates; which if they had done, that rich Town had been spoiled, and an infinite Treasure had come into his hands; whereby he would have repaired his own sinking state, setled his Tyranny over these people, and made them to bear that yoke which they have so tamely received from the hands of his Father and himself, although his Uncle laid the foundation of it in the blood of Barnevelt, that faithful Advocate of Holland, who out of his great wisdom, foresaw to what the Orange Tree would grow, and endeavored then to apply that Remedy which they were glad at last to use, though he was not able to bring it about, but must die as a Traytor, and the mercenary Priests proclaim him for an Heretique; his worst opinion being, that these people ought still to be free, and his worst action was, that he endeavored it: Besides, our Nation may see how the Providence of God hath watched over us in this disappointment of him, who is a most inveterate and irreconcileable enemy of our Nation; for had he obtained the money of the Bank at Amsterdam, he would have given great supplies to the King of Scotland[2] against us.

But I hope these people will see how neer they were to the brink

---

2. Charles II, who had been proclaimed king in Scotland.—*Ed.*

of danger, and put him into an incapacity of doing the like again: And indeed I perceive there is a general discontent amongst them, and it will never be made up again. He will now either make an absolute conquest of them, or they must otherwise dispose of him: The thing is yet but new, I cannot give more particulars about it; what was done at Amsterdam, you will hear thence; this is that I could learn at the Hague, whether several of us went for curiosity sake, to learn what we could of so strange an attempt. By my next you shall have more, it is Post time, and I cannot enlarge.

38. Holland's Vindication against Orange

The unexpected death of William II in November, 1650, opened the way for the Holland regents displaced from power and all the others made fearful by his summertime stroke of state, to take in their hands the complete control of government in the Dutch republic. The "Loevestein Six," as the arrested deputies were called, were now returned to office, for the promise of self-exile from politics which William had exacted for their release had lost its point. The States of Holland took the initiative in persuading the other provinces (except Friesland and Groningen, where Count William Frederick of Nassau became stadholder) not to name the infant William III to the late Prince of Orange's offices. But the tension with the English Commonwealth worsened all the same. Cromwell continued to demand measures against the Royalist exiles in the United Provinces and their Orangist supporters. He even proposed a union of the two states which would make the United Provinces a protectorate of the English Commonwealth, but it was rejected out of hand. Cromwell therefore approved economic assaults upon Dutch interests, embodied particularly in the Act of Navigation of 1651, which led in 1652 to war. This first Anglo-Dutch war was a disaster for the Dutch; not only were they at a strategic disadvantage, but the Dutch navy was in neglect while the English fleet was new and composed primarily of full-time warships, unlike their opponents' ships, mainly converted merchantmen. The Dutch thereupon sought peace in 1653, but the negotiations finally stuck on the issue of the House of Orange. Cromwell insisted that the States General forever bar the Princes from the stadholdership and captaincy-general because of their marriage connection with the Stuart dynasty; when it proved impossible to obtain this exclusion from the States General, the Lord Protector was persuaded to accept a similar but secret promise from the States of Holland alone, the famed "Act of Seclusion" of May 4, 1654, and to conclude peace. Word of existence of the "Seclusion" soon leaked out, and it was denounced as private diplomacy of the province of Holland, in unconstitutional violation of the rights of the States General. Amid the furious debate which ensued, the States of Holland instructed their executive secretary, the young Councilor Pensionary John de Witt (son of one of the "Loevestein Six") to prepare a defense of its right to adopt the "Seclusion" resolution. This was adopted on July 25 and published as the *Demonstration* ("Deductie"). It was an affirmation of the provincial sovereignty of Holland and a defense of the exclusion of the Prince of Orange as legal and necessary to end a disastrous war. Key passages are translated here from the *Demonstration*, which became one of the central statements of Dutch republican doctrine.

Source: Deductie, ofte Declaratie van de Staten van Holland Ende West-Vrieslandt . . . Ingestelt ende dienende tot Justificatie van't verlenen van seeckere Acte van Seclusie . . . Na da copije (The Hague: De Weduwe, ende Erfgenamen van wylen Hillebrandt Jacobsz van Wouw, 1654), pp. 1–2, 14–15, 47–50, 55, 71–72. Translated from the Dutch by Herbert H. Rowen.

THE STATES of Holland and West Friesland have sorrowfully and not without considerable heartache observed and meditated upon the fact that Their Noble Great Mightinesses,[3] ever since Almighty God in his fathomless mercy was pleased to open the way to the first establishment of the free government of this country (whose foundations were laid down only by the aforesaid Province of Holland and West Friesland with the help of the province of Zeeland, besides the miraculous guidance and gracious direction of his Divine Majesty), have always demonstrated without trouble, their true-hearted and steadfast concern for the preservation of the state of these United Provinces and for the unblemished conservation of its dearly-bought liberty, with so many proofs above all the other allies,[4] and especially during the recent difficulties caused by the bloody war with the Republic of England as well as during the subsequent negotiations for peace, together with the occurrences that took place in connection with it. But these States of Holland and West Friesland have experienced the frequent and only too common misfortune to see their sincere intentions and most praiseworthy actions, even those without which the noble edifice of this free state in all human probability would have been long since overthrown, taken amiss and made the object of much misinterpretation, especially by some of their allies, and now again suffer the misfortune that some of these same allies are pleased to pass

3. The States of Holland.—*Ed.*
4. Other provinces.—*Ed.*

unfavorable judgment upon Their Noble Great Mightinesses because, at the behoof of the Lord Protector of the Republic of England, Scotland, and Ireland, they passed a certain obligatory law, declaring that Their Noble Great Mightinesses would never elect the Prince of Orange or anyone of his line as stadholder or admiral of this province, or allow, so far as its vote was concerned, that they would ever be elected to the captaincy-general over the army of the States General. Indeed, things went so far that this aforementioned unfavorable judgment of these allies was made public by the States General of these United Netherlands.

Therefore the abovementioned States of Holland and West Friesland, being unable to conceive that this unfavorable judgment of some of their allies can have any other cause than that they, or some of their members, are not fully informed of the true situation and grounds of the aforesaid affair and the events connected with it, and of its essential circumstances, and that everyone who reads a detailed and well-reasoned account of what happened will beyond doubt consider it to be one of the usual results of Their Noble Great Mightinesses' good measures of precaution on behalf of the welfare of the common state. . . .

[Statement of the objections to the Act of Seclusion.]

In order to present a solid refutation of arguments or alleged reasons, and to demonstrate first of all that their Noble Great Mightinesses had power and the right to resolve upon and adopt the aforesaid Act of Seclusion without anyone's permission, there must be taken into consideration above all that the firm foundation of the relations among all the provinces is beyond controversy the complete and absolute sovereignty of the respective provinces in their own business as well as the indisputable right and unlimited power to decide, dispose, and decree by themselves, or to do or have done whatever they consider necessary or otherwise of service to their province or its inhabitants, in all matters which are not deferred to the Generality by the aforesaid Union [of Utrecht] or the individual consent of the provinces, and that no other province or anyone else in the world has any right to interfere, as this is claimed by the aforementioned writings of the above-mentioned three provinces, and especially in specific terms by the declaration presented on behalf of the States of Zeeland on July 30 last to the assembly of Their High Mightinesses.[5]

5. The States General.—*Ed.*

From this flows the matter which is in debate, that each province individually possesses the absolute and sovereign disposition over the election of stadholders in its province, or, to express it better, over the granting and conferring of such power and authority as was granted heretofore to previous stadholders by the dukes, counts, or lords of these aforesaid provinces, or such greater or lesser authority as the States of that province may decide according to the situation; and more specially to grant or exclude from these offices such persons as the States consider desirable, without being required to hear anyone else's opinions or have prior communication about it with any other provinces, unless some individual agreement made with other provinces applies, of which we shall speak hereafter. This is all applicable to the election or exclusion of governors and captains-general in the individual provinces as well as of admirals for the provinces which they will serve, unless it has been decided to give the disposition of all or some of the said matters to the Generality either by the terms of the said Union or by the individual consent of the provinces.

[Detailed argument in support of right of the province of Holland to negotiate separately with Cromwell and to adopt the Act of Seclusion under the provisions of the Union of Utrecht.]

These two points having been absolutely established as they are understood by Their Noble Great Mightinesses, we may now pass on to the alleged reasons presented by the aforementioned provinces why, even if it had been in the power of the province of Holland to proceed in the matter of the aforementioned exclusion in the way that it did, Their Noble Great Mightinesses nevertheless ought not to have done so.

And first, as concerns the allegation that the passage of this Act is contrary to and a violation of our dearly-bought freedom, Their Noble Great Mightinesses wish to declare first of all that they are as sensitive in this matter as any of the protesting provinces, and that they are intent and determined to protect this freedom both for the state in general and for their province in particular, as the apple of their eyes; and that they were the first and foremost in procuring freedom for themselves and their allies, and will never tolerate that it could be truthfully said that anyone else excels or surpasses them in zeal for its preservation.

It is true and Their Noble Great Mightinesses readily concede that by passing the said Act they have given up the faculty or the freedom (as it can be called) to promote the present Prince of Orange or his descendants, or to give their vote toward his promotion, to the high offices named above; but on the other hand, these provinces must also concede the truth that every war is a limitation upon the exercise of freedom, and that the war just waged against the Republic of England not only took from the government of a single province the faculty and the power to dispose of certain matters according to its own desires and opinions, but also deprived the whole state, each province, and the inhabitants of the country in general and in particular of the faculty and freedom to decide a great many matters of considerable importance, especially concerning shipping and trade which are the soul and the inward subsistence of the state.

If anyone, in order to restore a great number of freedoms, including those concerning his subsistence and the preservation of his own soul, gives up other and lesser freedoms, it cannot be said that he has abandoned his freedom but rather that he has preserved and restored it. Therefore it cannot be said without great error that Their Noble Great Mightiness did anything in this affair which violated our dearly-born freedom.

Indeed, if this argument were to be accepted, then all kinds of promises, obligations, contracts, treaties, and especially all confederations or alliances would have to be disapproved to the highest extent and never entered into; for it is common knowledge that none of these can be made without the reduction and loss of some freedom.

But to reveal more clearly the secret meanings and true aims of these so-called zealots of freedom, and in order to test their ideas on the touchstone of true and unfalsified freedom, Their Noble Great Mightinesses cannot let this occasion pass without a frank declaration that they have indeed taken note that these complaints and the expostulations of some provinces against them are not made in order to preserve the Union and protect freedom, as is falsely given out, but that the whole affair is aimed to putting the Prince of Orange in the high offices which his forefathers held in this country. This has been admitted by one of them in the express statement that the Prince had been deprived by the Act "of the prerogatives to which, as it were, he was born," without any merits of his own, and another province openly declared in his declaration "that the captaincy and admiralty-general should properly be given and granted to the Prince of Orange *de facto*." Their Noble Great Mightinesses cannot understand how these can be the signs of true lovers and zealots of freedom, or how it can be called freedom that anyone is born to the highest offices in a republic. Indeed, would it be a proof of free election to confer the highest offices upon children?

On the contrary, eveyone should realize, according to the judgment of all political writers of sound mind, that such charges cannot be given in a republic to those whose ancestors held these posts without considerable peril to freedom.

[Historical examples of the loss of power in republics to those who held command of their armies for life or even for an extended period of time.]

Therefore these self-proclaimed but confused zealots of freedom should be able to see upon the basis of and in the light of these examples and reasons, and they must admit, that by their arguments they not only contradict all the wise men in the world but also reject the examples of Holy Scripture, and that they should therefore at once abandon this false maxim that in a free republic children can be born to the offices of their fathers in any way.

Coming now to the aforementioned alleged reasons concerning the person of the Prince of Orange and his House, and first to the allegation that the Prince is deprived by this exclusion without regard for his merits from prerogatives to which he is in a sense born, their Noble Great Mightinesses call upon and beseech the aforementioned provinces to take into consideration the principal results and foremost fruits of a true freedom and undefiled liberty, which consists, according to the judgment of their Noble Great Mightinesses confirmed by the unanimous opinion of all political writers, that the highest offices should stand open to virtue, and that more regard should always be taken for piety and the merits of the person himself than for the wealth, family, ranks, or ancestors or other accidents of fortune.

Therefore all healthy republics, at least so long as they somehow maintain a government without corruption, and therefore in particular their Noble Great Mightiness, have always taken into consideration the nobility of houses and illustrious families, but have never given it as much weight as the nobility of the persons themselves who are to be called to the leadership of the Republic. . . .

We come now to the painful reproach that we are ungrateful

toward the House of Orange which is made against their Noble Great Mightinesses by these writings. They can assert with a good conscience that they have so shunned the fault of ingratitude on all occasions that they can maintain in equity and truth that in the display of gratitude they have not only always kept step with the other provinces but can say without boasting that often went far beyond the other provinces.

39. A Vindication of Orange against Holland

Thanks to the peace concluded with England, Holland was able to ride out the storm over the Seclusion Act. John de Witt proved to be a supple and superb leader for Holland and for the republic as a whole, but one who was stubborn in the defense of "republicanism"—that is, the rights of Holland within the Union and of government without a stadholder. There was no effective resistance to this policy until the English republic collapsed in 1660 and King Charles II, who was the uncle of William III, came to the throne. The Dutch sought to make him a friend by a magnificent reception in The Hague before his sailing to England, and Holland in particular repealed the Act of Seclusion and promised to promote the Prince some time in the future. As long as William's mother, Princess Mary, lived, this policy seemed to be working; but on her death in December, 1660, her royal brother assumed the guardianship of his nephew which Mary gave him by testament, and now Holland saw a new peril, domination of the United Provinces by England through the instrument of the Prince of Orange. The compromise of 1660, by which the Prince would become a "Child of State" educated to take over the captaincy-general, broke down, and Holland cast loose from responsibility for his future, refusing to name him captain-general with a lieutenant-general to command the army until he came of age. This meant a direct conflict with the Orangists, who demanded such an office for the Prince as a matter of right and of policy. Their central arguments on his behalf were stated by the States of Zeeland when they came as a body to The Hague in September, 1660, to urge Holland to make the Prince captain-general. The major passages of their statement before the States of Holland on September 10, on behalf of designation of William III as captain-general, are given below.

Source: Lieuwe van Aitzema, *Saken van Staet en Oorlogh*, 6 vols., (The Hague: Johan Veely *et al.*, 1669–1672), Vol. IV, pp. 637–639, 641. Translated from the Dutch by Herbert H. Rowen.

. . . A remarkable transformation took place in the body of this state, especially in the form of its government, as a result of the death of his Highness, Prince William II. Often it even ceased to function because many of the driving forces which made the wheel of government go round readily ceased to operate, which caused a notable change in the ordinary course of affairs.

There were many earnest conferences and discussions between these two provinces both before and during the Great Assembly, in the years 1650 and 1651, but they did not result in any final decision at that time because of discordant opinions and because the nature of the business seemed to permit putting off the affair until a later time, when the situation would be more favorable and it would be possible to examine it more closely and with fewer difficulties; for the two provinces were at that time principally concerned with the determination of other matters concerning the common Union which could not suffer any delay.

But afterwards the misfortune of various perplexing and unfortunate events abroad completely interfered with these efforts and for many years made it not only impossible to resume them, but also very unlikely that they would have been able to succeed.

But now that it has pleased God Almighty in His merciful and incomprehensible providence to dispose the affairs of the world at this time so that these difficulties have completely ceased, and a more favorable situation has arisen, as is well known, for the advantage of all Christendom and especially of these lands, the Lords States of Zeeland have judged it useful and proper to bring the matter up again for consideration. . . .

The Lords States of Zeeland therefore declare as a *first* firm and principal basis for this discussion that the repose and peace of the Low Countries in general and individually can never be maintained without employing heads and lords of eminence in the leadership of the common cause. They assert this not upon the basis of the maxims and teachings of various foreign governments and writers, but upon the judgment and decisions of our own forefathers and of all who throughout the ages have had the best knowledge of the character and constitution of the government of these lands. . . .

It is therefore no wonder that these lands, considered in general and as part of the German nation from ancient times, not just during the past 800 years but for centuries before, have not had any other form of government than one which gave these heads power and authority which was sometimes greater and more absolute and sometimes lesser and more limited. They always considered it necessary to have over them persons of excellent reputation and dignity, restricting and furnishing them with necessary laws and ordinances against all excesses.

The wisest men in the world have always praised this form of government as the safest, fairest, and most honorable. . . .

But we do not wish to be found guilty of imprudence or ingratitude and are bound to maintain steadfastly the form of republican government which has been left us by our forefathers down through the generations, and which has been praised not only by the ancients but also by reason and experience (to which special consideration should be given in matters of government).

However, it is nonetheless a fact that this form of government like others is subject to difficulties; yet it continues to be the most fitting for this state; especially since the advantage of a situation should be judged not by abstract speculation but by seeing what will serve best and what has given best service to the respective nations in all ages.

It is well known to the entire world that since the absence of an eminent head as a result of the death of Prince William II, various defects have arisen in the government which apparently can be remedied only by restoring and re-establishing an eminent head to lead it.

These shortcomings exist in various parts of the government, especially in the questions of military movement orders and the common army, the conduct of secret correspondence, the proposal and supply of quotas for the Union, and other points, as our delegates described them extensively to Your Noble Mightinesses in the year 1652.

Furthermore, whenever in these times disputes or disturbances arise between some of the provinces, the state is deprived of the means of conciliation, which the earlier Princes of Orange as heads of the provinces were able with great success and vigor to employ in overcoming these dissensions.

And because it is usual in all communities and societies to entrust the conduct of affairs to a few, so we can now clearly see that many parts of the functions which were exercised by the aforesaid heads have now fallen into the hands of a few who are not qualified to perform them, or do not have authorization to do so, and hence are not responsible for their conduct of them. . . .

Your Noble Great Mightinesses during conferences on this affair have considered it not improper to say that attention should be paid to the interests attaching to the present Prince of Orange. But these are such at the present time that the state need have no anxieties concerning them.

First, His Highness is connected by blood to the House of Orange and Nassau, to which these provinces, as has already been said, are in debt for their expenditure of life and property and their indomitable courage which so mightly contributed to the victory of these lands and the vindication of their freedom, their rights, and privileges, and the practice of the true Reformed religion.

Second, this state has a special interest in the alliance of the House of Orange with the House of Brandenburg, because of its possessions and places on the frontier of these provinces, as well as in Pomerania and Prussia on the Baltic Sea. Furthermore, the Elector of Brandenburg is not only one of the most powerful and eminent Imperial princes but is also the only one remaining who professes the Reformed religion. In various situations he has not refrained from risking everything, at the instance of and alongisde this state, to repress ruinous and far-reaching designs directed, it appears, principally toward the destruction of the trade of this country, which is its life and soul.

Among the other alliances on the side of the Princess Royal[6] is the crown of France, which has always had many interests in common with this state and which cannot be separated from it without notable difficulty and hurt for both sides.

But most important in this connection is the family tie with His Majesty, the King of Great Britain, and his brothers. For anyone with ordinary and healthy understanding has sufficient knowledge of how much this country needs the friendship and good understanding of that country and nation, as sad experience has brought painfully home to the good inhabitants of this country, as they still well remember. . . .

40. The Grounds of Holland's Welfare

The debate over the proper government for the United Provinces and the province of Holland was carried to a higher level of generalization by Pieter de la Court (1618–1685), the best political thinker of his

6. Princess Mary Stuart, sister of Charles II of Great Britain and widow of Prince William II.—*Ed.*

generation (apart from Baruch Spinoza, who was one of the greatest philosophical minds of all time). De la Court was trained in the law but followed his father in the business of textile manufacture at Leiden. However, like his elder brother John, he was most committed to concern for the political and economic welfare of his country, and advocated such principles as freedom of enterprise within the country, the primacy of Holland's interests, and a vigorous republicanism. In 1662 he published a work called *The Interest of Holland, or Grounds of Holland's Welfare*, under the semi-anonymity of the initials V. D. H. (Van den Hove, the Dutch form of De la Court). John de Witt, the Councilor Pensionary of Holland, read over the manuscript, toned down some of its most forthright passages, and contributed parts of several chapters. The work aroused a furious controversy, which was resumed when it was republished in expanded form in 1669 as *Indication of the Sound Political Grounds and Maxims of the Republic of Holland and West Friesland*. Because some Machiavellian declarations in it denied that it was necessary to adhere to disadvantageous treaties and the like, and it included as well assaults upon the Calvinist preachers, the work was banned by the States of Holland. It was translated into French and English in the early eighteenth century as coming from the pen of De Witt "and other Great Men in Holland"; it is from the excellent English translation that the following selections are taken.

Source: [Pieter de la Court], *The True Interests and Political Maxims of the Republic of Holland and West Friesland . . .* Written by John de Witt and other Great Men in Holland. (London: n.p., 1702), pp. 2, 6–13, 16–18, 45, 58–61, 66–67, 74–79, 242–246.

. . . Seeing the true Interest of all Countrys consists in the joint Welfare of the Governors and Governed; and the same is known to depend on a Good Government, that being the true Foundation whereon all the Prosperity of any Country is built; we are therefore to know, that a good Government is not that where the well or ill-being of the Subjects depends on the Virtues or Vices of the Rulers; but (which is worthy of observation) where the well or ill-being of the Rulers necessarily follows or depends on the well or ill-being of the Subjects. For seeing we must believe that in all Societies or Assemblies of Men, Self is always preferred; so all Sovereigns or Supreme Powers will in the first place seek their own Advantage in all things, tho to the prejudice of the Subject. But seeing on the other hand true Interest cannot be compassed by a Government, unless the generality of the People partake thereof;

thereof the Public Welfare will ever be aimed at by good Rulers. All which very aptly agrees with our *Latin* and *Dutch* Proverb, that, *Tantum de publicis malis sentimus, quantum ad privatas res pertinet, i.e.* We are only sensible of publick Afflictions, in so far as they touch our private Affairs; for nobody halts of another Man's Sore.

. . . Since it appears from the said Maxims, that the Publick is not regarded but for the sake of private Interest; and consequently that is the best Government where the Chief Rulers may best obtain their own Welfare by that of the People: It follows then to be the duty of the Governours of Republicks to seek for great Cities, and to make them as populous and strong as possible, that so all Rulers and Magistrates, and likewise all others that serve the Publick either in Country or City, may thereby gain the more Power, Honour and Benefit, and more safely possess it, whether in Peace or War: And this is the reason why commonly we see that all Republicks thrive and flourish more in Arts, Manufacture, Traffick, Populousness and Strength, than the Dominions and Cities of Monarchs: for where there is Liberty, there will be Riches and People.

To bring all this home, and make it sute with our State, we ought to consider that *Holland* may easily be defended against her Neighbours; and that the flourishing of Manufactures, Fishing, Navigation, and Traffick, whereby that Province subsists, and (its Natural Necessities or Wants being well considered) depends perpetually on them, else would be uninhabited: I say, the flourishing of those things will infallibly produce great, strong, populous and wealthy Cities, which by reason of their convenient Situation, may be impregnably fortified: All which to a Monarch, or one Supreme Head, is altogether intolerable. And therefore I conclude, that the Inhabitants of *Holland*, whether Rulers or Subjects, can receive no greater mischief in their Polity, than to be governed by a Monarch, or Supreme Lord: And that on the other side, God can give no greater temporal Blessing to a Country in our Condition, than to introduce a free Commonwealth Government.

But seeing this Conclusion opposeth the general and long-continued Prejudices of all ignorant Persons, and consequently of most of the Inhabitants of these *United Provinces*, and that some of my Readers might distaste this Treatise upon what I have already said, unless somewhat were spoken to obviate their Mistakes, I shall therefore offer them these Reasons.

Altho by what hath been already said, it appears, That the Inhabitants of a Republick are infinitely more happy than the Subjects of a Land governed by one supreme Head; yet the contrary is always thought in a Country where a Prince is already reigning, or in Republicks, where one Supreme Head is ready to be accepted.

For not only Officers, Courtiers, idle Gentry, and Souldiery, but also all those that would be such, knowing, That under the worst Government they use to fare best, because they hope that with Impunity they may plunder and rifle the Citizens and Country People, and so by the Corruption of the Government enrich themselves, or attain to Grandeur, they cry up Monarchical Government for their private Interest to the very Heavens: Altho God did at first mercifully institute no other but a Commonwealth Government, and afterwards in his Wrath appointed one Sovereign over them. Yet for all this, those Blood-suckers of the State, and indeed of Mankind, dare to speak of Republicks with the utmost Contempt, make a Mountain of every Molehill, discourse of the Defects of them at large, and conceal all that is good in them, because they know none will punish them for what they say: Wherefore all the Rabble (according to the old Latin Verse) being void of Knowledg and Judgment, and therefore enclining to the Weather or safer side, and mightily valuing the vain and empty Pomp of Kings and Princes, say *Amen* to it; especially when kept in Ignorance, and irritated against the lawful Government by Preachers, who aim at Dominion, or would introduce an independent and arbitrary Power of Church-Government; and such (God amend it) are found in *Holland*, and the other United Provinces, insomuch, that all vertuous and intelligent People have bin necessitated to keep silence, and to beware of disclosing the Vices of their Princes, or of such as would willingly be their Governors, or of Courtiers and rude Military Men, and such ambitious and ungovernable Preachers as despise God, and their Native Country.

Nay there are few Inhabitants of a perfect Free State to be found, that are inclinable to instruct and teach others, how much better a Republic is than a Monarchy, or one Supreme Head, because they know no Body will reward them for it; and that on the other side, Kings, Princes, and Great Men, are so dangerous to be conversed with, that even their Friends can scarcely talk with them of the Wind and Weather, but at the hazard of their Lives; and Kings with their long Arms can give heavy blows. And altho all intelligent and ingenuous Subjects of Monarchs, who have not, with lying Sycophantical Courtiers, cast off all Shame, are generally by these Reasons, and daily Experience, fully convinced of the Excellency of a Republic above a Monarchical Government; yet nevertheless, many vertuous Persons, lovers of Monarchy, do plausibly maintain, that several Nations are of that Temper and Disposition, that they cannot be happily governed but by a single Person, and quote for this the Examples of all the People in *Asia* and *Africa*, as well as *Europe*, that lie Southerly. They do also alledg, that all the People who lie more Northerly, are more fit to be governed by a single Person, and with more Freedom; as from *France* to the Northward, all absolute Monarchical Government ceaseth; and therefore maintain or assert, with such ignorant Persons as I mention'd before, that the *Hollanders* in particular are so turbulent, factious, and disingenuous, that they cannot be kept in awe, and happily governed, but by a single Person; and that the Histories of the former Reigns or Government by Earls [Counts], will sufficiently confirm it.

But on the other side, the Patriots, and Lovers of a Free-state will say, That the foregoing Government by Earls is well known to have bin very wretched and horrid, their Reigns filling History with continual Wars, Tumults, and detestable Actions, occasioned by that single Person. And that on the contrary, the Hollanders, subsisting by Manufacture, Fishing, Navigation, and Commerce, are naturally very peaceable, if by such a Supreme Head they were not excited to Tumults. Whether this be so or not, may be learned and confirmed too in part from those Histories.

But here it may be said, That things are much altered within these 100 Years last; for *Holland* then subsisted mostly by Agriculture, and there were then no Souldiery, Treasure, or fortified Places to be at the Earl's disposal. But when he had Wars, it was with the help of his Homagers and Tenants, only Subsidies or Money being given him at his Request by the States of the Country: And moreover, the Cities of *Holland*, and Castles of the Nobility were (according to the then Method of War) so strong, that they could not be taken by the said Earls, without great forces imployed against them; so that the States of *Holland* in their assemblies, have boldly contended for their Rights against the Earls Encroachments. Therefore these Earls, on the other side, by reason of their great Dignity, had many Adherents that depended on them, which must needs make that Government by Earls every way unsteady, weak, and tumultuous.

To this an approver of Monarchical Government may further add, that *Holland* now wholly subsists by Traffic, and that one Supreme Head, Captain-General, or Stadtholder, would have his own Life-Guards at the *Hague*, the Place of Assembly, and likewise the assistance of a great and well-paid Army, and of all the Preachers, and by them the love of the whole Populace; and that at his Pleasure he may dispose of all the impregnable Frontier Towns of those Provinces that have no suffrages or voices in the State, tho he should not increase his Strength by any foreign Alliances, or by Collusion and Flattery with the Deputies of the other Provinces of the Generality, insomuch that the States of *Holland* would not dare, no not in their Assemblies, to open their Mouths against the Interest of such a Supreme Head, or if they did, he would order his Souldiers to take them by the Collar, and might easily overpower most of the Cities of *Holland*, the People being unaccustomed to Arms, and moreover divided, Fortifications but slight and mean in comparison to the present way of Fortifying: So that one may truly say, That the *Hollanders* by setting up one Supreme Head over themselves, may now with Ease, and without Tumult, be govern'd like Sheep, by an irresistible Sovereign, against whom they durst not speak one word, when he should think fit to sheer, flea, or devour them. . . .

By this you may perceive, that the Supposition of the *Hollanders* being flegmatick and dull, and of a slavish Nature, is altogether groundless; for seeing they became not free but by the death of the last Stadholder and Captain-General, and that it was unseasonable and imprudent before that time, for them to shew their commendable Zeal for their Freedom, and their Skill in point of Government: And seeing it is evident, that a General of Men that are in Freedom, must be overcome, before we can pass a right Judgment thereof, and stop the mouths of Opposers; we must therefore leave it to God and Time: and if such as like Monarchical Government, and those base and slavish opposers of Liberty survive those times, they will then be able to discern which of the two Governments is founded on best Reason. . . .

For if inquiry be made into the Polity of all established Governments, we shall always find, that there are ever an incredible number of ignorant and malevolent People, Enemies to all Speculation, and Remedies, how good soever, which they conceive or really foresee will be prejudicial in any wise to themselves; and rather than admit them, they will press hard to imbroil the State more than it was before. Besides, there is an endless number of Political Maxims which have so deep a Root, that it is great folly to think any Man should be able, or indeed that it should be thought fit to root them out all at once: And consequently it would be yet a greater piece of Imprudence, if in *Holland, tanquam in tabula rasa*, as on a smooth, and in a very clean and good piece of Ground, we should go about to sow the best Seeds, in order to make it an Angelical or Philosophical Republick: So true is that good and antient Political Maxim, That in Polity many bad things are indulged with less inconveniency than removed; and that we ought never in Polity (as in playing at Tenis) to set the Ball fair, but must strike it as it lies; it being also true, that on every Occurrence a good Politician is bound to shew his Art, and Love to his Native Country, that by such constancy the Commonwealth may by degrees be brought to a better condition. I do therefore conceive my self oblig'd to consider *Holland* in the State as it now is, and hope that those Thoughts will produce the more and better Fruits, since those that duly consider the present State of it, will find that they agree for the most part with the Climate, Soil, Rivers, Meers [lakes], Situation, and Correspondence which such a Country ought to have with other Dominions, and especially with a free Commonwealth Government, which we have now at present in being: And I hope I shall not digress from it. By the Maxims of *Holland's* Interest, I understand the Conservation, and Increase of the Inhabitants as they now are, consisting of Rulers and Subjects. I shall likewise diligently enquire by what means this Interest may be most conveniently attained. And tho in the first place the Interest of the Rulers ought to be considered, because distinctly and at large it always seems to occasion the Subjects Welfare and Prosperity; and a good form of Government is properly the Foundation whereon all the Prosperity of the Inhabitants is built: I shall nevertheless consider in the first place the Preservation, and Increase of the number of Subjects, not only because it is evident in all Governments, and especially in all Republics, That the Number or Paucity of Subjects is the Cause of an able or weak Government; but also because ambitious Spirits can seldom find a multitude of People living out of civil Society and Government that will subject themselves to them: And on the contrary, where many Inhabitants are, there will never want Rulers, because the weakness and wickedness of Mankind is so great, that they cannot subsist without Government; insomuch that in case of a vacancy of Rulers, every one would stand Candidates for it themselves, or elect others. . . .

It is not enough to know how happy in general this Country is, in finding Imployment for so many Hands, and affording them sustenance, seeing there have been many causes which would have hindred the Success of our Fishing, Navigation and Traffick, had there been but one Country among the many that are near us, well situated for Fishing, Manufactury, Traffick, and Navigation, which during our Wars and Troubles had seen and followed their own true Interest; most of our neighbouring Nations, all that time being in a profound Peace, seemed to have less hinderance for promoting Manufactures, Traffick, employing of Ships for Freight and Fishing, than our Nation. So that to pursue the true Interest and Maxims of *Holland*, we ought particularly to know the Reason, why the great inconveniences of Taxes and Wars that we have laboured under, have not occasioned the Fishing, Manufactury, Traffick, and Navigation, to settle and fix in other Countries; as for example in *England*, where if all be well considered they have had far greater Advantages of Situation, Harbours, a clean and bold Coast, favourable Winds, and an Opportunity of transporting many unwrought Commodities, a lasting Peace, and a greater freedom from Taxes than we have. . . .

In the first place it is certain, that not only those that deal in Manufactures, Fishing, Traffick, Shipping, and those that depend on them, but also all civilized People must be supposed to pitch upon some outward Service of God as the best, and to be averse from all other Forms; and that such Persons do abhor to travel, and much more to go and dwell in a Country, where they are not permitted to serve and worship God outwardly, after such a manner as they think fit. And also that as to Freedom about the outward Service of God, during the Troubles, and shortly after; when the Manufactures, Trading, and Navigation for Freight began to settle in *Holland*, the Magistrate was so tender and indulgent, that there were very few useful Inhabitants driven thence by any rigour or hardship, much less any Foreigners: So that it brings that Maxim into my mind, that the surest way to keep any thing, is to make use of the same Means whereby it was at first acquired.

And among those Means, come first into consideration the Freedom of all sorts of Religions differing from the Reformed. For in regard of all our Neighbours (except *Great Britain,* and the *United Provinces,* and for the most part all far remote Lands, are not of the Reformed Religion; and that the Clergy under the Papacy have their own Jurisdiction: And seeing, if not all those that are called *Spiritual,* yet the Clergy at least that differ from us, have in all Countrys a settled Livelihood, which depends not on the Political Welfare of the Land: We see that through humane Frailty, they do in all these Countrys think fit to teach and preach up all that can have a tendency to their own Credit, Profit, and Ease, yea, tho it be to the Ruin of the whole Country; and moreover, when the Doctrine, Counsel, and Admonition of these Men is not received by any of their Auditors, these Clergymen do then very unmercifully use to prosecute them *Odio Theologico.* Whereas nevertheless all Christian Clergymen ought to rest satisfied, according to their Master's Doctrine, to enlighten the Minds of Men with the Truth, and to shew them the way to Eternal Life, and afterwards to endeavour to perswade, and turn such enlightened Persons in all humility and meekness into the Path that leads to Salvation. It is evident that all People, especially Christians, and more particularly their publick Teachers, ought to be far from compelling, either by spiritual or bodily Punishment, those that for want of Light and Perswasion are not inclined to go to the Publick Church, to do any outward Act, or to speak any words contrary to their Judgment: For *Potestas coercendi,* the coerceive Power is given only to the Civil Magistrate; all the Power and Right which the Ecclesiasticks have, if they have any, must be derived from them. . . .

But notwithstanding all this, we see, that by these evil ambitious Maxims of the Clergy, almost in all Countrys, the Dissenters, or such as own not the Opinion of the public Preachers, are turned out of the Civil State and persecuted; for they are not only excluded from all Government, Magistracys, Offices and Benefices (which is in some measure tolerable for the secluded Inhabitants, and agrees very well with the Maxims of Polity, in regard it is well known by experience in all Countrys to be necessary, as tending to the common Peace, that one Religion should prevail and be supported above all others, and accordingly is by all means authorized, favoured, and protected by the State, yet not so, but that the exercise of other Religions at the same time be in some measure publickly tolerated, at least not persecuted) but are so persecuted, that many honest and useful Inhabitants, to escape those Fines, Banishments, or corporal Punishments, to which by adhering to the prohibited Service of God they are subject, abandon their own sweet native Country, and, to obtain their Liberty, chuse to come and sit down in our barren and heavy-tax'd Country. . . .

Next to a Liberty of serving God, follows the Liberty of gaining a Livelihood without any dear-bought City-freedom, but only of virtue of a fixed Habitation to have the common right of other Inhabitants: Which is here very necessary for keeping the People we have, and inviting Strangers to come among us. For it is self-evident that Landed-men, or others that are wealthy, being forced by any accident to leave their Country or Habitation, will never chuse *Holland* to dwell in, being so chargeable a Place, and where they have so little interest for their Money. And for those who are less wealthy, it is well known, that no Man from abroad will come to dwell or continue in a Country where he shall not be permitted to get a honest Maintenance. And it may be easily considered how great an inconveniency it would be in this Country, for the Inhabitants, especially Strangers, if they should have no Freedom of chusing and practising such honest means of livelihood as they think best for their Subsistence; or, if when they had chosen a Trade, and could not live by it, they might not chuse another. This then being evident, that Strangers without freedom of earning their Bread, and seeking a Livelihood, cannot live amongst us: and as it is certain, that our Manufactorys, Fisherys, Traffick and Navigation, with those that depend upon them, cannot without continual Supplys of Foreign Inhabitants be preserved here, and much less augmented or improved; it is likewise certain, that among the endless Advantages which accrue to *Holland* by Strangers, and which might accrue more, our Boors[7] may be likewise profited. For we see that for want of Strangers in the Country, the Boors must give such great yearly and day-wages to their Servants, that they can scarcely live but with great toil themselves, and their Servants live rather in too great plenty. The same inconveniences we are likewise sensible of in Citys amongst

7. Dutch "boer"–peasants, farmers.—*Ed.*

Tradesmen and Servants, who are here more chargeable and burdensom, and yet less serviceable than in any other Countries.

. . . It is besides very considerable, That for the most part all Trades and Manufactures manag'd by Guilds in *Holland*, do sell all their Goods within this Country to other Inhabitants who live immediately by the Fisherys, Manufacturys, Freight-ships, and Traffick: So that no Members of those Guilds, under what pretext soever, can be countenanced or indulged in their Monopoly, or Charter, but by the excluding of all other Inhabitants, and consequently to the hindrance of their Countrys Prosperity. For how much soever those Members sell their Pains or Commoditys dearer than if that Trade or Occupation was open or free, all the other better Inhabitants that gain their Subsistance immediately, or by consequence by a foreign consumption, must bear that loss. And indeed our Fishermen, Dealers in Manufactures, Owners of Freight-Ships, and Traders, being so burdened with all manner of Imposts, to oppress them yet more in their necessity by these Monopolies of Guilds, and to believe that it redounds to the good of the Land, because it tends to the benefit of such Companies, is to me incomprehensible. These Guilds are said indeed to be a useful sort of People; but next to those we call Idle Drones, they are the most unprofitable Inhabitants of the Country, because they bring in no profit from Foreign Lands for the Welfare of the Inhabitants of *Holland*. *Esop* hath well illustrated this folly by a Cat, who first lick'd off the Oil from an oiled File, and continued licking, not observing that she had by little and little lick'd her Tongue thorow [through] which was given her to sustain her Life, and carry Nourishment into her Body, nor that she fed not on the File which did not consume, but on her own Blood before her Tongue was totally consumed.

On the contrary, I can see no good, nor appearance of good, which the Guilds in *Holland* do produce, but only that Foreign Masters and Journeymen Artificers, having made their Works abroad, and endeavouring to sell them to our Inhabitants, thereby to carry the Profit out of our Country into their own, are herein check'd and opposed by our Masters of Guilds or Corporations. But besides that this is more to the Prejudice than Advantage of the Country, since by consequence our Fishers, Manufacturers, Traders, and Owners of Ships let to Freight, are thereby bereft of the Freedom of buying their necessaries at the cheapest Rate they can; it is also evident that this feeding of Foreigners upon the *Hollander* would be more strenuously and profitably opposed and prevented, in case of all handicraft Work, and Occupations were permitted to be made, sold and practised by all, and no other People, except such as have their setled Habitations in this Country.

It if be granted that the forementioned means of subsistence, namely, Fishing, Manufactury, Traffick, and Freight-ships, are so necessary in, and for *Holland*, as hath been above demonstrated; and if the *Hollanders* who have no native Commodities must yet hold Markets equally with other Nations, who may deal in their own Wares, or Manufactures made of their own Materials; then it follows, that our Rulers ought not, under any Pretence whatsoever, to charge or tax their own Inhabitants, Fishers, dealers in Manufactures, Owners of Freight-Ships, or Merchants as such. . . . I know that all such Impositions, through the Ignorance of those that are unacquainted with Trade, are counted very light and insignificant; but those that are more intelligent and concerned therein, do know that you may pull a large Fowl bare, by plucking away single Feathers, especially in *Holland*, where with light gains we must make a heavy purse. . . .

And indeed if we consider, that all Dutys levied on Consumption must at the long run be born by the Fishermen, Manufacturers, Traffickers, and Owners of Ships, who for the most part employ all the People here directly or indirectly, we acknowledg, that they alone are above measure burdened thereby, and discouraged by Imposts above all others.

. . . [It] is now true in Holland, War is much worse than an uncertain Peace. And among all pernicious things, except the intolerable slavery of being govern'd by the Will of a single Person, nothing is more mischievous than a War: for if War be the very worst thing that can befal a Nation, then an uncertain Peace must be bad, because a War is likely to ensue.

But some may further ask; seeing Peace is so necessary for *Holland*, whether out of a strong desire of a firm and lasting Peace, we ought not, when once engaged, to continue in War, till we have compell'd the Enemy to a well grounded Peace?

To which I answer: If we consider the uncertainty of this World, especially in *Europe*, and that we by Traffick and Navigation have occasion to deal with all Nations, we ought to hold for a firm and general Maxim, that an assured Peace is, in relation to *Holland*, a mere Chimera, a Dream, a Fiction, used only by those who like Syrens or Mermaids, endeavour by their melodious singing of a pleasant and firm Peace to delude the credulous *Hollanders*, till they split upon the Rocks.

There it is, and will remain a Truth, That next to the Freedom of the Rulers and Inhabitants at home, nothing is more necessary to us than Peace with all Men, and in such a time of Peace to make effectual provision for good Fortifications on the Frontiers of our Provinces; to keep a competent number of Men of War at Sea; to husband our Treasure at home, and as soon as possibly we may, to take off those Imposts that are most burdensom, especially that of Convoys; holding our selves assured, that without these means, whereby to procure a firm Peace, and to preserve our Country in Prosperity, as far as the wickedness of this World will admit, all other Expedients will be found prejudicial to *Holland;* and that we on the contrary, relying on these Maxims and Means, ought always to wait till others make War upon us, directly and indeed; because by our diligent and continual preparation, they would soon understand, that there is more to be gotten by us in a time of Peace and good Trading, than by War, and the ruin of Trade.

But because these Conclusions concerning the Prosperity of *Holland*, seem to oppose the known Rules of Polity; 1*st*, That a defensive War is a consumptive War; and 2*dly*, That no Rulers can subsist, unless they put on the Skin of a Lion, as well as that of the Fox; I shall give you my Thoughts upon these two Maxims. . . . But he who looks further into matters shall find, that in using these Maxims there is great distinction to be made. For tho it be true of Monarchs and Princes, who will suffer no Fortifications, that a defensive is a consumptive War; yet in Republicks which live by Traffick, and have fortified themselves well, all offensive war is prejudicial and consuming: So that such Countries can never subsist without good Fortifications in this World, where the lovers of Peace cannot always obtain their wish.

The truth is, great Monarchs are justly compar'd to the Lion, who is King of Beasts, never contented with the produce of their own Country; but living upon the Flesh of their Enemies, I wish I could not say Subjects; conquering and plundering their Neighbours, and burdening their own People with Taxes and Contributions. Yet tho they appropriate to themselves all the Advantages of the Country, they would still be deficient in Strength, if by means of the Fox's Skin they could not sometimes answer their Enemies, and even their own Subjects, and escape the Snares laid for them by others. Whereas Republicks governing with more Gentleness, Wisdom, and Moderation, have naturally a more powerful and numberless train of Inhabitants adhering to them than Monarchs, and therefore stand not in need of such Maxims, especially those that subsist by Trade, who ought in this matter to follow the commendable example of a Cat: For she never converses with strange Beasts, but either keeps at home, or accompanys those of her own Species, meddling with none, but in order to defend her own; very vigilant to provide for Food, and preserve her young ones: she neither barks nor snarls at those that provoke or abuse her; so shy and fearful, that being pursued, she immediately takes her flight into some Hole or Place of natural Strength, where she remains quiet till the noise be over. But if it happens that she can by no means avoid the Combat, she is more fierce than a Lion, defends her self with Tooth and Nail, and better than any other Beast, making use of all her well-husbanded Strength, without the least neglect or fainting in her Extremity. So that by these Arts that Species enjoy more quiet every where, live longer, are more acceptable, and in greater number than Lions, Tygers, Wolves, Foxes, Bears, or any other Beasts of Prey, which often perish by their own Strength, and are taken where they lie in wait for others.

A Cat indeed is outwardly like a Lion, yet she is, and will remain but a Cat still; and so we who are naturally Merchants, cannot be turned into Souldiers. . . .

41. The United Provinces: A Description and Analysis

Not a few foreign visitors, though few Dutchmen, gave an account of the remarkable country at the mouths of the great rivers flowing into the North Sea. Of all these descriptions of the Dutch republic, none is more penetrating in its analysis and more vivid in its ability to bring the land and its people alive even to the modern reader than a book by an English diplomat who twice served as ambassador at The Hague, Sir William Temple (1628–1699). Temple began his diplomatic career by bringing the bellicose bishop of Münster, Bernhard Christopher von Galen, into the war against the Dutch as an English ally in 1665. But he was also the chief negotiator on the English side of the Treaty of Breda (1667), which brought the war to an end in view of the French invasion of the southern Netherlands in the War of Devolution. Sent to The Hague as ambassador, he concluded the Triple Alliance among the Dutch Republic, Great Britain, and Sweden in January, 1668, which persuaded Louis XIV to close off the Devolution War. When Charles II joined Louis XIV in war against the United Provinces in 1672, Temple's policy of friendship with the Dutch seemed to be a failure; but the Peace of Westminster in 1674, by which Charles abandoned his French cousin, was its triumph, and Temple was sent back to The Hague, remaining until 1679 and helping to negotiate the Peace of Nijmegen (1678–79) which terminated the war. A brief venture of Temple into domestic politics failed, and he withdrew into private life as a man of letters, whom Jonathan Swift served as secretary. His *Observations upon the United Provinces of the Netherlands*, published in 1672, rested therefore upon direct observation, aided by his intimacy with the Councilor Pensionary of Holland, John de Witt, whose two decades of the management of the government of the country gave him unrivaled familiarity with its intricacies and special characteristics. Selections from the chapters upon the government and the people are given below.

Source: The Works of Sir William Temple, Bart., new ed., 4 vols. (London, 1814), Vol. I, pp. 94–95, 98–100, 113–114, 116–117, 133–139.

IT IS EVIDENT by what has been discoursed in the former chapter concerning the rise of this State, (which is to be dated from the Union of Utrecht) that it cannot properly be styled a commonwealth, but is rather a confederacy of Seven Sovereign Provinces, united together for their common and mutual defence, without any dependence one upon the other. But, to discover the nature of their government from the first springs and motions, it must be taken yet into smaller pieces, by which it will appear, that each of these Provinces is likewise composed of many little states or cities, which have several marks of sovereign power within themselves, and are not subject to the sovereignty of their Province; not being concluded in many things by the majority, but only by the universal concurrence of voices in the Provincial States. For as the States-General cannot make war or peace, or any new alliance, or levies of money, without the consent of every Province; so cannot the States-Provincial conclude any of those points, without the consent of each of the cities that by their constitution has a voice in that assembly. And though in many civil causes there lies an appeal from the common judicature of the cities to the provincial courts of justice; yet, in criminal, there lies none at all; nor can the sovereignty of a Province exercise any judicature, seize upon any offender, or pardon any offence within the jurisdiction of a city, or execute any common resolution or law, but by the justice and officers of the city itself. By this a certain sovereignty in each city is discerned, the chief marks whereof are, the power of exercising judicature, levying of money, and making war and peace; for the other, of coining money, is neither in particular cities or Provinces, but in the generality of the Union, by common agreement. . . .

In this city of Amsterdam is the famous bank, which is the greatest treasure, either real or imaginary, that is known any where in the world. The place of it is a great vault under the Stadthouse, made strong with all the circumstances of doors and locks, and other appearing cautions of safety, that can be: and it is certain, that whoever is carried to see the bank, shall never fail to find the appearance of a mighty real treasure, in bars of gold and silver, plate, and infinite bags of metals, which are supposed to be all gold and silver, and may be so for aught I know. But, the Burgomasters only having the inspection of this bank, and no man ever taking any particular account of what issues in and out, from age to age, it is impossible to make any calculation, or guess, what proportion the real treasure may hold to the credit of it. Therefore the security of the bank lies not only in the effects that are in it, but in the credit of the whole town or state of Amsterdam, whose stock and revenue is equal to that of some kingdoms; and who are bound to make good all monies that are brought into their bank: the tickets or bills hereof make all the usual great payments, that are made between man and man in the town; and not only in most other places of the United Provinces, but in many other trading parts of the world. So as this bank is properly a general cash, where every man lodges his money, because he esteems it safer, and easier paid in and out, than if it were in his coffers at home; and the bank is so far from paying any interest for what is there brought in, that money in the bank is worth something more in common payments, than what runs current in coin from hand to hand; no other money passing in the bank, but in the species of coin the best known, the most ascertained, and the most generally current in all parts of the Higher as well as the Lower Germany.

The revenues of Amsterdam arise out of the constant excise upon all sorts of commodities bought and sold within the precinct; or, out of the rents of those houses or lands that belong in common to the city; or, out of certain duties and impositions upon every house, towards the uses of charity, and the repairs, or adornments, or fortifications of the place; or else, out of extraordinary levies consented to by the Senate, for furnishing their part of the public charge that is agreed to by their Deputies in the Provincial States, for the use of the Province; or by the Deputies of the States of Holland in the States-General, for support of the Union. And all these payments are made into one common stock of the town, not as many of ours are, into that of the parish, so as attempts may be easier made at the calculations of their whole revenue; and I have heard it affirmed, that what is paid of all kinds to public uses of the States-General, the Province, and the city, in Amsterdam, amounts to above sixteen hundred thousand pounds Sterling a year. But I enter into no computations, nor give these for any thing more, than what I have heard from men who pretended to make such enquiries, which I confess, I did not. It is certain that, in no town, strength, beauty, and convenience are better provided for, nor with more unlimited expence, than in this, by the magnificence of their public buildings, as the Stadthouse and Arsenals; the number and spaciousness, as well as order and revenues, of their many hospitals; the commodiousness of their canals, running through the chief streets of passage; the mighty strength of their bastions and ramparts; and the neatness, as well as convenience, of their streets, so far as can be compassed in so great a confluence of industrious people; all which could never be atchieved without a charge much exceeding what seems proportioned to the revenue of one single town. . . .

The greatness of this State seems much to consist in these orders, how confused soever, and of different pieces, they may seem; but more in two main effects of them, which are, the good choice of the officers of chief trust in the Cities, Provinces, and State: and the great simplicity and modesty in the common port or living of their chiefest ministers; without which, the absoluteness of the Senates in each town, and the immensity of taxes through the whole State, would never be endured by the people with any patience; being both of them greater than in many of those Governments, which are esteemed most arbitrary among their Neighbours. But in the assemblies and debates of their Senates, every man's abilities are discovered, as their Dispositions are, in the conduct of their lives and domestick, among their fellow-citizens. The observation of these either raises, or suppresses, the credit of particular men, both among the people, and the Senates of their towns; who, to maintain their authority with less popular envy or discontent, give much to the general opinion of the people in the choice of their Magistrates: By this means it comes to pass, that, though perhaps the Nation generally be not wise, yet the Government is, because it is composed of the wisest of the Nation; which may give it an advantage over many others, where ability is of more common growth, but of less use to the publique; if it happens, that neither wisdom nor honesty are the qualities, which bring men to the management of state-affairs, as they usually do in this commonwealth.

Besides, though these people, who are naturally cold and heavy, may not be ingenious enough to furnish a pleasant or agreeable conversation, yet they want not plain downright sense to understand and do their business both publick and private, which is a talent very different from the other; and I know not, whether they often meet. . . .

The other circumstance I mentioned, as an occasion of their greatness, was the simplicity and modesty of their Magistrates in their way of living, which is so general, that I never knew one among them exceed the common frugal popular air: and so great, that, of the two chief officers in my time, Vice-Admiral De Ruiter and the Pensioner De Witt (one generally esteemed by foreign nations as great a seaman, and the other as great a statesman, as any of their age) I never saw the first in clothes better than the commonest sea-captain, nor with above one man following him, nor in a coach; and, in his own house, neither was the size, building, furniture, or entertainment, at all exceeding the use of every common merchant and tradesman in his town. For the Pensioner De Witt, who had the great influence in the government, the whole train and expence of his domestique went very equal with other common Deputies or ministers of the State; his habit grave, and plain, and popular; his table, what only served turn for his family, or a friend; his train (besides commissaries and clerks kept for him, in an office adjoining to his house, at the public charge) was only one man, who performed all the menial service of his house at home; and, upon his visits of ceremony, putting on a plain livery-cloak, attended his coach abroad: for, upon other occasions, he was seen usually in the streets on foot, and alone, like the commonest burgher of the town. Nor was this manner of life affected, or used only by these particular men, but was the general fashion and mode among all the magistrates of the State: for I speak not of the military officers, who are reckoned their servants, and live in a different garb, though generally modester than in other countries.

Thus this stomachful people, who could not endure the least exercise of arbitrary power or impositions, or the sight of any foreign troops, under the Spanish government, have since been inured to all of them, in the highest degree, under their own popular magistrates; bridled with hard laws, terrified with severe executions, environed with foreign forces; and oppressed with the most cruel hardship and variety of taxes that was ever known under any government; but all this, whilst the way to office and authority lies through those qualities which acquire the general esteem of the people; whilst no man is exempted from the danger and current of laws; whilst soldiers are confined to frontier garrisons (the guard of inland or trading towns being left to the burghers themselves); and whilst no great riches are seen to enter by public payments into private purses, either to raise families, or to feed the prodigal expences of vain, extravagant, and luxurious men; but all public monies are applied to the safety, greatness, or honour of the State, and tho Magistrates themselves bear an equal share in all the burdens they impose.

The authority of the Princes of Orange, though intermitted upon the untimely death of the last, and infancy of this present Prince; yet, as it must be ever acknowledged to have had a most essential part in the first frame of this government, and in all the fortunes thereof, during the whole growth and progress of the State: so has it ever preserved a very strong root, not only in six of the Provinces, but even in the general and popular affections of the Province of Holland itself, whose States have, for these last twenty years, so much endeavoured to suppress, or exclude it. . . .

The people of Holland may be divided into these several classes: the clowns or boors (as they call them) who cultivate the land: the mariners or schippers, who supply their ships and inland-boats: the merchants or traders, who fill their towns: the Renteeners, or men that live in all their chief cities upon the rents or interest of estates formerly acquired in their families: and the Gentlemen, and officers of their armies.

The first are a race of people diligent rather than laborious; dull and slow of understanding, and so not dealt with by hasty words, but managed easily by soft and fair; and yielding to plain reason, if you give them time to understand it. In the country and villages not too near the great towns, they seem plain and honest, and content with their own; so that if, in bounty, you give them a shilling for what is worth but a groat, they will take the current price, and give you the rest again; if you bid them take it, they know not what you mean, and sometimes ask, if you are a fool. They know no other good but the supply of what nature requires, and the common increase of wealth. They feed most upon herbs, roots, and milks; and by that means, I suppose, neither their strength nor vigour seem answerable to the size or bulk of their bodies.

The mariners are a plain, but much rougher people; whether from the element they live in, or from their food, which is generally fish and corn, and heartier than that of the boors. They are surly and ill-mannered, which is mistaken for pride; but, I believe, is learned, as all manners are, by the conversation we use. Now theirs lying only among one another, or with winds and waves, which are not moved or wrought upon by any language or observance, or to be dealt with, but by pains and by patience; these are all the qualities their mariners have learned; their valour is passive rather than active; and their language is little more, than what is of necessary use to their business.

The merchants and tradesmen, both the greater and mechanic, living in towns that are of great resort, both by strangers and passengers of their own, are more mercurial (wit being sharpened by commerce and conversation of cities) though they are not very inventive, which is the gift of warmer heads; yet are they great in imitation, and so far, many times, as goes beyond originals: of mighty industry, and constant application to the ends they propose and pursue. They make use of their skill, and their wit, to take advantage of other men's ignorance and folly they deal with; are great exacters, where the law is in their own hands: in other points, where they deal with men that understand like themselves, and are under the reach of justice and laws, they are the plainest and best dealers in the world; which seems not to grow so much from a principle of conscience, or morality, as from a custom or habit introduced by the necessity of trade among them, which depends as much upon common honesty, as war does upon discipline; and without which all would break up, merchants would turn pedlars, and soldiers thieves.

Those families, which live upon their patrimonial estates in all the great cities, are a people differently bred and mannered from the traders, though like them in the modesty of garb and habit, and the parsimony of living. Their youth are generally bred up at schools, and at the universities of Leyden or Utrecht, in the common studies of human learning, but chiefly of the civil law, which is that of their country, at least as far as it is so in France and Spain. For (as much as I understand of those countries) no decisions or decrees of the civil law, nor constitutions of the Roman Emperors, have the force or current of law among them, as is commonly believed, but only the force of reasons when alledged before their courts of judicature, as far as the authority of men esteemed wise passes for reason: but the ancient customs of those several countries, and the ordonnances of their Kings and Princes, consented to by the Estates, or in France verified by Parliaments, have only the strength and authority of law among them.

Where these families are rich, their youths, after the course of their studies at home, travel for some years, as the sons of our gentry use to do; but their journies are chiefly into England and France, not much into Italy, seldomer into Spain, nor often into the more northern countries, unless in company or train of their public Ministers. The chief end of their breeding is, to make them fit for the service of their country in the magistracy of their towns, their Provinces, and their State. And of these kind of men are the civil officers of this government generally composed, being descended of families who have many times been constantly in the magistracy of their native towns for many years, and some for several ages.

Such were most or all of the chief Ministers, and the persons that composed their chief councils, in the time of my residence among them; and not men of mean or mechanic trades, as it is commonly received among foreigners, and makes the subject of comical jests upon their government. This does not exclude many merchants, or traders in gross, from being often seen in the offices of their cities, and sometimes deputed to their States; nor several of their States from turning their stocks in the management of some very beneficial trade by servants, and houses maintained to that purpose. But the Generality of the States and Magistrates are of the other sort;

their estates consisting in the pensions of their public charges, in the rents of lands, or interest of money upon the Cantores, or in actions of the East-India company, or in shares upon the adventures of great trading merchants.

Nor do these families, habituated as it were to the magistracy of their towns and provinces, usually arrive at great or excessive riches; the salaries of public employments and interest being low, but the revenue of lands being yet very much lower, and seldom exceeding the profit of two in the hundred. They content themselves with the honour of being useful to the public, with the esteem of their cities or their country, and with the ease of their fortunes; which seldom fails, by the frugality of their living, grown universal by being (I suppose) at first necessary, but since honourable, among them.

The mighty growth and excess of riches is seen among the merchants and traders, whose application lies wholly that way, and who are the better content to have so little share in the government, desiring only security in what they possess; troubled with no cares but those of their fortunes, and the management of their trades, and turning the rest of their time and thought to the divertisement of their lives. Yet these, when they attain great wealth, chuse to breed up their sons in the way, and marry their daughters into the families, of those others most generally credited in their towns, and versed in their magistracies; and thereby introduce their families into the way of government and honour, which consists not here in titles, but in public employments.

The next rank among them is that of their Gentlemen or Nobles, who, in the Province of Holland (to which I chiefly confine these observations) are very few, most of the families having been extinguished in the long wars with Spain. But those that remain, are in a manner all employed in the military or civil charges of the Province or State. These are, in their customs, and manners, and way of living, a good deal different from the rest of the people; and, having been bred much abroad, rather affect the garb of their neighbour-courts, than the popular air of their own country. They value themselves more upon their Nobility, than men do in other countries, where it is more common; and would think themselves utterly dishonoured by the marriage of one that was not of their rank, though it were to make up the broken fortune of a Noble family by the wealth of a Plebeian. They strive to imitate the

French in their mien, their cloaths, their way of talk, of eating, of gallantry or debauchery; and are, in my mind, something worse than they would be, by affecting to be better than they need; making sometimes but ill copies, whereas they might be good originals, by refining or improving the customs or virtues proper to their own country and climate. They are otherwise an honest, well-natured, friendly, and gentlemanly sort of men, and acquit themselves generally with honour and merit, where their country employs them.

The officers of their armies live after the customs and fashions of the gentlemen; and so do many sons of the rich merchants, who, returning from travel abroad, have more designs upon their own pleasure, and the vanity of appearing, than upon the service of their country: or, if they pretend to enter into that, it is rather by the army than the State. And all these are generally desirous to see a court in their country, that they may value themselves at home, by the qualities they have learned abroad; and make a figure which agrees better with their own humour, and the manner of courts, than with the customs and orders that prevail in more popular governments.

There are some customs, or dispositions, that seem to run generally through all these degrees of men among them; as great frugality, and order, in their expences. Their common riches lie in every man's having more than he spends; or, to say it more properly, in every man's spending less than he has coming in, be that what it will: nor does it enter into men's heads among them, that the common port or course of expence should equal the revenue; and, when this happens, they think at least they have lived that year to no purpose; and the train of it discredits a man among them, as much as any vicious or prodigal extravagance does in other countries. This enables every man to bear their extreme taxes, and makes them less sensible than they would be in other places; for he that lives upon two parts in five of what he has coming in, if he pays two more to the State, he does but part with what he should have laid up, and had no present use for; whereas he that spends yearly what he receives, if he pays but the fiftieth part to the public, it goes from him, like that which was necessary to buy bread or cloaths for himself or his family.

This makes the beauty and strength of their towns, the commodiousness of travelling in their country by their canals, bridges, and cawseys; the pleasantness of their walks, and their grafts in and near all their cities: and, in short, the beauty, convenience, and sometimes magnificence, of all public works, to which every man pays as willingly, and takes as much pleasure and vanity in them, as those of other countries do in the same circumstances, among the possessions of their families, or private inheritance. What they can spare, besides the necessary expence of their domestique, the public payments, and the common course of still increasing their stock, is laid out in the fabric, adornment, or furniture of their houses, things not so transitory, or so prejudicial to health and to business, as the constant excesses and luxury of tables; nor perhaps altogether so vain as the extravagant expences of cloaths and attendance; at least, these end wholly in a man's self, and the satisfaction of this personal humour; whereas the other make not only the riches of a family, but contribute much towards the public beauty and honour of a country.

IX The Golden Age Loses Its Glitter

By the end of the seventeenth century the magnificent miracle of the Dutch Republic was giving way to a more commonplace existence. The country was still wealthy but declining in comparison with the great powers around it. The special conditions upon which Dutch preeminence had been built had gone or were rapidly disappearing. More spacious and populous neighbors like France and England had turned deliberately and effectively to breaking the Dutch quasi monopoly upon Europe's interregional trade; it would be only a slim exaggeration to call the mercantilism represented by the English Navigation Acts and Colbert's policies a riposte to Dutch domination of commerce and shipping. Once other nations began to ship and to trade directly in a substantial part of the products they imported and exported, the massive profits on which both Dutch prosperity and Dutch power rested ceased to flow in. Another burden, less visible but no less damaging to the Dutch position, was the load of debt and taxation created by the long series of wars. Dutch taxation, unlike that of other countries, did not rest primarily upon the land but upon external trade and internal consumption; as such, it represented a substantial competitive cost which other states faced to a much lesser extent. Yet the immense wealth of the Dutch, especially of the merchants and patricians, did not vanish overnight. The decline of Dutch trade, for one thing, was only relative, when it was compared to the expansion of commerce generally in Europe in the eighteenth century and to phenomenal expansion of English and French commerce in particular. The absolute volume of Dutch shipping and trade remained about the same or declined only slowly. Furthermore, Dutch capital holdings remained profitable; the capitalists of Holland were major investors in the bonds of foreign governments, not least of England and France, and when business opportunities opened up, as in the American republic after the declaration of the independence of the United States, Dutch funds flowed there as well.

In political life, the eighteenth century was an age of institutional rigidity under which new currents of ideas stirred and seethed, especially after mid-century. When William III died without a direct heir in 1702, Holland and the other principal provinces did not go to the collateral line of Orange-Nassau, which still held the stadholdership in Friesland and Groningen; instead, a second stadholderless period ensued. Like the first of 1650–1672, it was marked by conflict between the patrician regents and the Orangists, with popular elements throwing their strength to the Nassau line. The debacle of Dutch policy during the War of the Austrian Succession, in which the French struck across the Austrian (southern) Netherlands into Dutch territory, led to the downfall of the stadholderless regime and the restoration of the House of Orange under Prince William IV in 1747. But neither he nor his successor, William V, were advocates of a revolution-from-above; as long as they dominated the policies of the country, they were satisfied with the political system in which a few thousand regents governed in the towns and provincial assemblies. But the regents were a self-chosen, self-perpetuating aristocracy, without a shred of the implicit representation of the community as a whole which Vranck had lauded in his *Brief Demonstration* (see No. 22) when the republic came into being.

The ideas of the Enlightenment, entering the country from France and England, resulted in a new and typically Dutch amalgam—the combination of the rule of personal freedom which the regents had followed, and the notion of the common people as equal partners in the state which had lain beneath the surface in popular rioting against the regents and on behalf of the princes of Orange. The new force, which took the name of the Patriots, turned its fire upon both regents and the Prince of Orange, especially under the flaccid William V; but the reformers pushed the two camps of conservatives into alliance, the States party and the Orange party moved closer together, and joined in accepting foreign help from Prussia and England in 1787. But the re-established authority of the Prince of Orange was utterly inadequate to meet the challenge which came from Patriots who found both spiritual encouragement and military support from the French revolutionaries. In 1795 the Patriots, aided by a French invasion, overthrew the old regime in the United Provinces and created the Batavian Republic. At this point the history of the early modern Low Countries closes and the modernization of the (northern) Netherlands begins.

42. Decline Begins in the Dutch Republic

One of the best informed and most astute observers of the United Provinces in the early eighteenth century was a Dutch-born and educated Frenchman, Adrianus Engelhard Helvetius (1662–1727). The son of a Swiss doctor who settled in Holland in 1649, he went to Paris to carry on a business in medical supplies as well as to take his medical degree. He settled permanently in France, gaining naturalization as a subject of the French king and becoming one of the country's leading doctors, with members of the royal family and the highest nobility as his patients. His grandson, Claude Adrien Helvétius, was one of the most celebrated philosophers of the French Enlightenment. Because of his familiarity with the Dutch scene and his keen powers of observation and judgment, Adrianus Engelhard Helvetius was sent to Holland several times during the War of the Spanish Succession (1701–1713) as a secret agent. After the first of these visits, which lasted from September to December 1705, he wrote a *"Mémoire* on the present state of the Government of the United Provinces" which he submitted to the French foreign minister in February, 1706. The account of the declining forces of the republic which he gave, confirmed by later visits in 1707 and 1710, as well as the similar information given by other French agents, helped sway the French government to lower its estimate of the importance of the Dutch and to make direct negotiations with the English the center of its policy. The *Mémoire* was not published until 1966, when it appeared with an introduction by a Dutch scholar in a Dutch historical journal; it is from this modern edition that the following selection is taken.

Source: Adrianus Engelhard Helvetius, "Mémoire sur l'état présent du Gouvernement des Provinces Unies," ed. M. van der Bijl, in *Bijdragen en Mededelingen van het Historisch Genootschap,* Vol. 80 (1966), pp. 171–180. Translated from the French by Herbert H. Rowen.

THE COMMERCE of the United Provinces in Europe has never been in a worse condition than today. During the course of earlier wars, although Dutch vessels were also open to the attacks of privateers, at least they could take refuge in the Atlantic and in the Mediterranean in ports under Spanish rule, which now are closed to them. Furthermore, even when they were completely barred from the trade of France, they still continued to ply both the Baltic trades, which they continue to enjoy, and the trades of Spain, the kingdoms of Naples and Sicily, and Spanish Flanders, which now they have good reason to miss. Not only is the market greatly reduced for their cloth, both of their own manufacture as well as that made in India and in the Baltic, and for their other wares, spices, salt fish, etc., but they are also deprived of the profitable return trade in wool, wine and other necessary commodities.

It is true that their trade to the Indies has not fallen off as badly, yet the lack of consumers is causing difficulties like those in their European commerce. In the East Indies the Company has launched a violent war against the Mogul, and in the West Indies trade is possible only through intermediaries and hence is subject to many disturbances. In peacetime the Dutch used to earn as much as eighteen million from Cadiz when the fleets (from Spanish America) returned. Smuggling does not produce anything like that amount, and the delays discourage the richer merchants, who await better times to risk their wealth. As a result, there are frequent bankruptcies, word of which scares people and discourages them from entrusting their money to merchants, whose own funds are limited, as they are in the habit of doing in peacetime. This decline even affects the domestic commerce of the country, which is suffering badly, especially thanks to the cunning manipulations of the English, who take advantage of the opportunity to raise themselves upon the ruins of their allies.

The English, a people as fierce as they are capable, being convinced that the States General need their help so badly that they would not dare dispute anything with them, follow the maxim of making the Dutch pay their auxiliary troops, even when they are engaged in battle. They supply them with goods of every kind, sending cloth and Indian fabrics which are forbidden in England, butter, tallow, even manufactured candles, grain, etc., and in this way they manage to make a profit on the support of the troops which they ought to be paying themselves. Far from supplying their pay and sending money out of Great Britain, they ship out large quantities of superfluous goods, which when used to meet the pay of English soldiers brings more money from Holland to England, although this crafty conduct totally destroys what remains of trade within the United Provinces, where the abundance of foreign goods reduces the price of local products and the sale of English wares results in the decline of local manufactures, as the clothmakers of Leiden have found to their cost. For since the common people in Holland have taken to wearing light flowing serge and other English fabrics, which are very cheap, Leiden has lost more than three thousand of its workers. Most of them have crossed into Flanders, thanks to the endeavors of Count van Bergeyck,[1] who does all he can as well to interfere with Dutch trade. It does them no good, however, to shout against the injustices perpetrated by the English, for instead of obtaining any satisfaction they are treated worse than ever in England, where Parliament invents a thousand chicaneries at their expense and forbids the import of most of their goods at the same time as it floods Holland with whatever surplus of anything exists in the three kingdoms.

It might be thought that the opening of trade with France would bring some solace to the United Provinces. Yet it is not to be denied that while the reduction in the price of wine has increased its sales and improved the business of a few merchants, it has ruined others whose stores were well stocked. This is not the place to examine whether the trade between the two countries upon the present footing is more advantageous to Holland or France. What is certain is that since the ban was lifted, Dutch merchants have shipped into France a great supply of louis d'or, so that these coins, which had been quoted at only nine livres, have risen to nine livres five sous.

Considering all the wounds which Dutch trade has received from every side, one might naturally expect that money would be in very short supply in their provinces. But we know that it circulates easily, which is explained by the immense sums which were amassed by their customary trade to every part of the world. There are many individuals whose wealth has not been exhausted by continued warfare, because they are sparing with what they have and renew it in business, but it would be wrong to believe that the state, who has been exhausting itself by spending so much for so long, is as rich in proportion as some of its people. On the contrary, it is extremely encumbered with debt, and without speaking of the other provinces, most of which do not blush for their poverty, Holland alone owes 420,000,000 in interest-bearing bonds.

The States of this province, in order to discharge a part of these

1. The leading native official of the French-sponsored government of the Elector of Bavaria in the Southern Netherlands.—*Tr.*

enormous debts and to meet the exorbitant expenses of the present war, have recourse to two means which are always employed in such circumstances, that is, new taxes and more loans. There are few countries where the ordinary taxes are more numerous and heavier than in Holland; taxes are collected on everything, with harshness and violence.

The taxes on flour, beer, and turf produce the greatest revenue. Taxes are levied on each household according to its consumption of wine, salt, soap, tobacco, tea, and coffee, etc., as estimated by the town magistrates, to whom the heads of family are required to make a faithful declaration of the number of their children and their servants, under penalty of fines. This sort of tax is to be extended to candles; the edict has been adopted but not yet published. Furthermore, most of these commodities, as well as a multitude of others, pay entry duties before they come into the provinces if they are of foreign origin, and always before they leave the hands of the retail shopkeeper.

When real estate, which here includes seagoing ships, is sold, a tax of two and one-half percent of the price must be paid to the state. All legal documents of any kind whatever have no force in law if they are not drawn up on paper sealed with the small seal if they are of minor importance and the great seal if they are more important. Each sheet which bears the great seal pays four shillings, and each with the small seal pays two. Valets and servants are not exempt from paying an annual tax, nor are horned cattle and horses, either in pasture or when brought out for sale. Wagons must also pay a tax, cart-horses ten pounds a year, and carriages 25 pounds.

Finally, there are also taxes levied on weddings, and burials are taxed so cruelly that a cadaver will remain unburied unless the relatives of the dead pay ten crowns for the last rites. There is no escaping this injust tax except by bringing affidavits of poverty to be registered, and frequent scandalous disturbances have already occurred in the Protestant temples and Catholic churches.

We will skip over a large number of taxes, which it would be tedious to give in detail, to discuss the so-called Hundredth Penny, which provides the state with its readiest revenues. It is collected on a permanent basis from all real estate possessed by subjects of the States of Holland, which includes land, houses, contracts of indebtedness, interest-bearing bonds, shares in the East India Company, etc. Although this tax, which is set by estimate of the local magistrate, is called the "Hundredth Penny," in respect to first establishment, it should rather be called the "Eighth Penny," because in fact it provides to the state every year an eighth of all revenues from the property taxed. Once it has been collected, there is no way to be relieved of it, and it is demanded with such rigor that landowners have often been known to abandon their lands to the state because they could not pay the charges upon them.

If this tax seems hard in peacetime, it is infinitely worse during war. Then each possessor of real estate pays the eighth twice, that is, a quarter of his income, yet it is called the Two-Hundredth Penny. When a war takes a turn for the worse and the state is obliged to increase its expenditures, the funds are found by doubling the tax of the Two-Hundredth Penny, that is, each landowner is compelled to pay out half of his annual income. This is the current practice. Finally, when things are at their very worst, as during the war of 1672, this tax has been imposed as much as three times in a single year, which meant that each person was paying three quarters of his income.

Nonetheless, onerous as this tax is, the state prefers to have recourse to it because it affects only the wealthy, rather than introduce new personal taxes and run the danger of arousing the poor populace, who are much more susceptible to rebellion than those who have something to lose.

The second resource of the province of Holland is to borrow from its own subjects, to whom it continues to pay the interest on the sums lent. If its credit were to be judged by the debts with which it is overburdened, one would have to expect it to be quite weak; yet, as soon as a new loan is asked, people hasten to beat each other to invest their funds in the public treasury. This confidence of the people arises less from the plentiful supply of specie in Holland and even less from the exactitude with which the bonds are paid off when they fall due, than to a number of political tricks which the ministers use, and the absence of any other safe investment in wartime.

It is certain that when peace opens the way for trade, those who have money to invest do not fail to put it in the hands of merchants in order to make a greater profit, but when the risks are too great, either because of the raids by foreign privateers or because of domestic bankruptcies which are a usual consequence of war, everyone keeps his funds for himself, or at least prefers to take a modest profit rather than run too great risks. To employ funds in the purchase of land or existing bonds would be very foolish at a time when this kind of property is subject to paying the Two-Hundredth Penny two or three times a year. It is therefore preferable to lend one's money to the state, especially since the new bonds are exempt from all taxation for a term of six years from the date of issue. At the end of this time, they become subject to the Two-Hundredth Penny, so that it is usual to obtain repayment of the principal, which is never refused when the bondholders ask for it.

Another source of profit which the state uses to dazzle the public and to display its pretended opulence is to order the paying off of six millions of debt every year, even in the most difficult times. This sum is then used to pay obligations contracted at a higher rate than before.

Helmette,[2] the receiver-general who is in charge of this operation, handles it with such skill, choosing for repayment those who he knows have least need of the funds, that sometimes he is overwhelmed with requests and pleas to keep the money; even then, he pretends to grant this favor only to people whom he holds in high esteem, because he is obliged to reimburse the same sum every year. This reimbursement nevertheless is not without great advantage to the public, because the six millions are distributed among the people, so that money stays in circulation and does not become scarce.

Finally, while the state is repaying old loans with one hand, it opens the other to take in new loans. It is then that Helmette uses another trick to induce people to lend more, more easily and more quickly. At the moment when the new issue is about to be fully subscribed, he brings in persons, some of them leading figures in the Republic, and refuses the large sums which they present to him, claiming that the issue has been fully subscribed and that they are too late.

Crude as these tricks are, they do not fail to take in the unwary and thereby to increase the credit of the state to the point where he boasts he could borrow the last penny in the purse of Holland's subjects. Indeed, they have been fortunate enough to be able to

2. Cornelis de Jonge van Ellemeet.—*Tr.*

borrow as much money as they needed until now at four percent. Their receiver-general has even been able to obtain in his name four million at three and one-half percent.

But in the end this is not an inexhaustible stream; it must run out some day if the trade which is its source itself continues to suffer from a drought. The East India Company alone, which would seem enough to prevent poverty, is scarcely able to maintain itself. It can conduct its trade only with cash, which comes only from the sale of its goods, for which the market is extremely reduced. Furthermore, in addition to the fact that the conflict with the Mogul involves new expenditures, it also interferes with the ordinary course of its trade. So many attacks suffered at the same time have not failed to lower the price of the company's shares. Nonetheless, the specie which leaves the United Provinces by various routes does not come back by any of them, so that the work of coinage has been halted throughout the country. The States have even been obliged recently to support the Emperor, who pledged to them his quicksilver mines for a loan of several million at five percent; this was another bloodletting for Holland, because these sums were furnished by individuals who gladly made the loans because they were declared to be free of the Two-Hundredth Penny tax. Finally, the expenses of war continue to increase every day. Portugal and Catalonia seem to be two chasms which are ready to swallow all the treasures of the Indies, so that the States General are beginning to tire of sending their most essential subsistence there, and their subjects, who have been very patient until now, are beginning to become angry against the heavy burden of the Two-Hundredth Penny, which has lasted too long.

This is the present situation of the affairs of the United Provinces.

43. The New Patriots

During the seventeenth century the term "patriots" had been used by both sides in the great conflict between the States party and the Orangists to praise themselves at the same time as they were denouncing their opponents. Not until the rise of a democratic movement in the second half of the eighteenth century did "Patriot" become a party name. It represented the forces of those who, to anticipate the great formula of the French Revolution, wanted liberty, equality, and fraternity in the Dutch Republic. In more specifically Dutch terms, they advocated the limitation or even elimination of the power of the stadholder, now a hereditary and hence much more explicitly monarchical office, the opening of the ranks of the town governments to members elected from and by the ordinary burghers, and the ending of the hoary system of using public office for private profit. Their primary membership was drawn from the merchant and professional classes in the towns, particularly those who were excluded from office because they were not members of the few families of regents who had become a nearly watertight caste of officialdom. But the most eloquent spokesman for the Patriot movement was a nobleman from Overijssel, Joan —an old Dutch spelling of *Johan*, "John"—Derk Baron van der Capellen tot den Pol. Van der Capellen tot den Pol was one of those historical figures whom a modern editor of his work[3] has called the "Red Barons," aristocrats who had a falling out with their own class and gave leadership to its adversaries over on the far side. Obtaining his seat in the States of Overijssel only with difficulty, he gave his resentment against the powers-that-be the form of a deep commitment to political reform upon a democratic basis. He supported the cause of the American Revolution, as we can see in the first selections below from his correspondence with American officials in their country as well as with the English radical, Dr. Richard Price, whose work he translated into Dutch. In 1781 he published anonymously a bitter and biting pamphlet, *To the People of the Netherlands*, which furnished the programmatic basis for the more radical Patriots; our second selection is taken from a contemporary English translation.

a. Source: W. H. Beaufort, ed., *Brieven van en aan Joan Derck van der Capellen van de Poll* (Utrecht: Kemink & Zoon, 1879), pp. 84–91, 103–105, 190–191. Translated from the French and Dutch by Herbert H. Rowen.

b. Source: An Address to the People of the Netherlands, on the Present Alarming and most Dangerous Situation of the Republic of Holland . . . By a Dutchman [Van der Capellen tot den Pol]. Translated from the Dutch Original. (London: J. Stockdale, 1782). Pp. 37–41.

a.

1. Van der Cappellen to Jonathan Trumbull, Governor of Connecticut, from Zwolle, December 7, 1778. (In French)

3. W. F. Wertheim, introduction to edition of *Aan het Volk van Nederland* (Amsterdam, 1966), p. 19.

To His Excellency Mr. Jonathan Trumbull, Governor, Captain-General, and Commander-in-Chief of the State of Connecticut at Lebanon in New England.

Sir,

To be the object of the public esteem of the brave Americans, worthy and virtuous people, is so great a thing that all the reputation of your name and Mr. Erkelens' will not be able to persuade me that I have merited even the slightest part of the gratitude which you desire to express to me on their part for the small service that I have tried to render them.

It is true, Sir, that beginning with the year 1775 I espoused the good cause of your compatriots with a zeal inspired in me by love of freedom, esteem for those who dare to defend it, and horror for all kinds of oppression. But, after all, what I did was no more than an act of pure justice. By my birth a member of the nobility of my province and (just like the lords in England) called in this capacity to sit in the Assembly of States (not the States General, as is erroneously believed in foreign countries, but those of the Province of Overijssel), I would have felt responsible for the innocent blood spilled by our troops if I had let them depart without taking a stand against it. Because I have been disturbed to see faulty translations published in Holland of the little speech which I had hastily composed, to which I owe the honor of being known and applauded in America, I take the liberty of offering you a very correct French translation.

The results of this action, the hardship and pinpricks it has caused me, and an unequivocal proof that I have not cooled since in my affection for the American people, are to be found in the appended copy of a letter of April 28 of this year which I could not refrain from writing to Mr. Ambassador Franklin. Until now I have received no answer to it or to that of September 6 following. Nevertheless, I so revere this great man that I am convinced that he has good reasons for not replying.

As for your kind letter, which Mr. Erkelens tells me was sent at the instructions of the President and members of the honorable Congress, you may be sure, Sir, that, placed among my family papers, it will be forever more precious to me than the most illustrious order of knighthood with which any monarch could have decorated me. My ancestors have been counted since time immemorial among the members of noble bodies and chapters. My house has given knights to Malta and the Teutonic Order; but this testimony of the approbation with which the American people is pleased to honor my efforts, which were well intended but too weak indeed to be helpful, is more valuable to me than any such things. It is my heart which speaks, for it has been touched. Be so kind as to convey what it says to those in whose name you have done me the honor of writing to me.

As for the good offices which you do me the honor of asking that I continue "as far as will consist with my duty to my own country."—My influence in this Republic in fact amounts to what can be achieved by the weak voice and the pen of a magistrate who has nothing to favor him but reason embattled against interests, prejudices, and passions. What could I do as an individual in this country, when even the voice of the mighty city of Amsterdam has counted for naught in a case which, under our form of government, absolutely requires unanimity? Faithful to its principles, enlighted as to its own interests and those of the Republic, and disdaining to bow beneath the English yoke, it sought a few days ago to communicate some of its own fire to other members of our state in order in prevent acceptance of the absurd and imperious proposals of England that it refrain from using its right, which is founded upon the law of nations as well as upon treaties, *to furnish building timber to France:* proposals which they dare to make to us, or rather laws which they dictate to us after having deprived us by force of a hundred ships and committed every kind of cruelty against our sailors, for whom there is no protection. But, alas! the truly patriotic endeavors of this worthy city, which is a friend to America and did not hesitate to declare during the month of October last that it was all necessary to fit out a fleet (these are its precise words) "at a time when the independence of America will soon be recognized and trade with the colonies will be in great need of protection against the envy of those who might wish to deprive the inhabitants of this state of it";—these endeavors were all fruitless. The English party has won out; by a plurality of voices we have abandoned the most important advantage which neutrality offers us and have sacrificed at the despotic demand of our eternal rival in trade one of its richest branches!

What, then, are the services which America may expect from me? In my capacity as a magistrate, as you can see, Sir, I can give none.—As an individual, I shall strive (if this is a service) to support by my example and my encouragement, as far as I am able, the negotiation undertaken for the Congress by Messrs. Horneca and Fizeaux at Amsterdam. I am not a capitalist: my patrimony consists completely in landed property. I will nevertheless invest a rather substantial sum which has come into my disposal by the death of my mother-in-law, although I could have made use of it to pay off debts which I had to contract in order to obtain a noble estate and thereby a seat in the States Assembly.

Furthermore, the ties which still bind me to my native country but which are beginning to become burdensome and by their nature are nothing less than indissoluble, prevent me, as long as they subsist, from putting forth my energies as I should wish for the interests of America and to devote myself to its service without reservation. Nonetheless, there are societies[4] which do their best service when they are dissolved: a civil society which does not protect its most useful members, such as businessmen, sailors, and farmers, a society whose directors may not perform their duties according to the light of their consciences and work for the public good without being exposed to ruinous persecution—such a society which, as you may guess, Sir, is in the position of which I speak. Satisfied to live in obscurity, and even without a well-known name, I decided, in entering the Order of the Nobility, to undertake (as I did) a vigorous attempt to arouse open and declared *opposition*—an ingredient which there is the greatest need to preserve in a constitution like ours, which has a large dose of monarchy in it. In its very nature my purpose required that I renounce entirely any idea of making a fortune. I have calculated upon being able to do without one. Several years of retreat in the countryside plus a little philosophy had entirely weaned me from the attractions held by offices and the favor of the powerful. A rigid frugality, a very bourgeois style of living, without a coach or numerous servants or hunting dogs, etc., assured my independence. Who should know better than you, Sir, the annoyances inseparable from such an undertaking! Having foreseen them, in part, I accepted them with patience, in the constant hope that eventually I would be useful to my country. . . .

I should bring to a close here a letter which is already imper-

4. *Société* is an ambiguous term meaning both a business company and the political and social organization of a country.—*Ed.*

missibly long. I cannot do so, however, without informing you that I have observed that the negotiation of Messrs. Horneca and Fizeaux would probably be more successful if Congress issued bonds in proper form, *signed in the name of the entire assembly by its president and secretary, and under its seal,* instead of the promises signed by Messrs. Franklin, Lee, and Adams. This is approximately what the Dutch expect in contracts from their States. Congress should bind itself in the *most explicit* manner (and this is the cardinal point upon which all public credit rests) never to reduce the rate of interest during the promised terms. The term of ten years seems somewhat short to me. I would suggest 20 years at the option of the lender. The commissioners of Congress should be authorized to give receipts when they receive money, with a promise to furnish as soon as possible duly signed bonds to replace the receipts. Congress, to my way of thinking, should not omit anything which can contribute to its credit in this country. What resources does England find in her credit in critical circumstances! How much more vigorous would the naval operations of France be if she had not taken the imprudent step which has perhaps lost her forever the confidence of the Dutch! She ought to attempt to regain it at any price, even at the cost of complete compensation for the losses which the Dutch suffered during the most recent reduction of interest on government bonds. How easily the aid provided by a firm credit would enable United America to rid itself of a war which continues to interfere with its trade and sometimes still makes its friends tremble! Please excuse these reflections, Sir. They are the result of the most sincere affection for a people whom I have held dear since childhood, whom I held dear even before it existed.

Another cause of distrust which affects the credit of America is the false news reports which the English constantly put into circulation and the friends of the Americans cannot refute for lack of information. It is a matter of the highest importance to enable them to give an idea of what is really happening on that side of the ocean and the present state of affairs by means of authentic accounts, containing nothing which is not *exactly* true, not dissimulating even the mishaps inseparable from the chances of war. If you choose, Sir, to honor me with such a correspondence, you may be confident that I will put it to very good use. News reports communicated in semi-secrecy are more effective than those which are made public. Your letter, which I distributed among others in Amsterdam (with discretion, to be sure, and until now without providing copies) made a strong impression upon all those who read it. They are all sorry that such a fine and vigorous defense of the American cause remains buried in the correspondence file of an individual. A description of the present state of United America, its pleasures, the form of government of its various Republics, the ease with which foreigners can settle and earn a living, the cost of wild and cultivated land, food, supplies, etc., with a brief history of the present war *and the cruelties committed by E. . . . . .*—this would work wonders in a country where America is known only by what appears in the gazettes, but where there are, I assure you, a great number of honest people who. . . . But I was almost forgetting to be a Dutchman myself.

You may continue to write to me in English. As I have read a great deal in this language, I am quite at home in it, although I have never had occasion to write it. I believe, nonetheless, that I would soon be able to express myself intelligibly in it, for it is only recently that I began to write in French, which I had cultivated only by reading. I hope, indeed, Sir, I pine to make our exchange of letters serve as a base for a friendship which, founded upon our common affection for freedom and the interests of mankind, could only be of the firmest. I will strive to deserve such friendship while I beg you to believe that I am, with all the respect due to your virtue, your talent and your position, etc.

2. Van der Capellen to Dr. Richard Price, July 1, 1779.

Dear Friend,

Mr. Dentan has handed to me on your behalf the sermon mentioned. I have also received your letter of May 28. I am infinitely indebted to you for so much kindness. The marks of friendship with which you honor me are a great solace in my present situation. My affairs are so embroiled that it is impossible to predict how they will turn out, or at least that they will turn out well. I am the first whom they have dared to attack in this way. The privileges of the nobility were respected until now, but in the end nothing is sacred. They persist in refusing to try me according to the laws of the country, which my antagonists earlier had declared to be their intention; when they came to see that they would not be able to crush me by legal procedures, and that if they brought me to trial as they had threatened, they would certainly lose in a *fair* trial, they have changed their weapons and invented the expedient of attaining their goal (which is to expel me from the States Assembly of my province) without being compelled to institute an *action for slander* against me. . . .

Here is the letter of G[overnor] T[rumbull], of which you asked to have a copy. I have taken the liberty to add another by G[overnor] L[ivingston, of New Jersey], which I received recently. A Dutch translation is now in press. These letters have strongly impressed all who read them. That of G. L., being more recent, convinced many persons that the disunity which was said to be reigning in America and the widespread disposition to return to British rule are lies invented by those who find their profit in throwing a veil over the events in America. You can make whatever use of these letters you please; you are the master. Only, be so kind as not to say in public that you have got them from me. I believe that they would do good work published in several newspapers. Your sermon will be translated into Dutch. Everything which comes from you is well received here.

America is free and independent. Nothing seems more certain. But I am sorry, as you are, that intolerance should have had so much influence in the establishment of this new Republic. I hope nevertheless that in the future they will endeavor to broaden its base in this respect, and that even the Americans, as soon as they will be free and safe, will not lose from sight the interests of the poor Negroes who still groan under the yoke of slavery among them. Under present circumstances, it would be dangerous to give them freedom all at once; but not to do it when the situation is opportune and to perpetuate slavery in the thirteen States would be an action which would give the lie to the principles which America has always professed. A people which can bear the sight of human creatures treated like animals does not deserve to be free—the Dutch today have this callousness.—For three years now the Negroes have been no freer than before if they live in this so-called Republic. I am the only one to have protested against this revolting law. How happy I would be to quit this fatal continent! My nation, dear friend, has not become the enemy of England. It does not seek and does not want anything but freedom of trade based upon the Law of Nations and treaties—but England has violated treaties endlessly, despite all our protests, so that they no longer exist. Henceforth only the Law of Nations should control the actions of the two powers. . . .

b.

Ah! my countrymen! once more arm yourselves, and exert the interest of the republic; or, in other words, your own. The republic is your common property, not only the property of the Prince and his grandees, who deem us all, the whole nation of the Netherlands, the descendants of the free-born Batavians, their hereditary vassals; their sheep and cattle, which they have power and right to fleece, or to put to death, as their avarice or resentment may impel them; and they treat us agreeably to this estimation of us. The inhabitants of a country, the landholders, the burghers, and boors [peasants or farmers], the poor and the rich, the great and the *small*, all these together, are the true owners, Lords and masters of their country; these ought to appoint governors, and to establish laws. A nation is a great society, in political partnership; the rulers, the chiefs, the magistrates, the Prince, those, in short, who constitute the acting sovereignty, are but directors, commanders, and treasurers of that society; and in their respective capacities, or collectively, they are of less consequence than its members, that is, than the collective body of the nation. For instance, the East India Company is a great association of merchants, united for the purpose of trading to India. They are too numerous, and they live at too great a distance from each other to meet constantly when it is necessary, and to direct, by personal attendance, the business of their company, which besides requires more skill and knowledge than all the members may individually possess; therefore they very wisely appoint directors, commanders, and treasurers, whom they pay for their trouble, and to whom they give no greater share of power than the business requires, for which they are engaged. The directors have naturally a greater authority than any single member, or even any great number of members, which makes not a *majority;* but if all the members, or a decided majority, insist on having an alteration in the government or direction of the company's, that is, of their own affairs, then it is the duty of the having an alteration in the government or direction of the commands of the latter, a majority of whom are the real owners, masters, and lords of the company.

It is just as with the great society of a nation. The great one who rules over you, the Prince, or whoever has any power in the public affairs, exercises that power in your name, and their authority is derived from *you*. You are the members, the owners, and masters of the national society which bears the title of the *United Nether-lands*. The great ones, on the contrary, are but directors and treasurers of this society. You pay them out of your own, i.e. out of the public purse. They are thus in your service; they are your servants; they are accountable to the majority of numbers, and in duty bound to obey your commands.

Besides, all men are born free: by nature, no one is under the command of another. Though some have brighter talents, more bodily strength, or a greater share of fortune than others, yet these accidents do not give them who are more intelligent, stronger and richer, any right to lord it over the simpler, weaker, and poorer people. God, our common Father, created man to be happy; and ordered every one, without exception, to promote the happiness of his fellow-creatures to the utmost of his power. To obtain this great object of the Creator, that is, to promote our common happiness, mankind has found it necessary to join in great societies, and to associate even by millions. Observe that in these societies, all the members are equal by nature; no member is subject to another. In these great societies, commonly called civil societies, the members join together to promote the mutual happiness, to defend their property and other rights, legally acquired.

44. Conservative Suggestions for Reform

The realization of the need for reforms and ideas about what measures could be taken for improvement in the condition of the country were not the monopoly of the Patriots, although they were by inclination and by situation an intrinsically reformist party. One of the most acute analyses of the reason, character, and extent of the decline of the Dutch Republic in the nineteenth century came from the pen of a conservative politician, Laurens Pieter van de Spiegel (1736–1800) in 1782. At that time Van de Spiegel had been secretary of the States of Zeeland for two years, but he was named Councilor Pensionary of Zeeland in 1785 and then was named to the same office in Holland in 1787. In international affairs Van de Spiegel was a strong advocate of the alliances with England and Prussia, thanks to which the Patriot movement was crushed by Prussian military intervention in 1787. In domestic politics Van de Spiegel combined vigorous support for the maintenance of the power of the hereditary stadholder, William V, with considerable understanding of the reasons for the country's difficulties and the need to take measures to remedy them. He was therefore part of the general movement of advocates of enlightened reform from above, carried through by consolidated princely author-ity, that marked not only such rulers as Joseph II of Austria but such ministers of state as Struensee in Denmark and Pombal in Portugal. While the chief political officer of Holland, and hence in effect William V's prime minister, he was able, with the help of the stad-holder's wife, Wilhelmina of Prussia, to stir the indolent Prince of Orange to accept reform of the system of provincial contributions to the expenses of the national government (1792) and the taking over of the second West India Company by the state (1793). Van de Spiegel was imprisoned upon the establishment of the Batavian Republic in 1795, was released in 1798, and went to Germany to serve the exiled stadholder until 1800, when he died. His *Sketch of a Remonstrance on the Intrinsic and Relative Power of the Republic* was written in June, 1782; although it remained in manuscript until published by a Dutch scholar in 1958, it seems to have been widely read in its time by an inner circle of Dutch political leaders.

Source: Johan de Vries, "Van de Spiegel's 'Schets tot een vertoog over de intrinseque en relative magt van de Republijk' (1782)," *Economisch-Historisch Jaarboek*, XXVII (1958), pp. 87–96. Translated from the Dutch by Herbert H. Rowen.

IF WHAT we hear and read every day about the declining situation of the Republic were only half true, it would be marching steadily toward its downfall. This decline is presented in the strongest light and in all sorts of ways, even in public documents of state, so that almost no one doubts that it is happening. Yet it is worth looking at carefully, for if it is true that the Republic is moving toward its ruin, then quick means must be sought to resist this decline as much as possible; but if it is not true, we must put a stop to such com-plaints, which only diminish us in our own eyes and make our neighbors scorn us. The great question then, is this: whether the Republic has suffered a real loss in domestic prosperity and strength, and how, and to compare its strength to that of other powers. Therefore, we need to consider: 1. the domestic strength of the Republic, not so much to determine its precise present level as to compare it with the situation when it was prosperous; 2. to consider this strength in relation to that of other powers and in this way to determine its natural position among the sovereign states.

I calculate that the Republic was at its most prosperous at the time of or shortly after the Peace of Münster.[5]

Almost the only trading nation in Europe, thanks to her navy mistress of the seas, respected on land thanks to possession of the best-trained armies, and still close to that purity of morals which adorns rising Republics in their beginnings, it saw itself confirmed by a glorious peace in the enjoyment of all the privileges achieved by eighty years of struggle. Its old enemy, Spain, continued at war with France, leaving trade with both kingdoms to the Republic. The Baltic powers were divided among themselves, and wise policy indicated that we should feed this fire so that we would remain masters of the Baltic trade, with the Hanseatic towns having only their small share. The only power which could stand in our way was England, which in the time of Charles I possessed not even three ships of 300 tons but counted four hundred ships of this size under Charles II. This was the result of the Navigation Act adopted by Cromwell in 1652 and renewed under Charles II in 1660.

Trade therefore flourished and because there was little competition from other nations profits could not but be great. But the objects of trade were nowhere near as varied as at present. The refinements of luxury have increased their number many-fold: civilization penetrated countries which had been almost barbarous, and its progress has opened up new channels of trade. The colonies in the West Indies, either just born or in their infancy, doubled the supply of necessities. Therefore, the competition of the other nations of Europe could not do us as much harm as is usually thought, because trade expanded and the branches of trade increased at the same time as their competition grew.

As for profits, it is certain that a merchant had to make more than now in order to maintain himself. First of all, the interest rate on money was much higher. In 1649, the bonds of the States General still had to pay six and a quarter percent and businessmen therefore had to pay even higher rates. Secondly, the services at the disposal of trade have increased greatly in the Republic since then. Think of the mails, the deposit banks in the large trading towns,

5. 1648.—Ed.

the easy availability of insurance, the low interest on commodity loans, the discounting of bills of exchange, and the like. All of this shows that a merchant can be satisfied now with smaller profits.

Let us examine more closely our relative strength and prosperity in that era of prosperity and at the present time. The strength of the nation, as was argued very perceptively by the Council of State in its presentation of the military budget of the Union for 1766, consists in having a numerous people and in their being put to wise use by the government. Our first question will be directed to the first point, and the second point will be the subject of our second question.

Whether or not a nation is populous is purely relative to the space which it must fill: twenty million people are too few for the extensive Russian empire, while two million are a great many for a tiny country like our Republic and make us the most crowded country in the world, probably not excepting China. We must consider the population of the Republic as consisting not merely of so many persons considered individually, but as so many persons of substance, each owning wealth of his own, large or small, or able to gain property by his activity. Their prosperity constantly attracts foreigners who wish to share in it; their wealth enables them to take other men into their service in time of need unless prevented by external circumstances, and they are therefore always able to bring the population to the size which they find to be necessary in the circumstances. Examples of this are to be seen in shipping, the army, sometimes in agriculture and in dike work, and especially, in the settling of colonies.

Is the population smaller now than in the happy times which are the first term in our comparison? It actually appears that it is not smaller but larger. How many cities in the Republic have not greatly extended their boundaries in that time? Amsterdam numbers about 100,000 inhabitants more than then. Villages in Holland and some other provinces have grown into small towns. The countryside between the principal cities is filled with people. It is true that fewer houses seemed to be occupied in many other cities, particularly further inland, but if we bring these cities back within their old ring walls, take away the growth usually undertaken with imprudent expectations on the basis of temporary prosperity, we shall see whether in fact they have lost so much. Besides, their loss, even if true, cannot weigh heavily as against the increase in other cities.

But is it possible that the people's means of subsistence have diminished? I see, at bottom, three ways the people of this country support themselves: agriculture, handicrafts, and commerce. I include the colonies and fisheries in agriculture, because their products can be considered as growing out of the soil of the fatherland. It cannot be denied that there is a great decline in some of these branches of activity, but on the other hand there is great growth in others, and we are considering prosperity as a whole and not in its components. The fisheries and handicrafts have suffered the most, the former indeed principally as a result of the competition of other nations, but the latter because of various inevitable causes which in my opinion leave some reason for hope, but not definite assurances of improvement. First of all, the unending struggle between domestic manufactures and free (foreign) trade and experience has taught everywhere that one expands at the expense of the other. Secondly, the abundance of money and its resulting decline in value have so increased wages of artisans in this country that our countrymen cannot sell their wares in competition with foreigners. In the third place, it must be admitted that the progress of other nations in this field has been greater than ours and that they surpass our workshops in the appearance and variety of styles of their products. It is beyond the purpose of our demonstration to go further into this matter. Let us see how the other branches of economic activity have fared.

Domestic agriculture has undoubtedly grown much larger, and it continues to expand by bringing new lands into cultivation in the provinces north of the rivers and in States Brabant for the production of grain, buckwheat, and timber; by the diking of thousands of acres in States Flanders which were flooded during the Spanish War and remained under water long after peace was made; and finally by the reclamation of polders [low-lying land] from the sea in Flanders and Zeeland, and by drainage in Holland. The treasures which have been won by these dikings, especially in Zeeland, would exceed our dreams if we could make an accurate count of them. Foreign agriculture has grown even more vigorously in the new colonies acquired or established since the Peace of Münster; their produce—sugar, coffee, cocoa, tobacco, cotton—are new crops which did not previously grow on any part of the soil of this country.

Let us now turn our attention to commerce. Here too we recognize that some branches of trade have declined, for it would be absurd to claim that all have prospered equally. The nature of the business is opposed to it. The question, however, is whether these losses are not greatly compensated by the establishment of new branches of trade and by the growth of others.

1. The West Indian colonies require a mass of necessities in which there was formerly no trade.

2. They send back annually about 200 ships laden with crops, not one of which used to be carried.

3. The trade in tobacco, which this present war[6] has caused to settle so strongly in Amsterdam, is a wholly new and important branch of commerce, and it extends to all Europe.

4. Coffee and tea have also become new articles of commerce.

5. Increased wealth in Europe and the colonies has brought into trade hundreds of commodities our ancestors never thought of.

6. The mass of gold slowly accumulated in the Republic has created a new commodity which, although it is not material, nonetheless gives employment to a very large number of people; I mean trade in shares and other credit instruments drawn upon this land, the colonies, foreign powers, etc.

7. Add to this the business of monetary exchange, which similarly is a result of the abundance of money.

If anyone still doubts whether the prosperity of the country has gone forward or backward in a good hundred years, let him explain the origin of the immense treasures which the Republic now possesses in larger quantities than at the time of the Peace of Münster. I calculate these treasures at 1,000 million guilders. This is the basis of my calculation:

England, which had no debts a hundred years ago, now owes about £200 million sterling; of this, the Republic has at least £30 million but because this capital is not all paid in, I put it at only 280 million guilders.

The Republic has in France somewhat over rather than under 50 million livres, [or] 25 million guilders.

Spain, the German princes, Denmark, Sweden, Russia, 30 million guilders.

Transactions with colonies, our own and foreign, 140 million guilders.

6. The Anglo-Dutch War of 1780-1784.—*Ed.*

Bonds issued by the provinces, cities, admiralties and other corporations in the Republic (not including shares in the East and West India Companies), issued more than a hundred years ago, about 425 million guilders.

N. B. In 1648 Holland a bonded debt of only about 120 millions.

In the exchange business and credit to foreign merchants; little has been known until now and it can be determined only very approximately, but certainly it is not set too high a figure if calculated at 50 million guilders.

Total: 950 million guilders.

Add to this the increased display of worked gold, silver, and jewelry, the much greater mass of idle money (proof of this is that the interest rate, which was still six and one-quarter percent shortly before the Peace of Münster and was reduced to four percent seven years after the Peace, is now two and one-half percent as a result of the abundance of money), and we shall not be far off if we set the increase of capital in the Republic at 1,000 millions. Let us now take this thousand million to be only 900 million, with an average interest rate of three percent; then the inhabitants of the Republic have an annual income from this accumulated capital of twenty-seven million guilders. Can we not believe that such great earnings outweigh the loss of some branches of commerce, and that a land where such profits are made does not have good reason to complain about general decline? It is obvious that I do not wish to consider these securities as real property; I want to point out that they are paid for with money and that before these immense sums can be spent, they must first be earned.

It is this that I consider to be the intrinsic strength and prosperity of the Republic in comparison with its situation when it was at its recognized height of prosperity.

How long this prosperity will last is hidden in the decisions of Providence. Events loom in the distance whose consequences no one can foresee. Will the new Republic of the Thirteen States of North America bring as much profit to our commerce and manufactures as many persons hope? Or will it steal from us the trade in Baltic goods to southern Europe which also grow in North America? Shall we then be compelled to pay a negative balance in our trade to both northern and southern Europe? Will the Republic [of the United Provinces], after the simulated sale of its ships during this war, ever recover the same extensive trade it had under its own flag? And will not other states take measures to make it difficult to re-establish this shipping? And even if this doesn't happen, haven't foreigners learned more than enough of the fine points of commerce to be able to conduct it now by themselves? Won't the Baltic powers, which now have erected a bridge for the protection of their shipping,[7] build their own merchant fleet and protect them? The answer to these and similar questions must come from time, which solves all political riddles.

Let us now consider the strength of the republic from the side of government, which also has to play its part. In this respect we must make our comparison not with the strength of the former prosperous time but with the exigencies of the present time; we must investigate whether the domestic strength and prosperity of the Republic, which on the whole remains the same as they have always been, now provide sufficient resources to support it against the might of other powers which are possible enemies. This is a question which is very difficult to answer. If the efforts of powers in wartime were all proportional to their intrinsic strength and income, then a parallel could be drawn. If we know, for example, that France has an income of 200 millions, the Emperor 100 million, and the Republic not quite 40 millions, then we can easily establish the situation of our commonwealth relative to these powers. But the forces of almost all the powers of Europe are extended far beyond their real resources. Some have arrived at a situation for which the only cure is a violent revolution in their finances. The Republic cannot and may not measure itself against such states. It must also be observed that if we ask whether a state possesses the strength to defend itself against its enemies, we do not assume that this defense must be conducted alone and by its own resources; neither the strength nor the numbers of aggressors can be defined in advance and hence the necessary forces of resistance cannot be either.

There have been writers who maintain that the Republic can defend itself against any foreign attack without alliances or the help of friends, thanks to its local situation and strength. They add specious arguments which can be confuted by investigation, however, and were in fact refuted by the Council of State in the

7. The so-called League of Armed Neutrality, made in 1780 by Russia, Denmark, Sweden, and Prussia.—*Ed.*

general military budget for the year 1724. In this regard the Republic stands in the same position that other states do; if an attack is greater than can be resisted by one's own strength, one must seek the help of friends. When danger is at the door, however, such friendship and alliance cannot always be found as quickly as they are needed. Who should be the natural allies of the Republic is another question which is better answered by particular circumstances than by deductive reasoning. Our forefathers joined in the closest alliance with France in order to humble the House of Austria[8] and when this aim had been achieved, they concluded the Peace of Münster which had as one of its political purposes to throw off the bonds of French influence. Afterwards the state joined with England to oppose the ambition of Louis XIV, and since then England has been considered as our natural ally. Now the "system" has been reversed once more: England passes for our hereditary foe and France for our natural friend. The way people think about the constitution of the form of government in the Republic contributes not a little to such changes of "system."

Let us return to the question we posed. To answer it honestly, we must say that the Republic has fallen far below the situation which it used to have relative to other powers, and that all the prosperity and strength of the inhabitants, even if wisely employed, can no longer provide it with the resources which it formerly derived from them.

45. An Argument against Popular Rule, by a Former Patriot

The Patriot movement forced political debate to look more closely at fundamentals of political life—the purposes of power, the best means of achieving them, the place of various groups in the state. One of the most closely argued defenses of the traditional regime came in 1792 from the pen of a former Patriot. Joachim van Rendorp, Vrijheer (Baron) of Marquette (1728–1792), had entered political life on the side of the democratic wing of the Patriots, but this wealthy Amsterdam regent and patrician, who was four times a burgomaster of the city, broke with the Patriots when they turned to the French monarchy for external support during and after the Fourth Anglo-Dutch war (1780–1784). He became in turn an advocate of a stadholdership more effectively limited by the power of the States, and then a staunch Orangist. Not surprisingly, the Patriots against whom he had turned attacked him as an "Aristocrat," a term which still had its Aristotelian

8. Habsburg.—*Ed.*

sense of one who participated in government by a few, but later, during the revolutionary period, came to mean a member of the nobility or other class of hereditary privilege.

In 1792, Rendorp published two volumes of memoirs "to explain what happened during the most recent war with England." In the introduction, a section of which is translated below, he sets forth his apologia for his shift of opinions. His arguments are interesting for the way in which they combine the principle that government exists to bring the greatest prosperity to the people as a whole, which is central to Enlightenment political thought, with the assertion that this aim was best achieved through the power of a stadholder and the regents. His arguments have something of the shape of Edmund Burke's in the *Reflections on the French Revolution*, the thoughtfulness of an intelligent conservative with a reformer's past, and the founding of the utility of traditional government upon the weaknesses of men.

Source: Joachim Rendorp, *Memorien dienende tot Opheldering, van het Gebeurde, Geduurende den laatsten Engelschen Oorlog*, 2 vols. (Amsterdam: Johannes Allart, 1792), Vol. I, pp. 12–21. Translated from the Dutch by Herbert H. Rowen.

ONE OF the principal accusations made against me was that of *Anglomania*. I freely confess that I wholly disapproved the war with England when it began, while it was being waged, and when it ended, because it was undertaken recklessly, fought badly, and concluded shamefully; that I would rather have seen an attempt made to obtain a better peace through separate negotiations, or at least that we had not trusted the Court of Versailles so rashly that we found ourselves compelled to accept a peace like this when that Court forced it upon us; and that I never was able to watch with approval while the Republic was subjected to the whim of the French Court in pretended recognition for its services during a war which in part it brought upon our heads, and while an effort was made to make the Republic more dependent upon France than it had ever been upon England.

But if I had developed any special predilection for England, any concern for special advantage or for increasing or just confirming influence, any base indulgence for the stadholder's way of thinking, I would despise myself: as I despise those who first fed the flames of this war out of a concern for their own advantage and to promote their private businesses, their political opinions, or anything else; who then catered to the wishes of France and discussed the most secret affairs of state with the French ambassador, and protected a number of seditious foreigners who helped them increase the agitation of popular feelings; and who further employed every kind of wile to achieve their aims, which, as later became evident, were none other than to change the form of government and to turn everything topsy-turvy.

The name of *Aristocrat* which was later conferred upon me was not yet in fashion. We can be sure that it was used as a taunt; but if it meant someone in whose judgment the citizens of our country had a right to no more or greater influence in the election of members of the government or in the conduct of its business than they had had ever since the foundation of the Republic in accordance with the privileges of the cities during the periods with and without stadholders, then I cannot deny it is a *title* which I deserve.

The only goal of all governments is to obtain the greatest possible prosperity of all members of society. If they are happy and their felicity is confirmed by continued experience, then the question *whether another and different form of government is better than that under which they live* is purely speculative. The leaders of those obviously bent on changing the constitution during the recent troubles should have given some thought to this, at least if they were acting in good faith.

Who will deny that there are many faults in our form of government? That the stadholders too often went beyond the bounds of their legitimate but inadequately defined authority? That the members of government during the stadholderless periods often neglected the general welfare out of concern for the interests of their cities or even for their own personal interests? That the structure of our form of government often results in faulty conduct of the affairs of state?

I willingly admit, therefore, that it would be possible to invent a better form of government. But the question is, would making changes in the present constitution make our country and its people happier? Or supposing that this were indeed true, can we flatter ourselves that we are able to change the constitution as it has been established for more than two hundred years without inflicting such a shock upon the country that every part of public administration will be adrift and without bearings, at least for some time? And finally, will the inhabitants (I mean men of property and not the riff-raff) be happier with the influence it is intended to confer on them under the common but vague term of "influence of the people"? That is, will our trade be more prosperous, our persons and property better protected from all violence, in a word, will our civil freedom be any greater than during the two hundred years which the present constitution has endured?

There is a clamor against "government by the Families." I am far from approving that anyone should seek a place in government in order to advance his relatives, but will it be any better if the government is elected by the citizens? Are most ordinary citizens, who would surely form the majority in an election, in a position to judge the abilities which are needed to guide affairs of state? Won't the mass of the electorate be led by intriguers or by a few influential men? Have we not recently seen what kind of men are able to win the trust of the crowd? Can we therefore expect that those elected to office will be competent and worthy men? Are those who arouse the common man by their intrigues, or who are favored by those who would set themselves up as the leaders of the crowd, better fitted to govern than those who get offices now through the influence of His Highness[9] or their families? All things which require the intervention of human passions are usually, if not always, marked by faults: and that is always how it is with the grant of offices and positions, for favor will always play a part in it. Certainly there can be no better and more appropriate way to grant office than to entrust the task to *one* man, for he cannot help but have fewer personal relations to all members of society and hence will be more impartial. Has not experience taught that such relations are *multiplied* by the number of those who stand in his favor, and that in fact it is not the Prince but his favorites who grant offices?

Let us just look at the matter with an historical and impartial eye. Who did the shrieking during the various political revolutions which occurred in our country? I point to the friends of the House of Orange who were out of power during the stadholderless periods and wanted the Prince in power in order to increase their own authority, and to those who in the periods when there was a stadholder did not in their own opinion have as much authority in the government as they should or who had hardened their hearts against the stadholder because of some harm they had suffered.

9. The Prince of Orange.—*Ed.*

The former shouted (and it was they who gave the tone to the people's voice) that only self-interest was practiced and the country's business was being neglected. The others in turn shouted that freedom was in danger, that the stadholder was trampling on privileges and rights.

Meanwhile how did things go in our country? Our persons and our property were as safe when there was no stadholder as when there was one and the simplest inhabitant could lead a calm life in his status, safe from the supremacy of the notables.

The Republic experienced glorious moments when there was a stadholder and when there was none, but it is worth observing that the moments of greatest glory when there was no stadholder occurred when the leadership of the government was in the hands of one or a few men, who in fact had the authority of a stadholder and hence were able to make the numerous wheels of general government, which are turned by so many hands, all move to one and the same purpose.

This observation, which I believe is supported by the history of our country, brought me, during the time when I gained some insight into the country's affairs, to the conclusion that the office of stadholder is a necessary part of our constitution, and that, although there have been times when it was thought possible to do without a stadholder in his various capacities, these were always times which ended in revolts and violence. One reason was that the Dutch people as a whole learned devotion to the House of Orange from childhood; another, that those who did not have a share in the government let no opportunity pass to make use of this inclination by the people in the hope of enjoying the pleasure and advantage of governing in their turn.

This sort of selfish people (for such we must call them) must be distinguished from those who truly love their fatherland, seek neither private advantage nor public power, but use more exalted ideas to consider the conduct of government. They see the failings that do exist and they try to remedy them, but, alas! they lose sight of the fact that the perfect government which they want for their fatherland is not possible. Or they forget that even if it were possible, the means which would have to be used to establish it would put the commonwealth in danger of being turned topsy-turvy before the end they desired was attained. Hugo de Groot once rightly remarked that men should avoid making changes in old ways of government: *that such changes are dangerous and it is safer to accommodate oneself to faults to which the people are accustomed than to attempt to reform them.*

That is my way of thinking. Is it *Aristocratic?* So be it, unless by an *Aristocrat* we mean someone who seeks advancement in government for the sake of personal advantage or political power, who in office considers only himself and not the general good and devotes his authority and influence only to helping and favoring his relatives. In that case, I ask with a calm mind what honorable man dares give me that title?

46. Reform of the State: A Patriot Vision

The repression of 1787, which sent numerous leading Patriots fleeing into exile, did not halt their activity. France became their haven especially after the onset of revolution in Paris in 1789, and they drew upon their observations of a country deliberately and systematically revising its institutions to revise their own ideas on reform of the Dutch state. In general they favored for the Netherlands a unitary state such as had emerged in France; they too wanted to abolish or at least restrict the historic provinces, and hence they saw federalism, such as many Frenchmen had advocated in the early years of the revolution, as the bane of the traditional Dutch system of government. But they also envisioned a reform for the sake of efficiency, by putting a modern functional government through ministers with defined tasks and distinct legislative and executive powers in place of the cumbersome machinery of rule in the United Provinces. Obviously, they wanted no more part of a hereditary stadholder than the French republicans did of a king. Early in 1793, two Patriots resident in Paris, the nobleman Robert Jasper Capellen, baron van der Marsch, and the wealthy banker, Balthazar Elias Abbema, drew up a brief sketch of their ideas for a new constitution to be adopted by a "National Convention" of the Batavians, as it was fashionable among the Patriots to call the Dutch people. The document was published in Dutch with a French translation in February and sent to the Netherlands. Some of its ideas were eventually adopted in the constitution worked out under the Batavian Republic created in 1795.

Source: "Schets tot grondslag eener nieuwe constitutie voor de Republiek der Bataven," in *Gedenkstukken der Algemeene Geschiedenis van Nederland van 1795 tot 1840,* ed. H. T. Colenbrander (The Hague: Martinus Nijhoff, 1905), Vol. I, pp. 107–111. Translated from the Dutch by Herbert H. Rowen.

First Article: on Sovereignty

According to the immutable first principles of the rights of man, and of freedom and equality, the Batavian people must be recognized as the sole and only legitimate sovereign.

Life, personal freedom, and possessions stand under the protection of the whole people.

Since it is impossible for all the people to meet in a single body to deliberate upon its interests, it naturally follows that its power must be exercised by representatives, and that the people themselves must elect these representatives freely and for a definite time.

Each citizen who has reached the age of eighteen years completed; who has an independent livelihood from his possessions, his abilities, or the work of his hands, and therefore has an essential interest in the general welfare, must have the right to cast his vote in the elections and the deliberations of the primary or fundamental assemblies; this right must not be granted, on the contrary, to servants or those who have been driven by their poverty to the unfortunate necessity of living on public charity, for such persons cannot be considered as being fully independent.

Each citizen, whatever his religious persuasion, who has received the majority of votes according to the established procedures, shall be eligible for all public offices.

Second Article: on the Form of Government

The Republic must be one and indivisible.

The supreme power entrusted by the people to their representatives shall rest in a National Assembly, consisting of deputies from the various departments freely chosen by the people.

The first Assembly shall draw up the constitution of the Republic in all its parts.

When the National Assembly shall have completed this work, it shall present this constitution as a whole to the people to be examined in their fundamental assemblies, and the people will then themselves decide by virtue of their sovereignty the form of government which will be judged to be most suited for maintaining their natural rights and their freedom and independence.

When the constitution shall have been ratified in this way by the majority of the people, no change shall be permitted to be made in it during the period of six years; but after the expiry of such time, the National Assembly shall again review all points and deliberate upon the changes which experience shall have taught to be necessary for the general happiness.

All the changes in the fundamental laws of the constitution must in turn require new ratification by the sovereign people themselves according to the same procedure followed for the constitution itself.

The National Assembly shall be renewed every two years by new elections of representatives.

No citizens shall be reelected to it except after an interval of two years.

The National Assemblies which shall follow that which has made the constitution shall have the legislative power in all matters resulting from the fundamental principles of the constitution.

They shall principally keep a watchful eye upon the executive power; they shall pay particular attention to public administration, finances, peace, war, treaties, commerce, and in general all aspects of sovereignty.

Regulatory and administrative laws shall receive their force and effect from the approval of the Executive Council, which shall promulgate them.

· The National Assembly shall determine annually the manner, quantity, and distribution of public taxation.

No war shall be declared which is not defensive, because offensive wars are in conflict with the justice of a free people. In the event of war the Executive Council shall be required to present a reasoned proposal in favor of its declaration to the National Assembly, which shall decide upon it by decree.

Treaties of peace, alliance, and commerce shall be decided in the same way by the National Assembly upon the basis of a reasoned proposal of the Executive Council, but the treaties shall not enter into force before they have been proposed to the people gathered in primary assemblies and approved by a majority of votes.

The Republic shall be divided into departments, the departments into districts, the districts into municipalities or urban Assemblies.

The colonies in Asia, Africa, the continent of America and the islands[10] shall be admitted in the same manner to representation in the National Assembly.

The number of departments, including the colonies, shall not be higher than twenty-four.

The representation of each department shall be determined by its size and population: provided, that a single department shall not be able to send more than five nor less than three deputies to the National Assembly, so that the number of deliberating members shall not be over one hundred.

Third Article: on the Different Religious Persuasions

All religions shall be permitted; and whenever a specified number of citizens shall meet at one place, the national treasury shall pay the costs of whatever ministry they shall choose or accept.

No one may be excluded from public offices because of his religious convictions.

Fourth Article: on the Executive Power

The executive power shall be subject to and dependent upon the Legislative Power of the National Assembly, which shall choose the ministers individually by vote.

The ministers shall be responsible individually and as a group.

The executive power shall consist in seven ministers, who shall meet each day and keep a watchful eye upon each other.

All constitutional laws ratified by the people shall be promulgated and applied by the Executive Council and by each of its members in his department.

The regulatory laws of the National Assembly shall be examined in the Executive Council, which shall have the right to present its obervations upon them to the said Assembly; but if a law contains nothing which is contrary to the constitution, and if the Legislative Assembly persists in its decision, then the Executive Council shall be obligated to promulgate and apply it.

In case of hostile attack or war preparations from the side of other peoples, the Executive Council shall present a reasoned proposal for war to the National Assembly.

10. The Dutch islands in the Caribbean.—*Ed.*

The same shall be done with regard to proposals for treaties of peace, alliance, and commerce.

The Executive Council shall likewise examine all general and particular matters which the National Assembly shall put into its hands, whether to transmit its opinions thereon or to issue a reasoned report.

The Minister of Foreign Affairs shall maintain all political relations with free peoples, friends, and allies; and since the Batavian people by their situation and relations are principally a trading people, he shall devote himself principally to promoting the commercial interests of the people with other trading peoples.

He shall have the nomination of all agents sent abroad in the name of the nation.

The Minister of Justice shall have supervision over all courts, judges in criminal cases, as well as juries for the examination of the charge and the verdict.

No death sentence shall be executed before he has signed it and given his order.

He shall have the nomination of all judges trying capital crimes.

In case the National Assembly which shall establish the new constitution shall not be able to complete the work of preparing a new code of civil and criminal law (which is most necessary because of the present differences in civil law and the arbitrary element in criminal laws), he shall busy himself without delay with bringing the law code into order, so that the second National Assembly can adopt these laws which are so necessary for the general welfare.

The Minister of the Navy shall have the administration and supervision of the maintenance, repair, construction, and equipment of the warships of the Republic, to the end that a formidable fleet shall always be ready in order to be able to protect vigorously commerce and colonies, which are rich sources of national prosperity. He shall be responsible for the supplies for the ships and their crews. He shall name the officers, including the ships' captains.

The Minister of War shall have administration over the regular army, the volunteers, and the national guards; over fortifications, inundations, and arsenals; over the arming, clothing, and equipment of the troops; over the quartering, payment, and discipline of the armed forces. He shall have the nomination to military posts up to the grade of colonel, but following the rules on promotion which shall be determined later.

The Minister of Colonies shall maintain a continuous correspondence with all colonial administrations and keep a watchful eye over them; he shall provide the necessary supplies for the military forces and other public establishments in the colonies which are paid out of the national treasury. He shall examine all requests made to him for assistance, and work in this respect in combination with the Minister of War and the Minister of the Navy, so far as each is specially involved; in general he will have charge of all matters concerning the interests and affairs of the Colonies. He shall furthermore have the nomination to all representative posts of the nation in the colonies.

The Minister of Finances shall have supervision over the collection of public taxation, which the National Assembly will determine annually; he shall issue payment orders for all expenditures defined by law; he shall draft and propose taxes which are least burdensome in meeting the public needs, as well as for payment of the interest and installments of the capital of the national debt; in general he shall be responsible for everything relating to the finances of the state.

The Minister of Internal Affairs shall maintain a continuous correspondence with all the internal administrations of the departments of the Republic; he shall have supervision over the dispatch of all laws; he shall have the superior administration over dikes, sluices, marshes, reclamations, peat-digging, and over the mints, posts, stage-coaches, ships, and canal-boats; over public education, national property, public foundations, and buildings.

Each minister shall be held to account for the funds given to him for the maintenance of his department, and they must organize their offices in the least costly way and that most suitable for a rapid dispatch of business.

Each minister shall individually give an account annually to the Assembly of the Executive Council, which shall then give a general report to the National Assembly.

The negotiators at Arras in early January, 1579, who reached an agreement bringing back the Catholic rebels of the Walloon provinces of the southern Netherlands to the allegiance of Philip II had no notion that they were taking the first step in the creation of a new nation. They sought only to restore peace and repose in the Netherlands under Philip's authority, but with respect for the traditional political rights of the provinces and to end the "excesses" of the Calvinists, who had control not only of the principal provinces north of the river line of Rhine and Meuse, but also in many of the great Flemish and Brabant towns south of it, like Bruges, Ghent, and Antwerp. Just as the Prince of Orange and the rebels in Holland and Zeeland had not yet limited their vision to defending the North, far less to creating an independent state there, so the Duke of Parma and the reconciled Catholics did not yet accept the permanency of the rule of their opponents above the river line. But military and political events—the inability of Parma to sustain his northward course of triumph, the consolidation of political authority in an effectively independent regime in the North, the closing of the "garden" of the Dutch Republic and its conquests below the river line under Princes Maurice and Frederick Henry—led to the emergence of two states in the Low Countries. One—the independent United Provinces—has been observed in its development in the previous chapters of this book; the other—the provinces which remained under the sovereignty first of the Spanish Habsburgs until the Peace of Utrecht in 1713, and then of the Austrian Habsburgs until the conquest by French revolutionary armies after 1792—remained dependent upon what was essentially a foreign dynasty, but maintained its sense of distinctness, both from the other states under the rule of their Habsburg lords, and from the preponderantly Calvinist Dutch state to the north, and it became the basis of the modern nation of Belgium. It is its history from 1579 until 1789 which we trace, all too briefly, in this final chapter.

47. A Separate Union in the South

When leaders of the Walloon provinces and towns began to display second thoughts about the rebellion because of the conduct of the

Calvinists, especially in Ghent, and the depradations of troops in the service of William of Orange, Alexander Farnese, the Prince of Parma, offered the States of Hainaut and Tournaisis and the towns of Lille, Douai, and Orchies, the restoration of the situation as it had been under Charles V provided that the Catholic religion was maintained and the sovereignty of Philip II was accepted again. Discussions among the Walloons extended to include Artois, and an agreement—called the Union of Arras—was reached on January 6, 1579, to come to terms with Parma on these conditions. King Philip gave his approval, which meant abandonment of his absolutist aspirations for the Low Countries for the sake of the preservation of Roman Catholicism and his sovereignty. After several months of difficult negotiations, the leaders of the Union of Arras concluded a formal treaty with Parma, called the Treaty of Arras, on May 17, 1579; it was accepted by the king in September, and formally proclaimed in October. Even though the promised withdrawal of the Spanish troops did not occur, the agreement remained in force because blame was put on the leaders of the rebellion, which continued unabated. The chief provisions of the treaty of May 17 are given below.

Source: "Articles de la Paix concluë entre les Députéz du Prince de Parme et les Provinces Valonnes, savoir le Hainault, l'Artois, les Villes de Douai, l'Isle, Orchies, &c. à Arras le 17 Mai, 1579," in du Mont, Vol. V, part i, pp. 350–355. Translated from the French by Herbert H. Rowen.

I.

First, the negotiations of the Pacification of Ghent, the Union, Perpetual Edict and His Majesty's Ratification, will remain in full force and vigor and shall be put into effect in all points.

II.

And in order to maintain appreciably better confidence among the subjects of His Majesty by means of a good Union and accord in the service of God for the preservation of the Roman, Apostolic, and Catholic religion, and obedience to His Majesty, together with the repose and prosperity of the country, both parties consent to a perpetual amnesty for all things that may have been said or done in any way whatsoever since the beginning of hostilities, or in consequence of them; and these things shall not be made the subject of investigations or accusations by judges, prosecuting attorneys, or others, as if these events had never occurred; and to this end all sentences, decrees, and edicts rendered either in this country or in any other land under His Majesty's jurisdiction in connection with the former troubles, shall be nullified and erased from their records, with full release and indemnity for all persons included in this agreement. However, there shall be excluded all rebels, exiles, whether in exile, in prison, or ordered to trial by the governors and magistrates of the contracting lands, and they shall not be able to plead innocence of the crimes with which they are charged and will not be included in this present amnesty and pardon. But there shall be published, as necessary, edicts expressly forbidding all persons without exception to reproach anyone because of the past events.

III.

His Majesty will confirm and approve all the actions, donations, and agreements of the Archduke, the States, the Council of State, which are not contrary to the Pacification of Ghent, the Union which followed it, the Perpetual Edict, and the rights, privileges, and liberties of the provinces, in general and in particular.

IV.

No one shall investigate or cause to be investigated the demolition of castles and forts; which castles and forts may not be rebuilt or other new ones constructed without the express decision of the States of each province individually.

V.

His Majesty shall send out of all the aforesaid countries, including the duchy of Luxemburg, all Spanish, Italian, Albanian, Burgundian, and other foreign troops not acceptable to the country, within six weeks of publication of the present Treaty or earlier if the armies more fully described below can be reorganized and everything made ready for their departure. But in any case they will depart within the said six weeks (considering that the contracting States promise to work in all diligence with the commissioners of His Majesty without deception or dissimulation so that the said armies may be ready on the day that the said foreigners shall be required to leave), and six weeks later, they shall be gone from the county of Burgundy, nor shall they be permitted to return to the said countries or be sent into them, since His Majesty is engaged in no foreign war and in general has no need of them, as is well known to the said States. Likewise the said States will send out all the French, English, Scots, and other foreigners under their command. . . .

VII.

During the time until the departure of the said foreigners, His Majesty and the United Lands will raise an army of natives of this country and others acceptable to His Majesty and to the States of the provinces which now enter into the present Treaty or may enter it later, at the expense of His Majesty, but with the under-standing that the above-mentioned provinces will aid His Majesty by payment of taxes as provided in Article XX below, in order to maintain the Roman Catholic religion and the obedience due to His Majesty upon the footing of the Pacification of Ghent, the Union, Perpetual Edict, and the present Treaty in all their points. . . .

IX.

All prisoners held by the contracting parties will be released immediately on both sides after the publication of the present Treaty, so much as is in their power, and without payment of ransom.

Likewise, Monsieur d'Ognies and others will very humbly beseech His Majesty to consent to send back to this country in freedom the Count of Buren,[1] provided that he swears an oath to uphold the Roman Catholic religion, the Pacification of Ghent, the Union, Perpetual Edict, and the present Treaty. . . .

XII.

And for greater security, in conformity with Article XI of the above-mentioned Perpetual Edict, an oath shall be sworn by the

---

1. Philip William, Count of Buren, eldest son of William the Silent.–*Ed.*

contracting States, as well as by all persons in high office, governors, magistrates, burghers, and inhabitants of the cities and places under garrison, and by the soldiers, and persons in towns and places where there are no garrisons, and even by all others who hold any command or military office, or other post, to uphold both the Roman Catholic religion and the proper obedience due to the King, in accordance with the above-mentioned Pacification and subsequent Union and the Perpetual Edict, and not to receive, change, or permit entry to any garrison without the knowledge of the governor general and the governor of the province, with the advice of the States of each province or their deputies; with the understanding that in case of urgent necessity, the above-mentioned provincial governor may send soldiers into forts where garrisons are usually stationed, provided that they are under oath to and in the service of His Majesty in each province. . . .

XV.

His Majesty shall now and henceforth give commission to a prince or princess of his blood acceptable to the States to be governor and lieutenant-general in this country, and he shall be bound to swear solemnly to observe the Pacification of Ghent and the subsequent Union, the Perpetual Edict, and the present Treaty in all its points and articles, and specifically to uphold the Roman Catholic religion and the reasonable obedience due to His Majesty, and His Majesty is most humbly beseeched to accept and continue in this governorship Archduke Matthias, on condition that he will leave at once to come into these reconciled provinces, if not with a complete commission, at least for the period of three months. And immediately after the departure and exit of the above-mentioned Spaniards and foreigners from all the Low Countries, and the liberation of the cities, castles, forts as stated above, my Lord the Prince of Parma[2] will have the governorship general . . . for the period of six months. . . . And after these six months, if His Majesty has not yet provided for the government of this country, in order to avoid all disorder and confusion, it will be administered by the Council of State while awaiting the arrival of the new governor.

2. Alexander Farnese.—*Ed*.

XVI.

His Majesty will choose for his Council of State ten or twelve persons, or more where customary, including lords and nobles as well as men of learning, all natives of the country, of whom two-thirds shall be acceptable to the States of the said provinces and shall have been of their party from the beginning of this war until now.

XVII.

All correspondence and dispatches shall be drawn up according to the advice and decision of the councilors of state (who shall be required to take the prescribed oath), after drafting by one of them, on order to prevent the difficulties of which we have become aware.

XVIII.

When governorships, as well as the post of general of the army, become vacant from now on and during the next six years, His Majesty will fill them with persons born in this country as well as with foreigners, both to be acceptable to the States of the respective reconciled provinces, capable, fitting, and qualified under their privileges. And with respect to the Privy Council, the Council of Finances, and other important offices, His Majesty will name both natives of the country and foreigners who are acceptable to the aforesaid States, provided that before they are received they shall solemnly swear this Treaty and promise by oath that in the event that they become aware of any action prejudicial to it, they will inform the provincial States, under pain of being held perjurers and men without honor. . . .

XX.

They shall henceforth not be burdened in any way with taxes, tributes of impositions other than those which were in force during the time of the late Emperor Charles, and with the consent of the States of each province respectively. Each and all of these shall be maintained in their privileges, usages, and customs, in general and individually. And in the event that any be infringed it shall be made good and restored.

XXI.

Furthermore, the contracting Parties shall be required to renounce, as far as concerns them, all confederations and alliances which have been made since the beginning of these changes and troubles. . . .

XXIII.

And in order to increase the goodwill and affection which princes owe to their subjects, so that the said subjects may be all the more inclined to give their prince the respect and proper obedience which they owe him, it appears desirable and necessary (as His Majesty is most humbly beseeched to do) to be pleased to send here at the earliest possible opportunity one of his children who shall be his successor apparent in this country, to be brought up and instructed according to the manner of the land, with all proper piety and virtue.

XXIV.

All provinces, castellanies, cities, or private persons in these Low Countries who shall desire to be reconciled with His Majesty upon the same footing and the same conditions as in this present Treaty shall enjoy this benefit, provided that they come here voluntarily within three months after the effective departure of the Spaniards from these Low Countries. . . .

XXVII.

Both sides will confirm the present Treaty and settlement by solemn oath upon Holy Scripture, and His Majesty will accept and consider it valid within three months after its publication, or sooner if possible.

XXVIII.

Thus done, concluded and decreed in the Abbey of St. Vaast at Arras, the 17th day of May, 1579, etc.

48. *The Spanish and the Dutch Netherlands*

The separation of the southern and northern Netherlands, one a dependent country under a foreign dynasty, the other an independent state, was more than a political division. It rested to a large extent upon the antagonism of the dominant religious groups, Catholic in the South, Calvinist in the North, but it was also a growing-away spiritually. The diffuse but real sense of unity that had existed during the later Middle Ages, at least between the southern provinces and Holland, Zeeland, and Utrecht in the North, was dissipated; in its stead came a feeling of mutual suspicion, antipathy and—on the part of the southerners—even fear. Over the decades and centuries these attitudes created a powerful sense of apartness which was to become the basis of separate nationhood in the nineteenth century. The northerners began to look upon the Spanish Netherlands from a narrowly strategic and commercial standpoint. It was a country which put an invaluable barrier between them and France, the mightiest state in Europe. They were able to dominate its economy by barring seagoing traffic from Antwerp (the closing of the Scheldt), by compelling the Spanish authorities to fix import duties no lower than those set by the Dutch, and by levying import and export duties on the goods which the southerners bought and sold through Dutch intermediaries.

This favorable situation of the United Provinces was imperiled, however, when France won its freedom of action after the Peace of the Pyrenees in 1659. The claims of the French crown on all or part of the Spanish Netherlands upon the basis of hereditary rights of the queen of Louis XIV, the Spanish infanta Maria Teresa (Marie-Thérèse), were soon set forth, although not until the War of Devolution of 1667 were arms used to enforce them. During 1663, only a year after France and the United Provinces had formed an alliance directed against England, discussion began between the French Court and the Dutch leaders about the future of the southern Netherlands. There was talk of setting up a nominally independent republic there under a French-Dutch co-protectorate, or of partition; but behind the discussions lay a clear French insistence on making some territorial gain on its northern frontier. The Delegated Councilors of Holland—the permanent executive committee of the States of Holland—asked a well-informed merchant of Dordrecht, who had traded with the southerners and traveled much along the Maas, Herman Gijsen by name, to present a report on the situation in the Spanish Netherlands and what the results would be of a change in its political status. The full text of Gijsen's report remained in manuscript in the archives of Dordrecht and The Hague until published in the twentieth century. Its cool, business-like analysis is not only informative about the strategic and economic facts but reveals by its very tone the extent to which the two regions had already become separate nations.

Source: S. van Brakel, "Eene deductie en een reisbericht van Herman Gijsen uit 1663 betreffende de economische belangen der Republiek in de Zuidelijke Nederlanden," *Bijdragen en Mededeelingen van het Historisch Genootschap*, 45 (1924), pp. 50–58. Translated from the Dutch by Herbert H. Rowen.

A Discussion by Herman Ghijsen Concerning the Situation and Condition of Trade of the Netherlands, and How This Could be Changed and Diverted if the Remaining Part of the Spanish Netherlands Came Under France. Item, What Would be the Best Steps to be Taken for Such an Event.

1. Because Your High Lordships have been pleased to propose that I present to them for their most wise consideration a discussion of what harm which could be suffered by the commerce of this state if, in the event of the death of the present king of Spain, who is of great age, the Spanish Netherlands should fall to the crown of France, whether by right of inheritance or through the force of arms;

2. Therefore, in order to do so in accordance with my duty and my little knowledge, I present the following remarks in the most commodious manner and clearest order.

3. First, the situation and opportunities of the Netherlands in general, followed by the character of each individually.

4. Second, the natural inclination and the character of their inhabitants and peoples.

5. Third, what may be anticipated if the Spanish Netherlands came to pass from Spain to France.

6. Regarding the first, namely, the opportunities and situation of the Netherlands in general and that from the earliest times trade has had its seat and prosperity there above all the neighbors about, I can give no historical account but only say what we know of it that has come down to us from our fathers and forefathers by tradition.

7. I have found that in the province of Flanders immediately before the troubles in the Low Countries, when, I say, the Netherlands in general stood under one rule and each did his best to advance his own interest, the following three principal branches of trade were established there, to wit, the salting of herring and other fish, the refining of white salt, and the manufacture of all kinds of cloth.

8. Antwerp flourished then far above Amsterdam, for it was the site of the whole trade of the East and West Indies, Spain, and the Mediterranean Sea, as well as of a portion of the Baltic trade. Item, the English Court was there at that time too.

9. The name of the Netherlands language is a clear proof of this, for all Netherlanders were then called Flemings, just as now they are often called Hollanders.

10. These three aforesaid trades were almost completely diverted by the recent troubles of the Low Countries, as is known to the whole world, but some time before, while Flanders namely was still at war with several of its counts, the salting of herring and other fish began to come here to Holland, and part of the cloth trade went to England.

11. But the most important of the causes for the coming of trade here to this country from Flanders and Antwerp was not the character of the country but the force of arms, in respect to the oppression of religion and to the neglect of rule over the sea from the very first by the Spaniards, who did not give it proper attention, and although the city of Antwerp was reconquered by the Prince of Parma, it remained closed off nevertheless as a seaport.

12. The seaports in Flanders turned away from trade to privateering and piracy.

13. And, although these aforesaid southern Netherlands have been at peace some time now with this state, they have nonetheless been ruined almost everywhere by the war which continued with France, so that they have been incapable of restoring their lost commerce.

14. Although they have observed the correct method for such improvement, in the first place all import duties have been abolished throughout Flanders and Brabant, where they have kept the Maas River under the highest tariffs, with the intention of attracting trade to come directly through the Flemish ports to Brussels and then by land to Namur. These are not more than ten

hours apart, so that the journey can easily be made in eight days, except when the waterways are closed by ice, while the Maas journey ordinarily takes three weeks and often, when a contrary wind prevents sailing as far as the tow-paths, or when the Maas is too high or too low, it can take a good eight or ten weeks and even longer before Liège or Namur can be reached.

15. Furthermore, much consideration must be given to the fact that when that country was at the height of its prosperity, it did not yet have the use of this very convenient canal to Brussels, which was dug only a hundred years ago or a little more, with five locks which bring the waters to a height of sixty feet.

16. Having thus far spoken of the situation and advantages of the Spanish Netherlands, we shall come to the second part, about the inclinations and tendencies of their inhabitants.

17. That the Hollanders cannot excel them in this, because they are equal in everything, can be easily shown by the shape of the land.

For Flanders stretches as far as Holland along the same sea; it is also a level and low country, cut through by many natural and dug channels and waterways on the one side, with the Scheldt River on the other. And they also have the same climate and latitude in common with Holland; and since all inhabitants suck in their nature and inclinations from the country, which is their true mother, so it necessarily follows that the Flemings will differ little or not at all from the Hollanders.

18. The only inequality I find between the above-named provinces of Holland and Flanders is that Holland is crossed by two rivers, the Rhine and the Maas, which give it an outlet to the sea;

19. But on the contrary the seaports of Flanders are artificial, all having dug channels, like Blankenburg, Ostend, Nieupoort, and Dunkirk, which all have Bruges city as their neighbor, and have the same runoffs, which they keep deep and clean by dredging; and I find that the seashore there is better than in Holland, where the outlet of a live and strong-flowing river into the sea is completely stopped up, as can be seen near the city of Leiden and the Old Rhine.

On the other hand, the maritime village on the Maas near Den Briel has, as I have heard, lost a good foot in depth in our own time.

20. Furthermore, the province of Flanders also has an outlet to the sea through the town of Grevelingen[3] but it is useful only for inland shipping, which can travel to St.-Omer and Artois.

21. But the other four canals which I have named are completely adequate for travel by heavy-draft inland shipping, as they have tight locks at the above-named ports, which are not more than ten to eleven feet wide; but these ports can be reached by heavily laden ocean-going ships at high water.

22. Here I shall end the second part in which I present the inclinations of the inhabitants, after having done that of the situation of the country, in order to introduce the third part, and to determine the advantages which France could enjoy thanks to this situation if that country came under its obedience.

23. Having thus far demonstrated the advantages which might come to France from the character of land and people, I shall take note in this third part of what we could expect from its transfer from Spain to France.

24. I shall first speculate about the freedom of commerce which France might give and allow us, with all friendly good feeling, such as Spain now gives; and then the advantages which France could take away from us in preferring its own interest.

25. Even with the freedom of commerce which France might allow us in its Netherlands, permitting our nation to trade everywhere and requiring them to pay no more than the inhabitants, it would still be able to gain some advantages over us greater than those which Spain is able to.

26. One of these is freedom of religion, which France permits and Spain does not.

27. Second, France would bring together its new acquisitions in the Low Countries with the part it already has, resulting in a great advantage to its commerce, and with an end to the export and import duties which now must be paid on either side, there would be a profit which would annul the antipathy and difference of humors which have always prevailed between the French and the Netherlanders.

28. The change of state and government would attract many people in the hope of gaining profit there more easily than in our country, for change has been called a queen whom everyone finds they like.

3. The Flemish name of Gravelines, now in France.—Ed.

29. These four aforenamed advantages could be had by France to a greater extent than Spain, as we have already explained.

30. But now I shall consider at last the specific aims which moved Your High Lordships to put their questions to me;

31. And determine what remedies could be used if France were to push its interest against our state, as it can easily do even without breaking treaties or violation of good friendship, not to speak of any outright hostility or violence.

32. The Spanish Netherlands, ruined by war and having lost its principal frontier cities, presents no danger to our state and provides us instead with a bulwark against the great, rising power of France.

33. But if it comes under France and if that crown is strengthened by such a major conquest, it could encourage that country, which has been our good neighbor until now, to change its interest and to seek to draw away, thanks to its good situation which I have demonstrated, the commerce which is the sole salvation and source of prosperity of our state.

34. Thus they could forbid in the whole of the Low Countries under their authority the importation of white salt from this country.

35. Item, the importation of all kinds of fish, such as herring, stockfish, and other fish, and whale oil.

36. And they could forbid us to bring into their country the goods that we have first transported to our country by sea, as the English already did in Cromwell's time with their great Navigation Act.

37. They could similarly forbid the importation of all kinds of manufactures into their country.

38. And in order to create prosperity in the Flemish seaports and to attract their own shipping, they would impose upon all foreign nations, including our own, anchor fees or cargo dues, as they pleased, and by that means seek to attract French trade.

39. Having thus far set forth all the disadvantages which could occur to us with the changing of our neighbors, I shall set forth the remedies which, subject to correction, should be adopted, and which Your High Lordships have already presented the drafts to me.

40. Notably, in accordance with article 52 of the treaty of peace made with Spain, to take possession of the Upper Quarter of

Gelderland as an equivalent, together with the fort of Navaigne and Argenteau, in order to have the Maas River open to Liège.

41. It would also be very advantageous to have the town of Limburg with its environs, which are attracted to the lands Beyond the Maas, in order to have a gate to Trier in order to avoid the land of Luxemburg.

42. On the other hand, it would also be very necessary to have a place by which to cut off the canal to the cities of Mechelen [Malines] and Brussels, for which purpose we have proposed that a fort be erected opposite the castle of Ruppelmonde, by which the Scheldt River could be controlled by means of a warship.

Here we may consider whether or not it would be to our advantage to have the city of Antwerp. Item, whether the king of Spain as duke of Brabant and count of Flanders has the power to sell some of the cities and territories of Flanders and Brabant without the consent of the States and the members of these provinces, and whether these States and members would approve it.

And in this way the gates through Gelderland and Brabant and also to Ghent would for the most part be under the control of this country and the course of commerce could be directed at its pleasure.

43. To receive several ports in Flanders, such as Nieupoort, Bruges, and Ostend, would also be advantageous to us, and we could consider whether we could ot lease them from that king for money, to be returned only to a male heir.

44. I would let no difficulty remain which could prevent passage between Mons in Hainaut, to which the Scheldt River through Flanders is navigable, and Namur, where the Sambre River runs into the Maas, which distance must be traversed by land but amounts to only eight hours, although by a very bad road.

I have until now given an account of the advantages of Flanders over Holland due to the character of its land and people, as they are now under Spain; this has been discussed through article 22.

Second, what advantage there would be if it came under France, but with freedom of trade, as indicated in articles 23 to 29.

Third, the advantages which France would gain if she wished to seek them in her own, properly seen interest.

And since we have taken over their trade from the province of Flanders and the city of Antwerp, similarly we have taken from

Spain and Portugal the sea routes to the East and West Indies, and similarly from France and Biscay the fisheries of Greenland, and only recently from the English the manufacture of fine and light cloths, which are desired in France and Italy, and even in the Levant at Smyrna and elsewhere, much above those of England.

Because it is notorious that envy and jealousy grow along with one's blessings, like a shadow with its body, so we cannot imagine that our prosperity can escape suffering from the envy which it arouses on every side, as England and France are beginning to do.

I shall conclude now, High Lordships, and hope to have satisfied Your High Lordships with this information, and shall commend this tender and general foster child into the arms of the fathers of the fatherland.

49. A Forward and Backward Revolution

The transfer of sovereignty over the southern Netherlands to the Austrian Habsburgs still meant rule by an outside dynasty, but one much more concerned with the welfare of its Low Countries possessions. Although the country suffered from destructive military campaigning on its territory whenever Austria fought a war with a western European power, Austrian policy was generally milder and more respectful of historic institutions and practices. Internal improvements, notably canals and roads, helped to bring the parts of the country closer together and assisted the revival of industry. Attempts to favor direct participation in international trade by setting up an Ostend Company to evade the closure of the Scheldt River to seagoing traffic had to be given up under Dutch and English pressure in 1727; but later Joseph II forced a showdown with the United Provinces and won free movement on the waterway.

Yet it was this same ruler, the emperor of the good heart and perpetual failure, who provoked revolt in the Austrian Netherlands. His policy, the purest of "enlightened despotisms," offended all major groups. An edict establishing religious toleration in 1781 ran against the grain of the Catholic hierarchy but did not matter much when there were so few non-Catholics to be tolerated. The decree of a radical reform in administration and the courts on New Year's Day, 1787, replacing the traditional agencies of government rooted in the provinces with unified, systematic rule from Brussels, met opposition which finally led Joseph to revoke the "Joyous Entry" of Brabant in June, 1789. This act brought the country into an uproar; conservatives opposed to reform were joined by followers of Enlightenment who rejected the emperor's tyrannical defiance of the will of his subjects in the Low Countries. During the next months, the Austrians were driven out by armed rebels, and an independent state, the United Belgian States, was established in January, 1790. The key documents in this development—the declaration of unity between Flanders and Brabant of November 30, 1789; the missive of December 20 of the Brabant States to the other provinces on its declaration of independence from Habsburg dominion; and the treaty among the provinces establishing the new state on January 11, 1790—are reproduced below. The new regime, which was dominated by the conservative elements, fell under the Austrian military forces sent in by the new emperor, Leopold II, in December, 1790. Belgium, as we may henceforth call the country, eventually emerged from its modernization under the authority of the conquering French during the French Revolution and the Napoleonic era.

a. *Source:* "Acte d'union des États de Flandre et de Brabant . . . 30 novembre 1789," in L. P. Gachard, ed., *Documens politiques et diplomatiques sur la Révolution belge de 1790* (Brussels: H. Remy, 1834), pp. 2–5. Translated from the French by Herbert H. Rowen.

b. *Source:* "Lettre des États de Brabant aux États des autres provinces, leur notifiant la déchéance de Joseph II . . . 20 décembre 1789," in *ibid.*, pp. 1–2. Translated from the French by Herbert H. Rowen.

c. *Source:* "Traité d'union, et établissement du Congrès souverain des États belgiques unis, 11 janvier 1790," in *ibid.*, pp. 113–120. Translated from the French by Herbert H. Rowen.

a.

THE STATES of Flanders, sharing with the States of Brabant, with which they have long been united by intimate bonds of friendship and interest, a determination to preserve their sacred rights, usages, privileges, and the religion of their fathers against the violations which these have suffered for some years now from a despotic and tyrannical government, and having found no other recourse than by the use of arms to throw off its yoke and to recover their freedom and independence, have become convinced that they can achieve this aim and consolidate their freedom only by joining their fate with that of the province of Brabant and by concluding with them a treaty of offensive and defensive unity in all matters, with a proviso that they will never enter into any negotiation or make any compromise whatever with their foreign sovereign except by common action; and desiring to give to the States of Brabant every possible mark of friendship and to demonstrate by unequivocal deeds our unlimited desire to cement this union in unbreakable fashion:

The said States of Flanders, upon the proposal of Canon Van Eupen by authority of the Lords States of Brabant, agree and consent that this union shall be transformed into a single sovereignty of the two States, with all the power and the exercise of this sovereignty to be concentrated in a Congress to be established hereafter, to be composed of deputies named by both sides according to articles of organization to be agreed upon in accordance with the feelings which arise from principles of equity and dictated solely by the common welfare; except that it is the intention of the contracting parties that for the present the power of this sovereign assembly shall be confined to the single aim of a common defense, with power to make peace and war and hence to raise and maintain a common national army, to command and maintain the fortifications necessary for the defense of the country, and to contract alliances with foreign powers—that is, these things which concern the common interests of the two States and those who shall decide to join them afterwards. The States of Flanders dare flatter themselves that the States of Brabant will find in this declaration a certain guarantee of the loyal feelings of the States of Flanders and of their zeal for the common cause, and we have no doubt that the States of Brabant will respond for their part in the same spirit of frankness.

Decided in our assembly, November 30, 1789.

J.-F. Rohaert.

b.

Brussels, from the General Assembly
December 20, 1789

My Lords:

The happy revolution which we have just brought to a glorious conclusion under the visible auspices of God has placed the supreme power in our hands. By virtue of this power we have declared ourselves to be free and independent and have deprived and dismissed the former duke, Joseph II, from all sovereignty, supremacy, etc., in this our land and duchy of Brabant. We believed it to be in our common interest to inform Your Lordships of these actions as well as of the close union which we have concluded with the Lords States of Flanders, of which we sent a copy herewith. We are absolutely convinced that Your Lordships, in their wisdom, will first of all see how useful and even necessary such a union, and other even more intimate unions, will be for the preservation of our freedom. Therefore, at the request of the deputies of Flanders who are now in residence here, we call upon you to send deputies to us as soon as possible with such powers as Your Lordships agree upon, so that, in case of approval, they can contract with us, extend this union, and make the necessary arrangements that the emergency and welfare of fatherland require.

We are, My Lords,

Your most humble and most obedient
servants,

THE STATES OF THE COUNTRY AND
DUCHY OF BRABANT.

c.

After the death of the Dowager Empress and Queen, Maria Theresa of Austria, the peoples who today form the United States of the Low Countries recognized as their sovereign Emperor Joseph II, elder son of the empress, and placed themselves as subjects under his rule but with reservations and express stipulations such as had been dictated from ancient times by the constitution of these provinces.

These stipulations and reservations contained in the inaugural pact were more ancient than the house which governed the country and may be said to have been born at the same time as the nation itself. Therefore, they were solemnly accepted and sworn and nothing was lacking in the treaty which the people made with the prince in accordance with custom before they give themselves to him.

The preservation of the ancient Catholic, Apostolic, and Roman religion in its entirety; the maintenance of the constitution, liberties, franchises, customs, and usages as they were contained in the charters and consecrated by the immemorial possession of the nation and in what Brabant in particular calls its *Joyous Entry*—all these were agreed to and promised under oath.

The inhabitants had their hearts set on these points all the more because it had long since been their comforting habit to consider that they were the essential elements of their constitution and that this constitution was the bulwark of their freedoms and the safeguard of their happiness.

Nonetheless, despite the positive oath which the sovereign took to observe the inaugural pact, and the frequently reiterated remonstrances of all the orders of the state against innumerable infractions of this pact, the sovereign has followed a steady course for some years with a purpose which was nothing less than to change everything, to introduce constant innovations, and to deprive the inhabitants of a constitution which they held dear and he could not despoil them of without committing an injustice and breaking his oaths.

We have seen the appearance of a mass of edicts one after another, attacking religion in various aspects of its morality and its form of worship, in its dogmas and its clergy. The law courts of the nation have been subverted; laws have been wantonly changed or violated; property and personal freedom, for which Belgians have shown themselves so zealous in all ages, were no longer safe against unconstitutional ventures. The laws, their force lost, remained silent before the soldier's sword; everywhere ancient usages were changed or repealed; the old order was replaced by a new order, consisting of the fickle and arbitrary desires of the prince or those who governed in his name and acted upon his authority. Our ailments became too great and without remedy. The government, not satisfied with offering obdurate resistance to our complaints, closed the door to such remonstrances as such by a new and final act of authority, annulling the *Joyous Entry* and the ancient possessions and fundamental laws of the provinces, and abolishing along with the constitution the assemblies of deputies of these provinces, which until then had been the ordinary organ by which the people were represented.

Finally the political compact, which ceases to bind when it no longer binds both sides, was formally broken by the sovereign himself. When this happened, what was left for the people to do except to use the natural and inviolable right given to them by the compact itself to resist violence with force and to take back an authority which had been entrusted to the sovereign only for the common welfare and with many precautions and express stipulations and reservations?

This is what they have done, and it is in accordance with the principles that the different provinces have declared themselves *free* and *independent*. Heaven has visibly given its blessing to an undertaking made under its auspices; Europe and mankind have applauded its success. But to have obtained success is not enough; we must consider how to consolidate success and make it last.

For these reasons the Belgian States, having drawn tighter the ancient ties of close union and lasting friendship among them, have agreed upon the following points and articles:

Article 1.

All the provinces unite and form a confederation under the name of the United Belgian States.

Article 2.

These provinces place in common, unite and concentrate the sovereign power; which they limit and restrict, however, to the following objectives: a common defense; the power to make peace and war, and consequently, to raise and maintain a national army as well as to institute, construct, and maintain necessary fortifications; to contract alliances, both offensive and defensive, with foreign powers; to name, send, and receive residents, ambassadors and other emissaries whatsoever: but all only by the authority of the combined government and without any recourse to the respective provinces. Agreement is also reached at the same time on the proportionate influence which each province shall exercise by its deputies upon the deliberations and in the accomplishment of the objectives set down in the present treaty.

Article 3.

In order to exercise this sovereign power, they create and establish a Congress of deputies from each of the provinces under the name of *Sovereign Congress of the United Belgian States.*

Article 4.

As the above-mentioned provinces profess and wish to profess forever the Catholic, Apostolic, and Roman religion and desire to preserve inviolate the unity of the Church, the Congress will respect and maintain the relationships with the Holy See as they have been observed heretofore in the nomination or presentation of subjects of the said provinces for archbishoprics or bishoprics, in a manner on which the provinces will agree among themselves hereafter, as well as in all other matters, in conformity with the principles of the Catholic, Apostolic, and Roman religion and the concordats and liberties of the Belgian Church.

Article 5.

The Congress will have the sole power to coin money under the stamp of the *United Belgian States* and to fix its name and value.

Article 6.

The provinces of the Union will contribute to the expenditures required for the performance of the sovereign powers granted to the Congress in accordance with the ratio observed under the former sovereign.

Article 7.

Each province retains and reserves all its other rights of sovereignty: its laws, its freedom, its independence, in fine all the powers, jurisdictions, and rights whatsoever which are not expressly put in common and delegated to the Sovereign Congress.

Article 8.

It is further irrevocably agreed that with regard to disputes which may arise, either as to the common contributions or as to any other object of debate whatever, whether by a province with the Congress, or by Congress with a province, or by one province with another, the Congress will attempt to terminate them amicably, and if an amicable compromise cannot be reached, then each province shall name a person before whom the case may be summarily transferred at the request of either of the parties and it shall decide the case. The Congress shall have the right of enforcement and if the sentence is directed against the Congress; it shall be obliged to accept it.

Article 9.

The United States obligate themselves most strictly to assist each other; and as soon as any province shall be attacked by an external enemy, they will all make common cause and together defend the province under attack with all their forces.

Article 10.

No province shall be free to make an alliance or any treaty whatsoever with another power without the consent of Congress, and the individual provinces may not form unions, alliances, or contracts among themselves of any kind whatsoever without the consent of the Congress.

The province of Flanders, however, may unite with West Flanders provided that each shall have its own deputies to the Congress, that these deputies will vote freely and independently: and the deputies of one may never at the same time be the deputies of the other.

Article 11.

This union shall be firm, eternal, and irrevocable. No province or group of provinces, even if in the majority, shall be free to break this union or to secede from it under any pretext or for any motive whatsoever.

Article 12.

It is also irrevocably agreed that the civil and military power, or any portion of either, will never be conferred upon the same person, and that no one having a seat or a vote in the Congress may be employed in the military service, and similarly that no one in military service may be a deputy to Congress or have a seat or a vote in it. Similarly, no person in the employ or pay of any foreign power, under whatsoever name it is given, may be admitted to the Congress.

Also excluded from it are all those who after ratification of the treaty of union accept any military order or any decoration whatsoever.

To this purpose, all the States composing the Union in general, and each member individually, as well as all who hold seats in the Congress, all councilors and members of the provincial councils, all magistrates and in general all judges and civil officials will promise and swear precise and faithful observance of this Union and of each and every one of its articles.

Thus concluded, made and decided at Brussels in the general assembly of the United Belgian States by the undersigned, deputies of the respective states, subject to the ratification of their principals, on January 11, 1790, at two o'clock in the morning.

[Of the 47 signatures which follow, 10 are by churchmen, five by noblemen signing with their titles, and the others by apparent commoners. This treaty of Union was ratified by the States of the respective provinces by January 20, 1790.]

Suggestions for Further Reading

The history of the Low Countries has been written almost wholly in its own languages, Dutch and French. The reader with a command of these tongues will find the best guide to the literature of the history of the Netherlands (limited, however, to the northern Netherlands after 1579) in H. de Buck, *Bibliografie der Geschiedenis van Nederland* (Leiden, 1968); it must be supplemented for specifically Belgian history after that date by the bibliographies in *Algemene Geschiedenis der Nederlanden*, ed. J. A. van Houtte *et al.*, 12 vols. (Utrecht, 1948–1959), which is the most comprehensive survey by scores of modern scholars, and by Henri Pirenne *et al.*, *Bibliographie de l'histoire de Belgique*, 3rd ed. (Brussels, 1931).

The classic modern histories are Henri Pirenne, *Histoire de Belgique*, illustrated ed., 4 vols. (Brussels, 1948–1952), a survey of unsurpassed brilliance, of which there is unfortunately no English translation; and P. J. Blok, *The History of the People of the Netherlands*, 5 vols. (New York, 1898–1912), which does for the northern Netherlands what Pirenne does for the southern, but with sturdy solidity rather than Pirenne's extraordinary combination of detailed knowledge and encompassing analysis. The view adopted by both Pirenne and Blok that the separation of South and North into modern Belgium and Holland was the result of deep-lying historical forces traceable far back into the medieval period is rejected by Pieter Geyl, one of the most original of twentieth-century Dutch historians, notably in his *Geschiedenis van de Nederlandse Stam*, new ed., 2 vols. (Amsterdam, 1948–1949; paperback ed., the most complete, 6 vols., Amsterdam, 1961–1962), of which the parts covering the revolt of the Netherlands and the seventeenth century have been translated (*The Revolt of the Netherlands* [London, 1932] and *The Netherlands in the Seventeenth Century*, 2 vols. [London, 1936–1964]). Geyl's position is reaffirmed more succinctly in his *History of the Low Countries: Episodes and Problems* (New York, 1964). Other useful although brief accounts are G. Edmundson, *History of Holland* (Cambridge, 1922), G. J. Renier, *The Dutch Nation, An Historical Survey* (London, 1944), and B. H. M. Vlekke, *Evolution of the Dutch Nation* (New York, 1945). The survey of Belgian history in English, H. vander Linden, *Belgium: The Making of a Nation* (Oxford, 1920), is elementary. The series of volumes called *Britain and the Netherlands* (London and Groningen, 1960–) contains invaluable shorter papers in English, chiefly although not exclusively on the history of the Low Countries. The series *Acta Historica Neerlandica* (Leiden, 1966–) contains translations of articles and summaries of books originally in Dutch in English, French, or German.

The political history of the early sixteenth century, including the events in and affecting the Low Countries, is recounted with superb analytic and narrative gifts by Karl Brandi in his *The Emperor Charles V* (London, 1939). The fundamental works in English on the revolt and the events until the fall of Oldenbarnevelt are by the American historian John Lothrop Motley: *The Rise of the Dutch Republic*, 3 vols. (New York, 1856), *History of the United Netherlands; from the Death of William the Silent to the Twelve Years Truce 1609*, 4 vols. (London, 1860–1867) and *The Life and Death of John of Barneveld*, 2 vols. (London, 1874); Motley writes with passionate conviction as a Protestant liberal, but has not been excelled for the informative wealth of his story and its vivid clarity. In addition to the fundamental works of Geyl listed above, the following are important: C. V. Wedgwood, *William the Silent* (New Haven, 1944), G. Griffiths, *William of Hornes, Lord of Hèze, and the Revolt of the Netherlands* (1576–1580) (Berkeley, 1954), and Charles Wilson, *Queen Elizabeth and the Revolt of the Netherlands* (Berkeley, 1970).

For the Dutch Republic, the outstanding work, in addition to Geyl's, is J. Huizinga, *Dutch Civilisation in the Seventeenth Century* (London, 1968). Charles Wilson, *The Dutch Republic and the Civilisation of the Seventeenth Century* (New York, 1968), by an outstanding economic historian, is informative especially on Dutch influences in England. John J. Murray, *Amsterdam in the Age of Rembrandt* (Norman, 1967) is short but detailed. F. Vere, *Salt in Their Blood: The Lives of the Famous Dutch Admirals* (London, 1955) is a tribute to commanders, some of whom won their laurels against the English. P. Geyl, *Orange and Stuart* (London, 1970) is a masterly study of the involvement of the Orange family with the Stuart ruling house and the resulting complications in Dutch political life. J. Geddes, *History of the Administration of John de Witt, Grand Pensionary of Holland* (vol. I [all published]; The Hague, 1879), is old-fashioned political biography, extremely detailed but clear; A. Lefèvre-Pontalis,

John de Witt (2 vols.; London, 1885) is still the only full-length biography in French or English but is clumsily executed and anachronistic. It may be supplemented by P. G. Rogers, *The Dutch in the Medway* (Oxford, 1970), a study of the Dutch raid to Chatham in 1667. J. Beresford, *The Godfather of Downing Street: Sir George Downing, 1623–1684* (London, 1925) is largely devoted to Downing's work as ambassador at The Hague. H. H. Rowen, *The Ambassador Prepares for War: The Dutch Embassy of Arnauld de Pomponne, 1669–1671* (The Hague, 1957), illuminates the origins of the war of 1672. Stephen Baxter, *William III* (New York, 1966) is the only satisfactory modern biography of the stadholder-king; it may be supplemented by K. H. D. Haley, *William of Orange and the English Opposition, 1672–74* (Oxford, 1953) for the first years of his administration. V. Barbour, *Capitalism in Amsterdam in the Seventeenth Century* (Baltimore, 1950) is an informative introduction to the Dutch economic achievement. See also G. Edmundson, *Anglo-Dutch Rivalry during the First Half of the 17th Century* (Oxford, 1911), C. Wilson, *Profits and Power: A Study of England and the Dutch Wars* (London, 1957), as well as C. Wilson, *Anglo-Dutch Commerce and Finance in the Eighteenth Century* (Cambridge, 1941), G. N. Clark, *The Dutch Alliance and the War against French Trade, 1688–1697* (Manchester, 1923), and H. I. Bloom, *The Economic Activities of the Jews of Amsterdam in the Seventeenth and Eighteenth Centuries* (Williamsport, Pa., 1937).

For the Dutch overseas, in addition to the well informed and brilliantly written work of C. R. Boxer, *The Dutch Sea-Borne Empire: 1600–1800* (London, 1965), fundamental studies are E. S. de Klerck, *History of the Netherlands East Indies*, 2 vols. (Rotterdam, 1938), A. Hyma, *A History of the Dutch in the Far East*, rev. ed. (Ann Arbor, 1953) and B. H. M. Vlekke, *Nusantara: A History of Indonesia*, 4th ed. (The Hague, 1959).

Among the rare works in English on the Dutch in the eighteenth century are R. Geikie and I. Montgomery, *The Dutch Barrier, 1705–1719* (Cambridge, 1930), R. Hatton, *Diplomatic Relations between Great Britain and the Dutch Republic, 1714–1721* (London, 1950), and A. Cobban, *Ambassadors and Secret Agents: The Diplomacy of the First Earl of Malmesbury at The Hague* (London, 1954).

Index